The Nazi Machtergreifung

The Nazi Machtergreifung

Edited by
PETER D. STACHURA
University of Stirling

London
GEORGE ALLEN & UNWIN
Boston   Sydney

George Allen & Unwin (Publishers) Ltd,
40 Museum Street, London WC1A 1LU, UK

George Allen & Unwin (Publishers) Ltd,
Park Lane, Hemel Hempstead, Herts HP2 4TE, UK

Allen & Unwin, Inc.,
9 Winchester Terrace, Winchester, Mass. 01890, USA

George Allen & Unwin Australia Pty Ltd,
8 Napier Street, North Sydney, NSW 2060, Australia

First published in 1983

British Library Cataloguing in Publication Data

   The Nazi Machtergreifung.
1. Germany—History—1918–1933
2. Germany—Politics and government—1918–1933
I. Stachura, Peter D.
943.085   DD240
ISBN 0-04-943026-2

Library of Congress Cataloging in Publication Data

Main entry under title:
   The Nazi Machtergreifung.
Includes index.
1. National socialism—Addresses, essays, lectures.
2. Germany—Politics and government—1918–1933—
Addresses, essays, lectures. 3. Germany —Social
conditions—1918–1933—Addresses, essays, lectures.
I. Stachura, Peter D.
DD240.N35   1983   943.086   82-24322
ISBN 0-04-943026-2

Set in 10 on 11 point Plantin by Computape (Pickering) Ltd
and printed in Great Britain by Biddles Ltd, Guildford, Surrey

For Kay

Contents

Preface

The fiftieth anniversary of the advent to power in Germany of Adolf Hitler's Nazi Party, in January 1983, is an appropriate time to reflect on a historical phenomenon whose importance in modern German and European history can hardly be overemphasised. The origins and development of National Socialism from 1919 to 1945 has been the subject of a vast, exhaustively detailed publications industry, and while the ever-expanding literature has broadened our understanding of this political movement, it is necessary from time to time to stop and pause in order to take stock of its place in history, particularly as scholarly interpretations of Hitler and the Nazis have undergone significant changes over the years.

The present volume, written by a group of mainly younger historians based at Canadian, American and British universities, is designed to provide a perspective of the *Machtergreifung* (Seizure of Power) after half a century of international scholarship on the event. In trying to ensure that the volume has coherence and shape as a book – as opposed to a loose collection of essays – all contributions are built around a central theme: the dynamics of social and political mobilisation by the Nazi Party during the Weimar era. In other words, the volume is held together, or so it is hoped, by essays relating to the nature of, and principal reasons for, support from Germans for the Nazis before 1933. The relationship between the Party and various social categories (the middle classes, the industrial proletariat, women, students, youth, and industrialists) constitutes a major element in the book, as does the attitudes towards Hitler displayed by a number of influential institutions in the Republic (the Christian Churches and the army). Finally, the Party's successful mobilisation of support is illustrated through the medium of foreign policy on the one hand, and ideology/propaganda on the other.

As a further step towards the aim of achieving coherence in the book, all contributions are specifically of a critical, historiographical type, relying on an examination of published material relevant to the 1918–33 period. The aim, therefore, is to give an overview and evaluation of some of the fundamental reasons for the triumph of National Socialism in 1933. It has to be stressed that the book does not purport to provide comprehensive coverage of all the pertinent factors involved in this development. There are obvious gaps within our chosen sphere of investigation which must be immediately acknowledged; for example, the role of agrarian élites, the labour and trade union movement, and the ancillary organisations of the Nazi Party, excepting the Hitler Youth and Nazi Students' Association, are not considered here. Neither is Hitler. His central role in the Party's ascent is axiomatic and reference to him occurs in virtually every essay in this volume, but the emphasis here is on the mass appeal and mass character of National Socialism, that is, the underlying factors rather than the leading individuals which made for its success. The absence of a particular study of the Führer, therefore, is compatible with the format and general substance of the book. To have attempted to cater for these and other elements in the overall situation would have required a publication much larger and broader in scope than the present volume. These omissions, however, should not detract from the essential purpose and orientation of the book.

As well as representing a statement of past and current research, it is to be earnestly hoped that this work will act also as a pointer for future lines of enquiry in Nazi studies, especially as it is directed towards a broad academic readership encompassing not only specialists, but also undergraduates and those seriously interested in European history, politics and sociology of the twentieth century.

Bridge of Allan
June 1982   PETER D. STACHURA

Abbreviations

AEG:	*Allgemeine Elekrizitäts-Gesellschaft*
BVP:	*Bayerische Volkspartei*
DDP:	*Deutsche Demokratische Partei*
DDR:	*Deutsche Demokratische Republik*
DFO:	*Deutscher Frauenorden*
DNVP:	*Deutschnationale Volkspartei*
DVP:	*Deutsche Volkspartei*
HJ:	*Hitlerjugend*
KPD:	*Kommunistische Partei Deutschlands*
NSDAP:	*Nationalsozialistische Deutsche Arbeiterpartei*
NSDStB:	*Nationalsozialistischer Deutscher Studentenbund*
NSF:	*Nationalsozialistischer Frauenschaft*
RDI:	*Reichsverband der deutschen Industrie*
SPD:	*Sozialdemokratische Partei Deutschlands*
VfZ:	*Vierteljahrshefte für Zeitgeschichte*

1 Introduction: Weimar, National Socialism and Historians

PETER D. STACHURA

The establishment and collapse of the Weimar Republic embraced a period of only fourteen years, yet it is a story which has continued to fascinate historians and public alike down to present times. Despite the ongoing debate about the degree of continuity in modern German history, which sometimes depicts the republican era as a mere interlude in the authoritarian–nationalist tradition linking the Second and Third Reichs, and seeing a decisive break coming in 1945 rather than 1918 or 1933, the Republic has rightly staked a strong claim to be considered for what it itself actually was. In particular it has become an essential task of scholarship to ascertain the reasons for the ultimate failure of parliamentary democracy in Germany in 1933 and its replacement by an antithetical political philosophy, National Socialism. This is not to suggest that the history of the Republic is synonymous with the upsurge of National Socialism, but clearly the one was the most important consequence of the other, and study of the period as a whole must take account of their intimate and tragic connection. A full and realistic understanding of these momentous events becomes even more pressing when it is acknowledged that what happened in Weimar Germany sooner or later affected the rest of Europe. It surely would be no exaggeration to say that the Europe of the second half of the twentieth century was significantly shaped by developments in Weimar during the years 1918 to 1933. Above all, the victory of the NSDAP and its subsequent destruction of oppositional organisations and ideologies within Germany, and then its responsibility for unleashing the Second World War causing the death of many millions, has to be accounted for as precisely and deeply as possible by historians.

There is, of course, no settled consensus among scholars in their assessment of this historical problem. Interpretations during the last fifty years have revealed a multiplicity of various personal, political and ideological influences as well as widely differing standards of scholarship.[1] Few evaluations written in the 1930s survived the postwar era, but one notable exception has been Arthur Rosenberg's stimulating if tendentiously pro-Marxist account which ends in the year 1930 because he believed that with the collapse of the Hermann Müller coalition government in March 1930 the Republic and democracy were effectively at an end.[2] Rosenberg's hypothesis rested on the premiss that the Republic in any case suffered from the outset from fundamental structural weaknesses which made its demise only a matter of time. The book immediately laid down a major line of enquiry in Weimar studies which revolved around the question: was the Republic doomed from the beginning, or did it have certain advantages which were eroded only in the face of later, overwhelming problems?[3]

During the early postwar years, West German historians conspicuously failed to face up fully to the calamities of the Weimar and Nazi eras. This was shown not only in superficial, apologetic works such as those by Friedenberg, Hoegener, Braun, Stampfer, Brecht and Papen,[4] but also in the writings of historians with an established and respected reputation, particularly Friedrich Meinecke and Gerhard Ritter.[5] Both offered explanations of what had occurred during the 1920s and 1930s which are no longer taken seriously by most. Meinecke argued that Hitler achieved power because a series of unfortunate coincidences brought down the Republic and that National Socialism, therefore, was something of an aberration, an artificiality of a transient kind in Germany's historical experience. Equally dubious was Ritter's attempt to label National Socialism as merely the German version of a wider phenomenon which afflicted the rest of Western and Central Europe during the interwar period, that is, a rampant nationalism destructive of all democratic and parliamentary structures. Both interpretations played down, on the one hand, the grotesque evil of National Socialism and its seductive power among the German electorate before 1933, and on the other, wrongly denied the quintessentially German features of Hitler's movement: this was not just a German variant of fascism or of authoritarianism, it was something arising out of a peculiarly German development and location, as Ludwig Dehio, to his credit, confessed early on in the debate.[6] An arresting exception from a non-German source to the trend towards shirking from the enormity of the Nazi period among many German scholars was Scheele's work which was, in fact, ahead of its time in contending that the conservative élitist groups in industry, the civil service and army caused the downfall of the Republic.[7] This provocative book, which has not received the recognition it deserves, counts as the first revisionist interpretation of the problem.

One of the principal reasons for the widespread reluctance of many scholars during the 1950s to probe more inquisitively into the causes of the Weimar tragedy lay in the political and ideological shadows cast by the exigencies of the Cold War. The theories of totalitarianism of that era, in effectively reducing National Socialism and communism to the one common denominator, inhibited more thorough and meaningful research. Attention was deflected from examining the essence of National Socialism, and in highlighting the virtues of democratic government *vis-à-vis* communist dictatorship (as exemplified by the Soviet Union and the German Democratic Republic), the weaknesses of Weimar democracy and its institutional framework were suggested rather than conclusively demonstrated. Only with the publication of Bracher's monumental work in the late 1950s were the fundamental structural failings of the Weimar democratic system, including the bureaucracy, judiciary and parties, laid bare.[8] A new era in Weimar studies was thus inaugurated.

During the 1960s standards of scholarship in this field attained admirable heights of excellence as virtually every important facet of Weimar political life was subjected to intensive scrutiny. Leading the way were, first, the sequel to Bracher's *Auflösung*, which convincingly dissected the factors which led to the immediate fall of the Republic and the setting up of a Nazi totalitarian state, and secondly, the study of the major Weimar political parties which lucidly identified not only their hopeless feebleness and disorientation in 1932–3 but also, more strikingly, the sheer incompetence and myopia of their leaderships.[9] The book confirmed, in this important respect at least, earlier notions that one of the basic reasons why the Republic got nowhere was related to the abject mediocrity of its politicians and party chiefs.

The notable advances of the 1960s was paralleled by a rather depressing development – the somewhat grandiose attempt to situate the traumatic events of the early 1930s in a very sweeping perspective of German history. Shirer's prodigious bestseller, which saw Hitler and National Socialism as the apotheosis of nefarious trends in German history stretching back through Bismarck and Frederick the Great to Martin Luther, probably did more than any other publication to mislead the general public in Europe and North America about the real nature of the Weimar era.[10] It was not so much that Shirer's thesis was unoriginal, for Butler, Taylor and Vermeil among others before him had spouted similar nonsensical prejudice,[11] but simply that his book was fluently written and glossily marketed to an unsuspecting audience whose appetite for knowledge of the whole interwar German period had reached unprecedented levels. Shirer confirmed, ostensibly on the basis of solid documentary evidence, just about every prejudice which the ignorant and misinformed harboured towards Germany and the Germans.[12] At least his book performed one extremely useful function: it showed to those with any discernment the huge gulf between popular, sensationalist history of twentieth-century German history and sober, objective, scholarly studies.

These studies had also been concerned with the character and development of the Nazi movement before 1933. By the early 1970s a wealth of detail had been provided in a mountain of monographs, articles and dissertations. There were impressive contributions from German historians such as Bracher, Broszat, Horn, Tyrell and Schulz, and

American scholars like Orlow, Nyomarkay, Gordon and Turner, about the NSDAP's organisation, leadership, ideology and propaganda,[13] which were the necessary ingredients of its ability to exploit for its own political advantage the exacting problems confronting the Republic, especially after the onset of the economic depression. The NSDAP's emergence from the murky waters of Munich's petty beer-hall politics in the very early 1920s to a position of pre-eminence in German politics little more than a decade later was an astounding accomplishment by any standard. The so-called first *Machtergreifung* of July 1921 when Hitler asserted his leadership of the Party and began to mould it according to his own image was a necessary and decisive initial step. However, at this stage in his career Hitler regarded himself primarily as a propagandist or 'drummer' of the nationalist cause among the masses, and not as the potential future dictator of Germany. He pursued a violent putschist strategy against the Republic, contemptuously dismissing all methods related to the practice of parliamentary democracy. By 1923 the NSDAP was a prominent constituent of the Bavarian Right, and by the autumn of that year the Party's policy reached a logical but ignominious climax in the Beer Hall *Putsch*.[14]

The failure of the *Putsch* marked an important turning-point in the Party's history for with Hitler and other leaders imprisoned during the following year for their treasonable activities in November 1923, the National Socialist movement split into a series of warring factions. The NSDAP rebuilt by Hitler after 1925 was fundamentally different in character, strategy and organisation from the old Party. Hitler now consciously began to see himself as a future dictatorial leader of Germany but accepted that his objectives would have to be realised within the democratic apparatus of the Republic. A quasi-legal, parliamentary strategy was consequently followed, involving the NSDAP in national and local elections whereby it hoped to attract a mass following. Party organisation was further centralised and remodelled under Hitler's absolute control, and during these years of the mid-1920s a hard core of followers – the *Alte Kämpfer* – many of whom came from dissolved *völkisch* and right-wing paramilitary groups, was gathered together. At the same time, and somewhat paradoxically, the Party made a considerable effort, especially in northern Germany where Gregor Strasser was active, to spread its appeal to industrial workers. Even if this appeal was relatively unsuccessful, the NSDAP was broadening out from its essentially Bavarian base into other parts of the country.

The Party's disappointing performance in the *Reichstag* elections of May 1928 was another watershed in its early history, for thereafter it was commited to a more decidedly pro-middle-class nationalist course of action based mainly in rural and small-town areas of northern, central and eastern Germany, which laid the groundwork for its phenomenal electoral success during the early 1930s. The NSDAP was perfectly poised to take full advantage of the deepening economic depression and the profound crisis of political and social identity among the broad range of the Protestant lower *Mittelstand*. Temporary alliances with the traditional conservative Right in the campaign against the Young Plan in 1929 and then in the Harzburg Front two years later strengthened the NSDAP's attraction for the bourgeoisie and helped convince some industrialists that it was deserving of financial support. At the same time, the Party's successful infiltration and eventual domination of many middle-class professional interest associations in towns and in the countryside was a vital contribution to its maturing political stature. By mid-1932, just four years after its dismal showing in the *Reichstag* election of 1928, the NSDAP had become not only the largest party in parliament, but also the most powerful political movement in German history on a platform of strident chauvinism, anti-Marxism, anti-Semitism and the Führer-cult. Later that year when the Party found itself in considerable financial and electoral difficulties and when an alternative strategy of flexibility was being advocated by Gregor Strasser, the crisis was resolved in Hitler's favour by the intervention of élitist power groups representing the old-time conservative–authoritarian ethos in Germany who belatedly perceived in National Socialism the best chance of safeguarding their privileged interests. The NSDAP ultimately came to power, therefore, as the spearhead of a counter-revolutionary, anti-modernist groundswell of opinion which aimed to turn the clock back to attitudes associated with the Wilhelmine Reich, as many scholars would currently argue.

This brings us to a controversial and ongoing feature of the debate about early National Socialism: should the NSDAP be classified as intrinsically 'revolutionary' or 'counter-revolutionary'? A good deal depends, naturally, on the definition of these terms, and at least one historian has recently argued that the events of 1933 constituted a new type of revolution which was quite distinct from the classical pattern of revolution established in 1789 and adherred to throughout the nineteenth century.[15] Most scholars argue that the NSDAP was composed of an unusually large number of contradictions and ambivalences which may, in fact, preclude a definitive answer to this question.[16] It is tempting, and indeed convenient, to conclude that National Socialism was simultaneously revolutionary and counter-revolutionary, or rather, that it combined both reactionary/restorative and progressive/modernist elements in its make-up. As such, the Party could more deftly appeal to a broader section of the population, setting itself up as the embodiment of traditional, honest German virtues *vis-à-vis* the *arriviste*, decadent and Western values of Weimar democracy, and at the same time projecting a tantalising image of hope for a better future in an egalitarian national community (*Volksgemeinschaft*). The National Socialists themselves were strangely uncertain about the historical significance of their victory in 1933. While Goebbels triumphantly announced after a few months in office that 'the year 1789 is hereby eradicated from history',[17] thus stressing the counter-revolutionary character of the NSDAP, the regime was at pains to stress that the year 1933 opened up a new, revolutionary era in German history because National Socialism was, despite certain links with the past, a unique historical force. On the other hand, there is no disagreement among scholars on one basic point: that it was this extraordinary aptitude for appearing to be all things to all men which was a crucial factor in Hitler's success.

There was one very important aspect of the pre-1933 history of the NSDAP missing from scholarly accounts before the early 1970s: what were the underlying social and economic implications of the Republic's collapse and Hitler's triumph? How far were political developments determined by influences relating to social class and the economy? When institutions, organisations, doctrines, programmes and leaders had all been discussed and analysed, it still had to be clearly explained what kind of people, and for what specific reasons, were attracted to National Socialism before 1933. The outstanding service of scholarship in the 1970s and early 1980s has been to take the assessment of what happened in the Weimar years down to the level of the ordinary man and woman in the street. The explanation for his or her electoral choices, membership of this or that political organisation and support for this or that social or economic programme, has been emerging with increasing clarity, thanks to the contributions of scholars such as Michael H. Kater, Peter H. Merkl and Heinrich August Winkler.[18] National Socialism as a social phenomenon is the keyword of this latest approach, which is being more and more supported by the techniques of computer and quantitative analysis. To a considerable degree, also, the methodology and conceptual orientation of Marxism in a broad sense has been an important influence, and historians of the German Democratic Republic, freed to some extent from the rigid Marxist–Leninist orthodoxy of the 1950s and 1960s, have played a useful part in developments. The one event in the West which really put the socio-economic approach on the historiographical map was the 1973 Bochum Conference, and the resulting substantial volume of essays has had an enduring effect on scholars.[19] What this new trend has not challenged, however, is the awareness that the *Machtergreifung*, a term employed by the Nazis to give the impression of their having accomplished a revolutionary deed in 1933, was more prosaically a *Machtübernahme*, a take-over of power within the existing legal and constitutional framework of the Weimar state. There was no storming of the barricades, and no fully fledged civil war against the communists, liberals, Jews or anyone else. The coming together of traditional conservatives and the Nazis ensured that the Hitlerian option and no other, such as a military dictatorship or a presidential Cabinet backed by the army, would result from the chaos of 1932–3. It was an outcome, therefore, which was neither inevitable nor irresistible.

What then, in summary, are the main hypotheses concerning the collapse of the Republic and the success of the NSDAP? First, the intellectual–cultural theories, of which there are several, seek to establish a line of continuity between Hitler and Bismarck, or even Luther. It is argued that the German intellectual and cultural tradition, with an emphasis on authoritarianism, conservatism and militarism, prepared the ground for National Socialism, or, in extreme cases, made National Socialism inevitable. Germany, the argument continues, went its own way independent of the mainstream of Western civilisation – the concept of a German *Sonderweg* which, incidentally, has surfaced with renewed vigour in recent scholarly discussion.[20] The interpretation suffers from several basic weaknesses: it selects only certain aspects of Germany's intellectual–cultural tradition – those which *seem* akin to National Socialism – and ignores others; secondly, other Western countries also had elements of authoritarianism and militarism in their heritage without succumbing ultimately to something like National Socialism; thirdly, at its most absurd, this view in seeing Hitler and Luther in the same tradition overlooks the vast amount of historical experience separating the sixteenth and twentieth centuries. For instance, how does one account for the impact of the Enlightenment in Germany during the eighteenth century in this situation? Finally, the theory implicitly ascribes to Germans a degree of passivity, even docility, which cannot be reconciled very readily with the passionate political commitment shown by so many of them from the November Revolution in 1918 to the campaigns against democracy in the early 1930s. Long-term projections back into the distant past seem at best unconvincing, and at worst, sublimely ridiculous.

Refinements of this interpretation suggest that National Socialism was the final expression of the nineteenth-century Romantic tradition in Germany, or of a late-nineteenth-century chauvinistic, anti-modernist outlook as articulated in the writings of Paul de Lagarde, Julius Langbehn and Friedrich Nietzsche.[21] There is more plausibility here, provided the connection is made between this attitude of anti-modernism and the emergence before 1914 of a developing lower-middle-class radical nationalism. As Eley has underlined in his otherwise polemical and rather pretentious work,[22] the lower-middle class, who later provided the backbone of the National Socialist movement, was evolving its own ideology in opposition to traditional conservatism on the one hand, and to socialism on the other. The *Mittelstand* harboured deep anxieties about their social and economic status in a rapidly changing urban-industrial society, which before 1914 caused it to join racist and ultra-nationalist political organisations in conspicuous numbers. The loss of the war, revolution, economic turmoil and advances by labour all combined to intensify their fears until the point was reached where the NSDAP appeared to be their last hope for survival against big business and organised labour. In this respect, therefore, the more sophisticated intellectual–cultural theory does help to explain why particular sections of German society responded so eagerly to Hitler, so long as the socio-economic dimension of the situation is duly recognised. At the same time, the theory adds considerable weight to the 'continuity' school of thought which insists on German history from 1871 to 1945 being treated as a whole, whether related to the persistence of reactionary/ authoritarian ideas in domestic politics or to aggressive imperialist notions in foreign affairs. Clearly what this means is that the Weimar era cannot be properly understood without developments in Bismarckian and, even more, Wilhelmine Germany being considered.[23] But, of course, this approach does not provide the full story of the Republic's collapse.

The second major interpretation emphasises the Republic's failure to carry through an effective revolutionary transformation of the social, economic and political system in 1918–20, and thus to create an institutional order which would faithfully serve its interests. The old élites were left largely untouched in their positions of influence in the civil service, the judiciary, the military, churches and universities and finally, the economy, from which they helped undermine the Republic. The half-hearted commitment of the ostensibly democratic parties to the Republic and their timid and unimaginative leaders, the argument goes on, meant that sometime before 1933 there was a Republic with few Republicans. This interpretation, dating from the 1950s and early 1960s,[24] also criticises the scope given to its enemies by the liberal Weimar constitution, particularly in respect of its system of proportional representation, which made for permanent cabinet instability, and Article 48, which allowed the President of the Republic extraordinary powers in periods of crisis: under President Hindenburg, always a monarchist at heart, the constitution effectively sanctified actions inimical to the interests of parliamentary democracy.

There is much to be said for this interpretation, but there are at least three basic counter-arguments. Its stress on constitutional and political failures leaves no room for considering crucial social and economic factors such as have been spotlighted by current research. Moreover, constitutional and political structures can function, regardless of their formal character, only if the right kind of people use them, that is, people who basically believe in these structures and give them their unqualified allegiance. Changes in the Weimar constitution, including even the abolition of the system of proportional representation and Article 48, would have been no guarantee against the failure of the Republic while popular attitudes, especially among the middle and upper classes, remained to a large degree hostile to it. It is significant that as early as

June 1920 parliamentary elections produced a majority against the Republic. Finally, of course, this interpretation tells us nothing about National Socialism and why Hitler and not someone else was able to come to power in 1933.

A third view has it that there were certain developments associated with foreign affairs over which the Republic had little or no control and which caused in substantial measure the debacle of 1933. The imposition of the Treaty of Versailles with its war-guilt clause and provision for wholesale reparations, and the subsequent unhelpful even hostile attitude (for instance, the Ruhr occupation) of the Allies are seen as particularly deleterious. The political and psychological impact of these developments on Germans of every political shade of opinion was such that the Republic was immediately denied potential support, while its many enemies were presented with easy ammunition with which to attack her. It is argued that despite Locarno and Germany's entry into the League of Nations in the mid-1920s, and despite the easing of reparations through the Dawes and then Young Plans, the Republic never attained the degree of international esteem which would satisfy the expectations of many Germans. In short, through no great fault of her own, the Republic was regarded by many Germans as a failure in foreign affairs.

While not disputing the difficulties of the Republic in foreign matters, the consensus of opinion among scholars is that this explanation is of limited importance, as a leading foreign policy specialist has recently stressed.[25]

Fourthly, the contribution of economic developments, particularly the hyperinflation of the early 1920s and the Depression of the early 1930s, has been rightly stressed, though only in comparatively recent times has this factor been subjected to probing and refined analysis. Previously the link between economic catastrophe and National Socialism was assumed in a rather facile way rather than being empirically proved. Also, of course, older works on the economic theme had not begun even to consider the wide-ranging and important implications of a crisis-ridden system of organised and monopolistic capitalism and a failed political system. The only valid point which older studies made was that the success of National Socialism would have been inconceivable without the economic depression. The Republic cannot be blamed, of course, for the Depression but it can be for the way it, and particularly Chancellor Brüning, handled the crisis.

Fifthly, there is the argument that amidst the political, social and economic upheavals of the early 1930s, the NSDAP was able to emerge as a force because of its stand against the communists.[26] There are two strands of thought here. First, that the KPD helped smooth Hitler's path by its uncompromising anti-republican line, by splitting the working class through its ill-conceived ultra-leftist strategy, and by its slavish adherence to Moscow. Secondly, that the revolutionary language and style of the KPD facilitated the NSDAP's claim to be the most resolute defender of German national and bourgeois values and interests. The theory is not too compelling because, in the first instance, it ascribes to the KPD a political importance which it never had, and secondly, it unjustly minimises the responsibility for Hitler of the democratic parties and politicians, above all, the SPD. The contribution of anti-Semitism to the NSDAP's success is usually put in the same bracket as that of anti-communism, but is equally unconvincing.[27] Despite the fanaticism with which Hitler and other top Party leaders pursued this integral part of the National Socialist *Weltanschauung*, it is unlikely that many voters gave their support because of it. After all, the NSDAP pursued its violent anti-Semitism between 1925 and 1929 without achieving any significant electoral success.

A sixth interpretation is concerned to indicate the selfish and negatively anti-democratic role played in the early 1930s by the traditional German élites. Marxist-oriented historians in particular have been prominent here. Some of the Marxist–Leninist conspiracy theories coming from the German Democratic Republic, in which monopoly capitalists, imperialists and militarists are implicated, are obviously too far-fetched, but more subtle theories of this kind have developed convincing conceptual and empirical models of the connections centred around common interests between at least certain sections of the élitist groups and the National Socialists, especially in 1932–3.[28] Without such support the NSDAP would not have come to power. Hitler promised the élites not only an attack on Marxism and the Left in general at home, but also rearmament in preparation for economic and political imperialist expansion abroad. An important qualification which needs to be made, however, is that even before the élites could begin to intervene on behalf of the NSDAP, the Party had had to demonstrate to them that it commanded mass popular support. In the absence of such support, the intrigues and manoeuvrings of the élites would have been futile, or at least, of very limited and ephemeral effect. In other words, in rightly attributing considerable blame to the élites for finally allowing Hitler to achieve office, the responsibility of the middle classes who provided the NSDAP's popular support must not be overlooked or under-estimated.

Finally, earlier studies, in particular, ascribed much importance to the personal role of Hitler, underlining his brilliant opportunism and spellbinding oratory.[29] The Führer's pivotal and indispensable role and contribution to his Party's success is undeniable, and there may even be a case for saying that National Socialism was Hitlerism before 1933, though recent work on Gregor Strasser suggests that an alternative form of non-Hitlerian National Socialism was not entirely inconceivable in certain circumstances.[30] Besides this, though, and partly influenced by the current controversy between 'intentionalists' and 'functionalists' over Hitler's role in the governmental structure of the Third Reich,[31] no scholar would today seriously contend that the efforts of one man can be said to have been the most important element in a situation as complex as the Weimar Republic in the early 1930s. Hitler's personal contribution was conditioned and made successful by a range of factors outside his control. Furthermore, it is historically untenable to allow one man to be made the scapegoat for the failures and weaknesses of a whole generation of Germans.

No monocausal explanation of the Weimar Republic's collapse is possible because of the profound complexity and wide-ranging inter-action of a conglomeration of diverse factors. It remains a primary task of scholarship to bring these various explanations, including those emanat-ing from the research of the last decade, into a general, scholarly history of the Republic. Eyck's book, once considered the best political account of these years, is now patently out of date, not least because of its cursory treatment of those social and economic aspects which are the focal point of current research.[32] More recent general histories have signally failed to fill the gap. Nicholls produced a clearly written but brief and superficial account aimed at a non-specialist audience, and failed to take the opportunity in a second edition of the book to incorporate the fruits of scholarship in the 1970s which he incomprehensibly decided had not materially changed what he had written earlier.[33] During the last few years works by Köhler, Stürmer, Flemming, Gessner, Michalka/ Niedhart and Erdmann/Schulze have made little advance.[34] Indeed, in the latter work there is an unashamed dismissal of the importance of the approach which highlights social and economic factors, and as a whole it constitutes a veritable throwback to the analytical methods and priorities of a quarter of a century ago. The quest to determine the relationship between politics and social and economic developments within the general framework of the republican period, however, must continue.[35] The rise of the NSDAP has, of course, to form a critically important part of such a book, and the prevailing preoccupation of scholars with analysis of the Party's social character dovetails appropriately with similar trends in wider Weimar studies. The present volume aims, within the terms of reference already intimated in the Preface, to help prepare the way of this enterprise by establishing a clear and balanced historiographical vista on the Nazi component of the Weimar Republic's tragic history.

Notes

1   A useful overview is provided by Pierre Aycoberry, *The Nazi Question. An Essay on the Interpretations of National Socialism (1922–1975)* (London: 1981). Earlier historio-graphical works worth noting include Andrew Whiteside, 'The Nature and Origins of National Socialism', *Journal of Central European Affairs*, XVII, 1957, pp. 48–73;

12 *The Nazi* Machtergreifung

John L. Snell (ed.), *The Nazi Revolution. Germany's Guilt or Germany's Fate?* (Boston, Mass: 1959); Eric C. Kollmann, 'Reinterpreting Modern German History: the Weimar Republic', *Journal of Central European Affairs*, XXI, 1961/62, pp. 434–51; Bundeszentrale für Politische Bildung (ed.), *Rückschau nach 30 Jahren. Hitlers Machtergreifung in der Sicht deutscher und ausländischer Historiker* (Bonn: 1963); John S. Conway, '"Machtergreifung" or "Due Process of History": the Historiography of Hitler's Rise to Power', *Historical Journal*, 7, 1965, pp. 399–413; Wolfgang Ruge, 'Zur bürgerlichen Geschichtsschreibung der BRD über die Weimarer Republik', *Zeitschrift für Geschichtswissenschaft*, 22, 1974, pp. 677–700; Hans Mommsen, 'Aufstieg der NSDAP und nationalsozialistisches Herrschaftssystem. Eine Problemskizze', in Annelise Mannzmann (ed.), *Hitlerwelle und historische Fakten* (Königstein/Ts: 1979), pp. 14 ff.

2 Arthur Rosenberg, *Geschichte der Deutschen Republik* (Karlsbad: 1935).

3 cf. Kurt Sontheimer, 'The Weimar Republic: Failure and Prospects of German Democracy', in E. J. Feuchtwanger (ed.), *Upheaval and Continuity. A Century of German History* (London: 1973), pp. 101–15.

4 Ferdinand Friedenberg, *Die Weimarer Republik* (Berlin: 1946); Wilhelm Hoegener, *Die Verratene Republik. Geschichte der deutschen Gegenrevolution* (Munich: 1958); Otto Braun, *Von Weimar zu Hitler* (Hamburg: 1949); Friedrich Stampfer, *Die ersten vierzehn Jahre der deutschen Republik* (Hamburg: 1952); Arnold Brecht, *Prelude to Silence. The End of the German Republic* (New York: 1944); Franz von Papen, *Memoirs* (London: 1952). The latter's second set of memoirs, *Vom Scheitern einer Demokratie, 1930–1933* (Mainz: 1968), offers little improvement.

5 Friedrich Meinecke, *Die Deutsche Katastrophe* (Wiesbaden: 1946); Gerhard Ritter, *Europa und die deutsche Frage. Betrachtungen über die geschichtliche Eigenart des deutschen Staatsdenkens* (Munich: 1948).

6 Ludwig Dehio, *Deutschland und die Weltpolitik im 20. Jahrhundert* (Munich: 1955).

7 Godfrey Scheele, *The Weimar Republic: Overture to the Third Reich* (London: 1946).

8 Karl Dietrich Bracher, *Die Auflösung der Weimarer Republik. Eine Studie zum Problem des Machtverfalls in der Demokratie* (Stuttgart: 1956; new and enlarged edn, 1960). Bracher has recently reaffirmed the validity of his major thesis in 'Demokratie und Machtvakuum: zum Problem des Parteienstaats in der Auflösung der Weimarer Republik', in Karl Dietrich Erdmann and Hagen Schulze (eds), *Weimar. Selbstpreisgabe einer Demokratie. Eine Bilanz heute* (Düsseldorf: 1980), pp. 109–34.

9 Karl Dietrich Bracher, Wolfgang Sauer and Gerhard Schulz, *Die Nationalsozialistiche Machtergreifung. Studien zur Errichtung des totalitären Herrschaftssystems in Deutschland 1933/34* (Cologne: 1960); Erich Matthias and Rudolf Morsey (eds), *Das Ende der Parteien 1933* (Düsseldorf: 1960).

10 William L. Shirer, *The Rise and Fall of the Third Reich. A History of Nazi Germany* (London: 1960).

11 Rohan D'O Butler, *The Roots of National Socialism 1783–1933* (London: 1941); A. J. P. Taylor, *The Course of German History* (London: 1945); Edmond Vermeil, *Germany's Three Reichs* (London: 1944).

12 The classic critique of Shirer is Klaus P. Epstein, 'Shirer's History of Nazi Germany', *Review of Politics*, 23, 1961, pp. 230–45.

13 Karl Dietrich Bracher, *Die Deutsche Diktatur. Entstehung, Struktur, Folgen des Nationalsozialismus* (Cologne: 1969); Martin Broszat, *Der Nationalsozialismus. Weltanschauung, Programm und Wirklichkeit* (Stuttgart: 1960); Wolfgang Horn, *Führerideologie und Parteiorganisation in der NSDAP (1919–1933)* (Düsseldorf: 1972); Albrecht Tyrell, *Führer befiehl ... Selbstzeugnisse aus der 'Kampfzeit' der NSDAP. Dokumentation und Analyse* (Düsseldorf: 1969); Gerhard Schulz, *Aufstieg des Nationalsozialismus. Krise und Revolution in Deutschland* (Berlin: 1975); Dietrich Orlow, *The History of the Nazi Party, 1919–1933* (Pittsburgh, Pa: 1969); Joseph Nyomarkay, *Charisma and Factionalism in the Nazi Party* (Minneapolis, Minn: 1967); Harold J. Gordon, *Hitler and the Beer Hall Putsch* (Princeton, NJ: 1972); Henry A. Turner,

Faschismus und Kapitalismus in Deutschland (Göttingen: 1972). The full range of publications in the field can be consulted in Peter D. Stachura, *The Weimar Era and Hitler 1918–1933: A Critical Bibliography* (Oxford: 1977); Peter Hüttenberger, *Bibliographie zum Nationalsozialismus* (Göttingen: 1980); and H. Kehr and J. Langmaid, *The Nazi Era 1919–1945. A Select Bibliography from Early Roots to 1980* (London: 1982).

14 The most important study of these early years is Albrecht Tyrell, *Vom 'Trommler' Zum 'Führer'. Der Wandel von Hitlers Selbstverständnis zwischen 1919 and 1924 und die Entwicklung der NSDAP* (Munich: 1975). A useful bibliographical essay covering works on the same period is Hellmuth Auerbach, 'Hitlers politische Lehrjahre und die Münchener Gesellschaft 1919–1923', *Vierteljahrshefte für Zeitgeschichte*, 25, 1977, pp. 1–45.

15 Leonard Krieger, 'Nazism: Highway or Byway?', *Central European History*, 11, 1978, pp. 3–22, esp. p. 16.

16 Karl Dietrich Bracher, 'Tradition und Revolution im Nationalsozialismus', in Manfred Funke (ed.), *Hitler, Deutschland und die Mächte. Materialien zur Aussenpolitik des Dritten Reiches* (Düsseldorf: 1976), pp. 17–29; Eugen Weber, 'Revolution? Counter-Revolution? What Revolution?', in Walter Laqueur (ed.), *Fascism. A Reader's Guide* (London: 1976), pp. 435–68; Hans Mommsen, 'National Socialism: Continuity and Change', ibid., pp. 151–92.

17 Josef Goebbels, *Revolution der Deutschen* (Oldenburg: 1933), p. 155, speech of 1 April 1933.

18 Their work is referred to in detail in the first essay in this volume by Stachura. The book by Richard F. Hamilton, *Who Voted For Hitler?* (Princeton, NJ: 1982), was not to hand before this volume was completed in June 1982.

19 Hans Mommsen, Dietmar Petzina and Bernd Weisbrod (eds), *Industrielles System und Politische Entwicklung in der Weimarer Republik* (Düsseldorf: 1974).

20 cf. David Blackbourn and Geoff Eley, *Mythen deutscher Geschichtsschreibung. Die gescheiterte bürgerliche Revolution von 1848* (Frankfurt: 1980); David P. Calleo, *The German Problem Reconsidered. Germany and the World Order, 1870–Present* (London: 1979).

21 Fritz Stern, *The Politics of Cultural Despair. A Study in the Rise of the Germanic Ideology* (Berkeley, Calif: 1961).

22 Geoff Eley, *Reshaping the German Right. Radical Nationalism and Political Change After Bismarck* (New Haven, Conn: 1980). See H. A. Winkler's justifiably hyper-critical review of the book in *Journal of Modern History*, 54, 1982, no. 1 (March), pp. 170–6.

23 cf. Fritz Fischer, *Griff nach der Weltmacht* (Düsseldorf: 1961); H. U. Wehler, *Das deutsche Kaiserreich 1871–1914* (Göttingen: 1974).

24 cf. Theodor Eschenburg (ed.), *Die improvisierte Demokratie* (Munich: 1963). Taking a similar line despite being published quite a few years later, and clearly out of date historiographically is Anthony J. Nicholls and Erich Matthias (eds): *German Democracy and The Triumph of Hitler. Essays in Recent German History* (London: 1971).

25 Andreas Hillgruber, 'Unter dem Schatten von Versailles – die aussenpolitische Belastung der Weimarer Republik', in Erdmann and Schulze (eds), *Weimar*.

26 A view of conservative historians such as Karl Dietrich Erdmann. See his *Die Weimarer Republik* (Stuttgart: 1973, 9th edn).

27 cf. Eva G. Reichmann, *Hostages of Civilization. The Social Sources of National Socialist Antisemitism* (London: 1950). Stressing both anti-communism and anti-Semitism is Milton Mayer, *They Thought They Were Free* (Chicago: 1955).

28 One of the most stimulating of recent examples is David Abraham, *The Collapse of the Weimar Republic. Political Economy and Crisis* (Princeton, NJ: 1981).

29 Alan Bullock, *Hitler. A Study in Tyranny* (London: 1952).

30 Udo Kissenkoetter, *Gregor Strasser und die NSDAP* (Stuttgart: 1978); Peter D. Stachura, *Gregor Strasser and the Rise of Nazism* (London: 1983).

31   Klaus Hildebrand, 'Nationalsozialismus ohne Hitler? Das Dritte Reich als For-schungsgegenstand der Geschichtswissenschaft', *Geschichte in Wissenschaft und Unterricht*, 31, 1980, pp. 289–304; and for a contrary view, Timothy Mason, 'Intention and Explanation. A current controversy about the Interpretation of National Socialism', in Gerhard Hirschfeld and Lothar Kettenacker (eds), *Der 'Führerstaat'. Mythos und Realität. Studien zur Struktur und Politik des Dritten Reiches* (Stuttgart: 1981), pp. 23–42.

32   Erich Eyck, *Geschichte der Weimarer Republik*, 2 vols (Zurich: 1954–6).

33   Anthony J. Nicholls, *Weimar and the Rise of Hitler* (London: 1968); the second edn was published in 1979.

34   Henning Köhler, *Geschichte der Weimarer Republik* (Berlin: 1981), a very short general survey; Michael Stürmer (ed.), *Die Weimarer Republik. Belagerte Civitas* (Königstein/ Ts. 1980); Jens Flemming and Claus-Dieter Krohn (eds), *Die Republik von Weimar* (Düsseldorf: 1979); Dieter Gessner, *Das Ende der Weimarer Republik* (Darmstadt: 1978); Wolfgang Michalka and Gottfried Niedhart (eds), *Die ungeliebte Republik. Dokumentation zur Innen-und Aussenpolitik Weimars, 1918–1933* (Munich: 1980); Erdmann and Schulze (eds), *Weimar*.

35   Pointers in this direction have come from a number of edited volumes, including Karl Holl (ed.), *Wirtschaftskrise und liberale Demokratie* (Göttingen: 1978); Dirk Stegmann, Bernd-Jürgen Wendt and Peter-Christian Witt (eds), *Industrielle Gesellschaft und politisches System. Beiträge zur politischen Sozialgeschichte* (Bonn: 1978); Richard J. Bessel and E. J. Feuchtwanger (eds), *Social Change and Political Development in Weimar Germany* (London: 1981). A valuable reference work is Thomas Trumpp and Renate Köhne (eds), *Archivbestände zur Wirtschafts-und Sozialgeschichte der Weimarer Republik. Übersicht über Quellen in Archiven der BRD* (Boppard: 1979).

2 The Nazis, the Bourgeoisie and the Workers during the Kampfzeit

PETER D. STACHURA

Ideas concerning the social composition of the NSDAP's early membership and electoral constituency have begun to be refined only in comparatively recent times when, at last, scholars have shown a readiness to utilise a variety of methodological and conceptual tools drawn from a wide range of the social sciences. Until this initiative was taken, discussion in this important sphere of Nazi studies was somewhat vague and unscientific, and based for the most part on certain ideological perceptions or educated conjecture and observation. The precision which quantitative sociological analysis has now brought to the debate is striking, and has allowed significant empirical research to emerge. The course towards a more sophisticated and accurate comprehension of the nature of the Party's following before 1933 can be briefly outlined.

Communist or Marxist views of National Socialism during the 1920s and early 1930s were numerous, and although there was widespread appreciation of its links with the bourgeoisie, uncertainty about which particular sections of this amorphous class were directly involved was paramount.[1] A number of German Communist leaders had been aware from an early date of the potential attraction of National Socialism for the masses, including the proletariat, and Klara Zetkin for one had recognised that this situation was at least partly due to the deficiencies in the KPD's approach.[2] But her admonition went unheeded amidst the confusion which dominated communist discussion of the NSDAP for most of the pre-1933 period. From outside the KPD Trotsky postulated a clear connection between the Nazis and the petty bourgeoisie but, of course, he was unable to substantiate his judgement with empirical data.[3] The correlation of the lower-middle class with fascism none the less fitted in nicely with a general Marxist outlook which regarded this class as the embodiment of political and social reaction, and hence a principal adversary of the proletarian and labour movements.

The communist perception of National Socialism became hopelessly obscured by the development of the KPD's ultra-leftist strategy in the late 1920s which identified the Social Democrats as 'social fascists'. In the consequent universal and undiscerning denunciation of fascism virtually everything and everyone who was simply non-communist was labelled 'fascist'. Not until after 1933 when the Third Reich appeared to be consolidating rather than disintegrating, as the communists had prophesised, did the Comintern as a whole adopt a more differentiated view of National Socialism and its social base. Dimitrov's celebrated description of fascism at the Seventh Congress of the Comintern in 1935 as 'the open terroristic dictatorship of the most reactionary, the most chauvinistic, the most imperialistic elements of finance capital' was adopted as the official communist line and became the basis of the broad Marxist–Leninist standpoint on the subject. But it was if anything a handicap rather than a help in coming to terms with the hard realities of the NSDAP's mass following until long-overdue modifications surfaced during the post-1945 period.

Outside the communist camp reactions to the character of the NSDAP were similarly uninformed. Even those contemporaries directly in touch with the Party whether as active members or sympathisers, such as Albert Krebs, the one-time *Gauleiter* of Hamburg, Kurt Ludecke and Konrad Heiden, paid little attention to the question of who these Nazis really were that they were describing.[4] The first steps towards a keener understanding of the Party's social complexion came, in fact, from beyond the political world. In an important study published in 1932 Theodore Geiger surveyed the sociology of the German middle class, and in stressing differences of occupation and interest within this class identified the essentially petty bourgeois support for the NSDAP.[5] His conclusion was endorsed a few years later from an unofficial, independent Marxist source, Arthur Rosenberg's study of fascism as a mass phenomenon using the methods of electoral sociology.[6] The Columbia University professor, Theodore Abel, adopted a less rigorous approach when in 1934 he collected the autobiographical statements of some 581 Nazis who had submitted entries to an essay competition organised by him.[7] Unfortunately it was not until forty years later that his data was subjected to serious analysis by Peter Merkl.[8] During the early war years, finally, Erich Fromm noted the susceptibility of the petty bourgeoisie to National Socialism because of the defeat and collapse of Germany in 1918 and the subsequent hyperinflation and economic depression.[9] These studies collectively underlined a fundamental relationship between the early NSDAP and the lower-middle classes, but the complexities and details of that relationship as well as the motivating factors present in the situation awaited investigation. In other words, pre-1945 knowledge about National Socialism's early social character was still at an inchoate stage on both the communist and non-communist sides of the argument.

The early postwar literature on the NSDAP in the West was too preoccupied with the enormous task of coming to terms with the unprecedented enormity of Nazi barbarism to have much time for detailed enquiry into the people who made up the movement at the grassroots level. While works proliferated on diplomacy, war aims, concentration camps, the resistance, the machinery of terror and the top leadership of the Third Reich, historians neglected the broader sociological dimensions of their theme. One notable exception to this trend on an empirical level was Broszat's account of the Berlin NSDAP during the mid-1920s which emphasised the high percentage of unskilled workers in the Party membership, thus reflecting a certain pseudo-proletarian style in the propaganda methods employed by *Gauleiter* Josef Goebbels.[10] The most influential theory regarding the middle-class nature of fascism, however, was provided in Lipset's refined piece of electoral sociology published in 1959.[11] His thesis that National Socialism before 1933 represented a radicalism of the bourgeois centre was an important and stimulating contribution to the debate, even though it is no longer held to be valid. He took no account of new voters and previous non-voters in his calculations and ignored the crucial role of the upper classes in the rise of fascism. How these different sections of bourgeois society ultimately came together in support of Hitler was not explained. Consequently Lipset's theory did not address itself to the critical question of the functional relationship between fascism and capitalism which remains, of course, a highly controversial area of discussion. His brief character sketch of the typical NSDAP voter in 1932 as 'an independent member of the middle classes, male Protestant, living on a farm or in a small locality, an ex-voter for the centrist or regionalist party, hostile to big industry' takes us only so far, particularly as Winkler has shown that the broad middle-class voters had deserted the two major liberal parties, the German Democratic Party (DDP) and German People's Party (DVP), long before the rise of the NSDAP.[12]

In the German Democratic Republic (DDR), at the same time, the debate followed a predictable and generally unenlightening course. The rigid Marxist–Leninist orthodoxy which dominated East German historiography about Germany's recent past, and which was strengthened by the atmosphere of the Cold War, determined that the NSDAP be regarded above all as a tool of the grande bourgeoisie – the so-called monopoly capitalists, financiers, estate-owners and militarists. There was no room in this arid approach for the inclusion of the *Mittelstand*, a basic omission to which Andreas Dorpalen has rightly drawn attention.[13] By concentrating exclusively on the upper classes' alleged responsibility for bringing the NSDAP to power, the East Germans were simply distorting the whole social and political circumstances of that period in order to satisfy their preconceived ideological-political prejudices. Only from about the mid-1960s has a slightly less doctrinaire attitude appeared, thus giving rise to a more interesting conceptual position in some cases, and complementing the impressive empirical information which a number of East German historians have been assembling. This trend has come about for various reasons, but is mainly the result of a more settled political atmosphere in Europe generally once the Cold War ended, and also in response to the increasingly refined methods of investigation into National Socialism being displayed by Western historians.

Abandoning to a large extent the theories of totalitarianism which were so popular in the West during the 1950s and early 1960s despite their perfunctory treatment of National Socialism as a social phenomenon,[14] scholars began developing an understanding of newer disciplines relevant to this topic. The way was opened up for the advance of political science in particular, and in Germany valuable work was published. From this basis, supplemented by the new electoral sociology initiated by Lipset, developed a more probing attitude not only in relation to fascism's links with different social classes, but also with specific sub-groups, especially within the *Mittelstand*. Marxist methodology, often in adapted forms, was extensively applied. It was not long before the computer came into vogue, making possible detailed assessments of Party membership lists, or fragments of them, which are available in archives. The results of computer-aided analysis have been most impressive, as illustrated by the extensive and important contribution made by Michael H. Kater.[15] A fuller picture of the early Nazis than ever before has been produced, though this has had the overall result of enlarging upon in considerable detail earlier broad notions about the essentially petty bourgeois structure of the NSDAP before 1933. Current research is poised to launch into a more advanced stage of computer analysis. The advantages (as well as the limitations) of the quantitative method have been persuasively indicated by Kater, who has justified, in particular, the use of sampling from the huge, central personnel file of NSDAP members located at the Berlin Document Center.[16] To work through the 8 or 9 million members' files would be feasible, even with the aid of computers, only if there were a large team of researchers and an abundance of funds available. Realistically work has to proceed on the basis of representative samples, as Conan Fischer and Mathilde Jamin have done recently, on a lesser scale, for the SA (Stormtroopers).[17] The result is to accentuate the empirical foundations of research, but obviously where the details are more certain the pertinent conceptual models can be all the more securely constructed.

An allied aspect of the problem concerns the issue of the motives of those who supported the NSDAP before 1933. The point of the exercise is to explain the reasons for the responses of certain social groups at certain times. To date, results have been mixed, or at least incomplete. The variables in play are not always of a concrete nature: how can emotional impulses, for example, be properly evaluated? The gap cannot be said to have been filled by psychologically based historical studies which, as a whole, have not attained the scholarly level set by Merkl and Loewenberg.[18] A more promising avenue of research concerns the applicability of the Nazi phenomenon to theories of modernisation. The foundations were laid during the 1960s by the provocative studies of Barrington Moore, Ralf Dahrendorf and David Schoenbaum which suggest that National Socialism, despite being an anti-modernist movement, brought Germany by brutal means into the modern world.[19] This challenging hypothesis has more recently been tested, along the lines of statistical analysis, but with inconclusive results, by Matzerath and Volkmann.[20] The specific question of whether the pre-1933 NSDAP was supported in the main by 'losers' in the modernisation process has yet to receive a definitive answer, the excellent studies by Jannen and Rogowski notwithstanding.[21] Clearly, however, this is an interesting and important development which will undoubtedly help to sharpen our perception of the early phase of the movement.

Mention must be made of a number of particular difficulties which have arisen in research into the social character of National Socialism. There is, in the first instance, the problem of how to categorise social class in a period of history which was so extensively destabilised by the aftermath of military defeat, institutional collapse and profound economic dislocation. In these circumstances, it is not possible to assume an orderly, neat arrangement of people into social groups, and Merkl has been prominent in arguing that the middle-class thesis relating to early National Socialism is unacceptable for this reason, especially because, in his view, there was not a permanent, stable and easily definable lower-middle class.[22] During the Weimar Republic, the process of proletarianisation among the middle classes, which has yet to receive the in-depth examination it deserves, undoubtedly blurred the dividing lines between the respective classes. The loss of white-collar employment and the collapse of many small or family businesses during the early 1920s and then the early 1930s contributed substantially to a levelling-down among bourgeois groups, some of whom consequently discovered that they had to adapt to a working-class life style, income level and educational opportunities. But while Merkl's point can be recognised and conceded to some degree, it is one which requires sound quantitative support before it can be allowed to deflect from the task of ascertaining the nature of the *Mittelstand*–NSDAP relationship. Social categorisation cannot be absolute in a society as deeply torn by upheaval as the Weimar Republic, but allowing for the obvious imperfections it must continue as a valid and appropriate tool of investigation.

An allied problem is created by the very pronounced fluctuation in membership of the NSDAP before 1933. There was a surprisingly large turnover, especially in large cities during the depression years, which imposes certain constraints on research. In the same vein, the passage of the Party through various distinctive phases of development and involving major changes in organisation, ideology and propaganda, adds to the difficulty of achieving a precise definition of social class.[23] A further problem, highlighted by Genuneit and Kocka, relates to the question of which occupational groups are to be included under the headings 'middle class', 'lower-middle class' and 'working class': to which of these, for instance, do skilled workers (*Handwerker*) belong?[24] Kater's inclusion of this group in his lower *Mittelstand* category has been justifiably criticised, but otherwise this is an area in which hard and fast rules are impossible to formulate. Controversy is bound to continue.

The type of person attracted to the NSDAP during the years 1919 to 1923 has been well established by Kater and, to a lesser degree, by Douglas.[25] Their research, based on Party membership lists dated late 1923 and from 1919 to July 1921 respectively, shows convincingly that the NSDAP was a largely lower-middle-class movement, male, and rooted mainly in small-town or rural areas. The inadequacies of earlier studies of the pre-*Putsch* NSDAP by Werner Maser, Georg Franz-Willing, Dietrich Orlow and Robin Lemman, which suggested a lower-middle-class or vaguely bourgeois predominance on the basis of fragmentary or limited data, have now been strikingly revealed.[26] The character of the Party underwent a fundamental transformation following the failed *Putsch*. Whereas it had been constructed as an intrinsically counter-revolutionary, anti-democratic élitist movement before 1923 and pursuing a line of direct military activity against the Republic, it adopted a more cautious, long-term approach when it was refounded. The struggle was now taken along the parliamentary road, in practice if not exactly in spirit, and elections were openly and violently contested. The NSDAP sought to extend into all areas of public life in order to attract the mandatory mass support. One feature which did not change, however, was the social character of the bulk of the Party's following: whether during the relatively quiet years of the Republic in the mid-1920s, or during the Depression years later on it was the lower *Mittelstand*, comprising small businessmen, artisans, lower-ranking white-collar workers and civil servants, and small farmers, who provided the backbone. This is indisputably shown, above all, in excellent studies by Kater, Childers and Weber.[27]

The response to Hitler of the small business community (*gewerbliche Mittelstand*) and the reasons behind it have been convincingly analysed by Winkler.[28] The devastating effect of hyperinflation and Depression pushed this group, which had enjoyed considerable protection during the Wilhelmine era, increasingly towards the political Right throughout the 1920s. Whereas they had supported the liberal parties in the main at the beginning of the Republican period, their disillusionment at the failure of these parties to protect their economic and social status from organised, large-scale capitalism and labour resulted in a transient flirtation with the DNVP and a few splinter bourgeois organisations before the small businessmen arrived on the doorstep of the NSDAP.

What they were really looking for was a restoration of their former privileges, and in the NSDAP they perceived an agreeably reactionary, anti-modernist party which would put both the big capitalists and the workers in their place. These considerations, rather than any clear affinity with the Party's grandiose foreign policy aims, ultra-nationalism or even anti-Semitism, provided the major impetus behind the small businessmen's reaction. Only during the Third Reich when it emerged that the regime was favouring big business did the commercial middle classes realise how mistaken they had been in placing their hopes on Hitler.[29]

Other groups of the 'old' or traditional *Mittelstand* had by 1930, and more decidedly by 1932, demonstrated their commitment to the NSDAP for a variety of reasons. The artisan–handicrafts sector was conspicuously represented for very much the same kind of socio-economic reasons as the small businessmen, though there were distinctive regional variations in the degree of their support, as Krohn/Stegmann and Domurad have argued.[30] The growing resentment of primary schoolteachers over their diminishing social status in an increasingly materialistic society, poor salary levels, reduced promotion prospects and augmenting fears of redundancy brought many of them into the Party's following.[31] Another important and well-documented source of Nazi support was, of course, the small farming community which, afflicted by a severe agrarian slump before the onset of the industrial depression, perceived at an early date the deficiencies of their traditional political and occupational representative organisations and found little difficulty in accommodating themselves to the *Blut und Boden* hocus-pocus propagated by the NSDAP from the late 1920s.[32] By the time of the *Reichstag* election in July 1932 the Party's support among the old *Mittelstand* in small-town or rural parts of Protestant northern, central and eastern Germany was substantial and unmistakable.

Recent scholarship has stressed the need to distinguish between the old and new *Mittelstand*. The latter, consisting chiefly of white-collar salaried employees in industry, commerce and the civil service, were rather slower in opting for Hitler. Using a regressive analysis of voting in a sample of 135 'geographically distributed, socially diverse and predominately Protestant communities ranging in size from 15,000 to over a million inhabitants', Childers goes so far as to argue that the relationship between the NSDAP and the new middle class 'was surprisingly tenuous, even after the onset of the Depression'.[33] He stresses that civil servants gave more support to the Party between 1930 and 1932 than the *Angestellte*. On balance, it may be that Childers is underestimating the extent of *Angestellte* support for the NSDAP and his assertion that at the July 1932 election this group voted largely for the DNVP appears dubious. The doubts expressed by Coyner about the authentic bourgeois status of the *Angestellte* are surely unfounded.[34]

They usually had an exaggerated and tenacious notion of being middle class, and were anxious to preserve that status in the face of economic catastrophe. On the other hand, it was almost certainly the case that lower-ranking civil servants formed a more united and significant body of support for the Party than their counterparts in industry and commerce.

The response of the *Mittelstand* to Hitler has been detailed, with varying degrees of success, in a large number of regional studies involving many of the politically most important areas of Weimar Germany. Allen's classic study of Northeim ('Thalburg'), Noakes's heavily empirical analysis of Lower Saxony, Pridham's well-researched study of Bavaria and Heberle's pioneering survey of Schleswig-Holstein are probably the most illuminating.[35] Regrettably, scholarly studies of the situation in Saxony and Thuringia are still awaited. The fact that both areas now lie in the German Democratic Republic immediately poses problems of accessibility to archival material, while the communist authorities are usually not at all keen to allow Western scholars to examine sensitive documents relating to the Weimar period in general, and to the NSDAP in particular. Until this situation changes for the better, an important gap in the historiography of early National Socialism will remain unfilled.

The particular problems in extending this hypothesis of lower-middle-class preponderance to the membership of the NSDAP and its ancillary organisations have been outlined by Stachura.[36] While the membership of the entire movement corresponded by and large to the background of its electorate, this pattern was broken in specific leadership cadres, such as the *Reichstag* faction and *Gauleiter* corps,[37] and in certain ancillary groups, notably the NS Doctors' League and Lawyers' League. In these cases, upwardly mobile elements of the professional classes and of the upper-middle classes were more numerous. In broad terms, the reserve with which most sections of the upper-middle classes regarded National Socialism began to break down only in 1931/2.[38] The support given to it before that date by university students was exceptional in that class. But by the summer of 1932 the increasingly obvious ineptitude of the DNVP, coupled with the NSDAP's growing identification with traditional conservative and bourgeois interests (Harzburg Front, links with big business, decline of the Party's 'left-wing', and so on), produced a new disposition. It was not until Hitler was actually in office, however, that the upper classes came over in support of the NSDAP in anything like the scale of the lower-middle classes. Then, in 1933/4, they were inclined to do so for reasons of social and career opportunism rather than of genuine political and ideological conviction.

Into quite a different category come the élitist sections of German society. The large landowners and big industrialists, represented by organisations like the *Reichslandbund* and *Reichsverband der deutschen*

Industrie, awakened to the possibilities of power-sharing with the NSDAP at a very late date. Only following the collapse of the reactionary–authoritarian Papen government and as a result of the fears aroused by the *Querfront* strategy and pseudo-social concepts of the Schleicher administration did these powerful groups, acting through their figureheads such as President Hindenburg and his entourage and Papen, intervene in December 1932 to forge the Nazi–Nationalist alliance which a few weeks later put Hitler in the Reich Chancellory. By then the élites saw the NSDAP as a bulwark against the Left and a possible communist revolution, and also perceived the enormous advantages to themselves of Hitler's expansionist ambitions in foreign policy, his demands for extensive rearmament, and, as Volkmann has ably shown, his *Grossraumwirtschaft* ideas for the economy.[39] In 1932/3 the German élites backed Hitler in order to preserve and strengthen their own anachronistic privileges and power behind a smokescreen of chauvinism and spurious appeals to national honour.

The counter-argument to the proposition that the NSDAP was a party of bourgeois integration by 1933, albeit with a lower-middle-class substance and orientation, rests essentially on an evaluation of the nature and extent of its relationship with the working class. Involved here is a basic question: can the NSDAP be meaningfully described as a popular or people's party (*Volkspartei*)? Winkler argues the NSDAP emerged as an 'absolutist' or 'totalitarian *Volkspartei*', while Mommsen prefers the description 'negative *Volkspartei*'.[40] Other historians, like Merkl, Mühlberger and Falter, are simply content to call the NSDAP a 'people's party' on the basis of an alleged strong proletarian element in its following.[41] The discussion centres on the post-1925 period because no one has seriously contended that before the *Putsch* of 1923 the NSDAP was anything but a lower-middle-class party. Indeed, if anything, it had acquired a deserved reputation by 1923 for being positively anti-working-class in outlook: Cahill's study of the infamous May Day demonstrations in Munich that year makes this point absolutely clear.[42]

The NSDAP's ideological and propagandistic emphasis on what is quaintly referred to usually as 'German socialism' during the time between its refoundation in 1925 and the *Reichstag* election in May 1928, led many contemporary observers and some later historians, notably Kele,[43] to conclude that the working-class component of the Party was extensive and permanent. But although it may be acknowledged that industrial workers in certain parts of Germany where this socialistic appeal was at its strongest – for example, in Berlin, the Ruhr and Westphalia[44] – were attracted in relatively large numbers to Hitler, the Party retained its mainly lower-middle-class character across the country as a whole. Kater convincingly estimates that workers constituted a mere 7 per cent of Party membership 1925–9, while Tyrell puts it at 8·5 per cent for the period before 1930.[45] Several factors account for this pattern, beginning with the hollowness of 'German socialism' as an ideological concept. Based on a petty bourgeois *enragé*'s vision of a society in which the influence of organised capitalism and labour seemed to be increasing daily, this type of 'socialism' was totally divorced from the main currents of German and European socialist thought and tradition, and amounted to little more than a vacuous romantic–Utopian view of urban-industrial society. Naturally the organised and class-conscious working class were thoroughly unimpressed. Moreover, Turner has underlined the fact that Hitler was never seriously committed to this orientation in the Party's appeal. The Führer was unwavering in his belief that private property and capitalist enterprise should be untouched by revolutionary prescriptions, and he remained hostile to the idea of a Party-sponsored trade union movement.[46] His stance consequently did much to undermine what Orlow has called the NSDAP's 'urban plan' during the mid-1920s.[47]

A critical problem in the historiography of the early period of the NSDAP's history, and which relates directly to the role of workers in the Party, involves the status and meaning of the so-called 'Nazi Left'. The description, admittedly, implies a blatant contradiction in terms, but the matter is not that simple. Reinhard Kühnl focused attention on this subject in his untidy but pioneering and provocative monograph.[48] He argues that there was a coherent left-wing in the NSDAP between 1925, when the Strasser brothers became active with their radical brand of National Socialism in north Germany, and 1930, when Otto Strasser ostentatiously left the Party along with a few hundred other reputed 'socialists'. Kühnl goes into considerable detail about the organisation, ideology and personnel of this 'Nazi Left', but ultimately his hypothesis is unacceptable. He overestimates the coherence of this alleged grouping as an ideological force, although rightly stresses the intrinsically petty bourgeois nature of the alternative draft Party programme drawn up by Gregor Strasser and others in 1925. The Draft differed from the official programme of 1920 only in its greater emphasis on its vaguely socialist parts. By paying scant regard to the interests of either the industrial workers or agricultural labourers the Draft can be deemed a total failure only as a legitimate socialist statement. The obsession with extreme nationalism, racism, imperialism and anti-Semitism which was the hallmark of the 1920 programme also surfaced in stark form in the Draft. This document, therefore, has few claims for acceptance as a separate, independent ideological statement by a recognisable 'socialist' or 'left-wing' faction in the NSDAP; its only source of originality lay in its nebulous espousal of a fascist-style corporativism. When it is further taken into account that at both the organisational and personal levels there is clear evidence of deep disunity in the sub-group established to co-ordinate the activity of the radicals – the *Arbeitsgemeinschaft*

Nordwest – Kühnl's case evaporates. There was no basis here for a 'Nazi Left'.[49]

Kühnl's contention that a 'Nazi Left' functioned as a distinct and reasonably influential entity within the Party during the remainder of the 1920s is not supported by any real evidence. It is now clear that despite the radical anti-capitalist and anti-bourgeois rhetoric associated with the implementation of the 'urban plan', the Party's would-be radicals signally failed to clarify how, ideologically, they differed from the Hitlerian line of thought. Particularly culpable in this respect was Gregor Strasser who during the mid-1920s is rightly seen as the principal spokesman of the 'radicals'. His many public pronouncements and writings on the necessity of abolishing capitalism and eliminating the power base of the reactionary bourgeoisie also carried, significantly, frequent demands for a full-blooded assault on the power of international Marxism and Jewry which, he claimed, were primarily responsible for leading the honest German proletariat away from the national path. Strasser's exposition of his 'socialism' went no further than these vehement tirades, thus accentuating the intellectual poverty of his kind in the Party.[50] The *Kampfverlag*, which he founded and jointly owned, showed itself similarly incapable of cutting through its passionate denunciations to furnish a coherent definition of its conceptual position. There was, in consequence, no comprehensible ideological posture that can be described as 'Nazi leftism'. Furthermore there is substantial evidence that Gregor Strasser, having witnessed the utter failure of the urban strategy at the 1928 *Reichstag* election, and having accepted the need for a fundamental reorientation of the NSDAP's organisation, propaganda and ideology in favour of the middle classes, as Stachura has suggested,[51] was becoming more and more alienated from his brother Otto and others like him during the late 1920s. Gregor was politically astute enough to realise that the NSDAP could never hope now to become a major electoral force as a workers' party; the middle classes and their political organisations which, as Jones has repeatedly and convincingly demonstrated,[52] were in deep crisis anyway by that time, had to be attacked. In due course the NSDAP vote rose in almost the same proportion to the losses sustained by the traditional middle-class parties.

Kühnl is correct in saying that with the secession of Otto Strasser in 1930 radicalism was effectively at an end in the NSDAP.[53] The Party increasingly distanced itself thereafter from its earlier and ill-defined association with 'socialism', despite Kele's misconceived assertions to the contrary.[54] Only in a few ancillary organisations of the Party which recruited or attempted to recruit followers from the workers did a coarse anti-capitalist radicalism persist as a factor of importance, that is, in the Hitler Youth, the SA and the NS Factory Cell Organisation (NSBO).[55] In the NSDAP the process of embourgeoisment picked up momentum and soon came to dominate its personality. That having been said, however, Kühnl's conclusion is based in ignorance of the really critical development which proves the non-existence of a unified 'Nazi Left' during the early 1930s, namely, the continuing blunting and eventual disappearance of Gregor Strasser's earlier radicalism as he moved from a sectarian National Socialist understanding of Weimar politics to a more flexible, open-ended approach in line with a reasonably moderate neo-conservative, nationalist outlook. While he maintained a powerful position within the NSDAP as its Organisation Leader and *Reichstag* Deputy, Strasser was constructing, often unknown to Hitler, a labyrinth of important contacts with groups and personalities in industry, the trade unions, the bourgeois parties and neo-conservative circles which laid the foundations of his co-operation with General Schleicher in late 1932. By that time, disillusioned by Hitler's sterile opposition tactics and fearful in any event of what might become of a Germany led by the Führer, Strasser determined to leave his power base in the NSDAP altogether.[56] The crisis in the NSDAP resulting from his resignation of his Party offices in December 1932 has been misunderstood by historians such as Hentschel and Schulz.[57] The crisis did not signify a revolt of the Party's 'socialists' or of the putative 'Nazi Left', for by then there were no longer any committed radicals in the Party. It is to be hoped that, henceforth, in discussion of the pre-1933 NSDAP there is no reference to either Gregor Strasser the 'socialist' or to the non-existent 'Nazi Left'. With these myths safely buried, a more realistic appraisal of the Party's development, especially in 1930–3, can be made.

The deliberately pro-middle-class course pursued by the NSDAP after 1928, involving strident emphasis on themes likely to warm the hearts of the bourgeoisie, and the absence of a coherent 'Nazi Left', go a long way towards explaining why the industrial proletariat were greatly underrepresented in the Party's membership and electoral constituency before 1933. Attempts to argue otherwise are unconvincing because they are invariably based on regional statistics (Mühlberger for Westphalia, Hambrecht for Middle Franconia) which cannot be used for conclusions about the national situation.[58] More rewarding to some extent are works which analyse what kind of worker was attracted to National Socialism and for what reasons. Foremost among this genre is Mason's account.[59]

Marshalling his arguments and supporting empirical details in compelling fashion in the early stages of his work, Mason builds on previous studies, especially those by Weber and Pratt,[60] to explain that the minority of industrial workers who did follow the NSDAP usually operated from a position outside the parameters of working-class organisational life. In some cases these workers can be legitimately described as lumpen-proletariat, bereft of any binding social or economic links with their own class. More numerous, however, were better-off skilled workers, workers with supervisory responsibilities, auxiliary artisans and personnel employed in family or small businesses where the influence of owners was direct and strong. They were joined by non-unionised or weakly organised unskilled workers in the public service industries, and unskilled agricultural labourers in certain parts of Germany where social development was limited: the eastern provinces are a case in point. The younger members of these categories of workers were particularly susceptible to the NSDAP, Mason argues, though he does not provide the statistical data needed to substantiate what appears, certainly, to be a plausible assertion. He writes that the younger elements were likely to be taken in by certain prominent components of the Party's propaganda, including ultra-nationalism, pseudo-egalitarianism (the *Volksgemeinschaft* ethos), and its dynamism and sheer novelty. As an extension of these points, McKibbon and now Hagtvet have successfully argued that the NSDAP did not gain unduly from the working-class unemployed during the Depression; unskilled or semi-skilled unemployed shunned the Party in preference to the SPD and KPD, and only among some younger, long-term unemployed did it pick up a noticeable measure of support.[61] Merkl's point that some workers who supported Hitler because of their patriotism and innate conservatism – equivalent perhaps to working-class Tories in the United Kingdom – is also valid.[62] Finally, while the bulk of the pro-Nazi proletarians came from groups not under the influence of working-class ideology or organisation, the small number of fully unionised workers who did were also invariably located in regions, such as Chemnitz-Zwickau, where unusual socio-economic and industrial structures prevailed. They too, in a different way, were outside the mainstream of working-class life.

The industrial proletariat, like the Catholic population, had developed over a long period of years a secure immunity to the kind of transparent appeal made by the NSDAP. Both groups had established their own specific identity within German society on the basis of a closely knit organisational framework, cultural perception and political introspectiveness, as Winkler has lucidly intimated.[63] The resultant deep feelings of class and confessional solidarity, sharpened by persecution and ostracism, were the core of an attitude against which the Nazi battering-ram was bound to falter. In the case of the workers, the Depression of the early 1930s undoubtedly made weakening inroads into their sub-world as the trade unions and the SPD lost ground – a situation made much worse, of course, by the bitter hostility between them and the Communists. In general, however, and despite these important handicaps, the workers remained steadfastly loyal to their political convictions, finding little difficulty in perceiving the grotesque evil of National Socialism. At the same time, it cannot be seriously argued, as Mason does with his customary penchant for colourful overstatement, that the NSDAP was motivated above all by an anti-working-class impetus during 1928–33:[64]

in the final instance it was class antagonism which represented the unifying and harmonizing element in the confusing multitude of sectional interests and dogmas which comprised National Socialism before 1933. Without this unifying bond of anti-communist and anti-social democratic interests and ideas the movement would never have been able to develop so dynamic an integrative power . . . Though they might agree on little else, all activisits achieved unison about the identity of the internal enemy.

Further, by 1932/3 the NSDAP

was the most extreme and at the same time most popular political expression of a much broader economic, social and political reaction whose central aim consisted of repelling the working class movement.

The NSDAP's inclinations were certainly anti-labour and anti-socialist/Marxist, but to account for its rise and ultimately successful advent to power on these terms alone is totally misleading. The *Machtergreifung* was the climax of a complicated interaction of social, economic, political and historical forces of which the NSDAP's antipathy for the Left was but one. The Party was the spearhead of a broadly restorationist, anti-modernist movement of propertied, nationalist and Protestant Germany which had its genesis in the ideas and conventions of the Wilhelmine Reich. As such, the NSDAP could hardly be anything other than a product of a quintessentially bourgeois ideological and political ambience.

This conclusion does not obviate the need, of course, for further research into the sociological aspects of early National Socialism. There is considerable scope not only for more detailed analysis of the Party's growth in particular geographical locations, most pressingly in central Germany, but also for investigation of a whole range of variables relating to age, sex, generational conflict, marital status, mobility, religious beliefs and educational experience as well as of emotional–psychological impulses which conditioned the *Mittelstand*.[65] The extent of downward mobility among the middle classes and the applicability of modernisation theories also require much further work. As for the NSDAP–worker relationship, it would be helpful, of course, to have more details of the ideological and physical factors involved on both a national and local level, but the overall character of that relationship is now firmly established. In short, the picture we have of the NSDAP's social character is not yet complete by any means. On the other hand, the broad outlines of the Party's relationship to both the bourgeoisie and proletariat which this essay has tried to delineate are unlikely to be significantly altered by future research. The NSDAP was a predominantly lower-middle-class affair.

Notes

1 Interpretations of fascism by leading contemporary Marxists are usefully compiled in Wolfgang Abendroth (ed.), *Faschismus und Kapitalismus*. *Theorien über die sozialen Ursprünge und die Funktion des Faschismus* (Frankfurt: 1967).

2 Ernst Nolte (ed.), *Theorien über den Faschismus* (Berlin: 1967), p. 91.

3 Leon Trotsky, *The Struggle Against Fascism in Germany* (London: 1971), pp. 399–407.

4 Albert Krebs, *Tendenzen und Gestalten der NSDAP*. *Erinnerungen an die Frühzeit der Partei* (Stuttgart: 1959); Kurt G. W. Ludecke, *I Knew Hitler*. *The Story of a Nazi Who Escaped the Blood Purge* (London: 1938); Konrad Heiden, *Geschichte des National-sozialismus*. *Die Karriere einer Idee* (Berlin: 1932).

5 Theodore Geiger, *Die soziale Schichtung des deutschen Volkes*. *Soziographischer Versuch auf statistischer Grundlage* (Stuttgart: 1932).

6 Arthur Rosenberg, *Der Faschismus als Massenbewegung*. *Seine Aufstieg und seine Zersetzung* (Karlsbad: 1934).

7 Theodore Abel, *The Nazi Movement*. *Why Hitler Came to Power* (New York: 1935).

8 Peter H. Merkl, *Political Violence under the Swastika*. *581 Early Nazis* (Princeton, NJ: 1975).

9 Erich Fromm, *Escape to Freedom* (New York: 1941).

10 Martin Broszat, 'Die Anfänge der NSDAP in Berlin 1926/27', *Vierteljahrshefte für Zeitgeschichte*, 8, 1960, pp. 85–118.

11 Seymour Martin Lipset, *Political Man*. *The Social Bases of Politics* (New York: 1960), pp. 127–79.

12 Heinrich August Winkler, 'Extremismus der Mitte? Sozialgeschichtliche Aspekte der nationalsozialistischen Machtergreifung', *Vierteljahrshefte für Zeitgeschichte*, 20, 1972, pp. 175–91.

13 Andreas Dorpalen, 'Weimar Republic and Nazi Era in East German Perspective', *Central European History*, XI, 1978, pp. 218 f.

14 The most notable are: Carl J. Friedrich and Zbigniew K. Brzezinski, *Totalitarian Dictatorship and Autocracy* (Cambridge, Mass: 1956); and Hannah Arendt, *The Origins of Totalitarianism* (New York: 1951).

15 Among others, Kater's *Studentenschaft und Rechtsradikalismus in Deutschland, 1918–1933* (Hamburg: 1975); 'Zur Soziographie der Frühen NSDAP', *Vierteljahrshefte für Zeitgeschichte*, 19, 1971, pp. 124–59; 'Zum gegenseitigen Verhältnis von SA und SS in der Sozialgeschichte des Nationalsozialismus von 1925 bis 1939', *Vierteljahrsschrift für Sozial-und Wirtschaftsgeschichte*, 62, 1975, pp. 339–79; 'Sozialer Wandel in der NSDAP im Zuge der nationalsozialistischen Machtergreifung', in Wolfgang Schieder (ed.), *Faschismus als soziale Bewegung* (Hamburg: 1976), pp. 25–67; 'Ansätze zu einer Soziologie der SA bis zur Röhm-Krise', in Ulrich Engelhardt, Volker Sellin and Horst Stuke (eds), *Soziale Bewegung und politische Verfassung* (Stuttgart: 1976), pp. 798–831; 'Der NS-Studentenbund von 1926 bis 1928: Randgruppe zwischen Hitler und Strasser', *Vierteljahrshefte für Zeitgeschichte*, 22, 1974, pp. 148–90. Professor Kater is about to publish a social history of the NSDAP from the 1920s to 1945, which is eagerly awaited.

16 Michael H. Kater, 'Quantifizierung und NS-Geschichte. Methodologische Überlegungen über Grenzen und Möglichkeiten einer EDV-Analyse der NSDAP-Sozialstruktur von 1925 bis 1945', *Geschichte und Gesellschaft*, 3, 1977, pp. 453–84, esp. pp. 471 ff.

17 Conan J. Fischer, 'A Social History of the SA's Rank-And-File Membership, 1929–1935' (Doctoral thesis, University of Sussex, 1980); Mathilde Jamin, 'Methodische Konzeption einer quantitativen Analyse zur sozialen Zusammensetzung der SA', in Reinhard Mann (ed.), *Die Nationalsozialisten*. *Analysen faschistischer Bewegungen* (Stuttgart: 1980), pp. 84–97, esp. pp. 84 f, 94 f.

18 Merkl, *Political Violence*; Peter Loewenberg, 'The Psychohistorical Origins of the Nazi Youth Cohort', *American Historical Review*, 76, 1971, pp. 1457–1502.

19   Barrington Moore, *Social Origins of Dictatorship and Democracy* (Boston, Mass: 1966); Ralf Dahrendorf, *Gesellschaft und Demokratie in Deutschland* (Munich: 1965); David Schoenbaum, *Hitler's Social Revolution. Class and Status in Nazi Germany, 1933–39* (London: 1966).

20   Horst Matzerath and Heinrich Volkmann, 'Modernisierungstheorie und National-sozialismus', *Geschichte und Gesellschaft*, 3, 1977, pp. 86–116.

21   William Jannen, 'National Socialists and Social Mobility', *Journal of Social History*, 9, 1976, pp. 339–66; Ronald Rogowski, 'The Gauleiter and the Social Origins of Fascism', *Comparative Studies in Society and History*, 19, 1977, pp. 399–430. Rogowski concludes that the 'losers' of modern German society 'very likely' made up the majority of the Party's supporters before 1933 (p. 429).

22   Merkl, *Political Violence*, pp. 75–6; and Merkl, *The Making of a Stormtrooper* (Princeton, NJ: 1980), p. 153.

23   As indicated recently in Peter D. Stachura, 'The Political Strategy of the Nazi Party, 1919–1933, *German Studies Review*, III, 1980, pp. 261–88.

24   Jürgen Genuneit, 'Methodische Probleme der quantitativen Analyse früher NSDAP-Mitgliederlisten', in Mann (ed.), *Die Nationalsozialisten*, esp. pp. 35 ff, 40 ff, 44 ff; Jürgen Kocka, 'Zur Problematik der deutschen Angestellten 1914–1933', in Hans Mommsen, Dietmar Petzina and Bernd Weisbrod (eds), *Industrielles System und Politische Entwicklung in der Weimarer Republik* (Düsseldorf: 1974), p. 800, n. 13.

25   Kater, 'Zur Soziographie', esp. pp. 137–9, 149–52, 155; Donald M. Douglas, 'The Parent Cell: Some Computer Notes on the Composition of the First Nazi Party Group in Munich, 1919–21', *Central European History*, X, 1977, pp. 55–72, esp. 67–9.

26   Werner Maser, *Der Sturm auf die Republik. Frühgeschichte der NSDAP* (Stuttgart: 1973), pp. 254–5; Georg Franz-Willing, *Die Hitlerbewegung, I: Der Ursprung 1919–1922* (Hamburg: 1962), pp. 129–30; Dietrich Orlow, *The History of the Nazi Party, 1919–1933* (Pittsburgh, Pa: 1969), p. 56; Robin Lenman, 'Julius Streicher and the Origins of the NSDAP in Nuremberg, 1918–1923', in Anthony J. Nicholls and Erich Matthias (eds), *German Democracy and the Triumph of Hitler* (London: 1971), pp. 129–59, esp. p. 142 when he writes that the Party members were drawn from 'the aggrieved and the disorientated, to say nothing of adventurers and obvious lunatics'!

27   Kater, 'Sozialer Wandel', esp. pp. 27 ff; Thomas Childers, 'The Social Bases of the National Socialist Vote', *Journal of Contemporary History*, 11, 1976, pp. 17–42, esp. pp. 20 ff, 27 ff; Alexander Weber, 'Soziale Merkmale der NSDAP Wähler, (Doctoral dissertation, University of Freiburg i.B., 1969), pp. 15–108.

28   Heinrich August Winkler, *Mittelstand, Demokratie und Nationalsozialismus. Die politische Entwicklung von Handwerk und Kleinhandel in der Weimarer Republik* (Cologne: 1972), pp. 54 ff, 76–83, 112 f, 165–79.

29   Heinrich August Winkler, 'Der entbehrliche Stand. Zur Mittelstandspolitik im Dritten Reich', *Archiv für Sozialgeschichte*, XVII, 1977, pp. 1–40.

30   Claus-Dieter Krohn and Dirk Stegmann, 'Kleingewerbe und Nationalsozialismus in einer agrarisch-mittelständischen Region. Das Beispiel Lüneburg 1930–1939', *Archiv für Sozialgeschichte*, XVII, 1977, pp. 41–98, esp. pp. 56 ff, 60 ff; Frank Domurad, 'The Politics of Corporatism: Hamburg Handicraft in the Late Weimar Republic, 1927–1933', in Richard Bessel and E. J. Feuchtwanger (eds), *Social Change and Political Development in Weimar Germany* (London: 1981), pp. 174–206, esp. pp. 196 ff.

31   Rainer Bölling, *Volksschullehrer und Politik. Der Deutsche Lehrerverein 1918–1933* (Göttingen: 1978), pp. 203–8; Wilfried Breyvogel, *Die soziale Lage und das politische Bewusstsein der Volksschullehrer 1927–1933* (Königstein/Ts: 1979); Hildegard Casper, 'Die Deutsche Lehrerverein in der Weltwirtschaftskrise 1930–1933', in Dietfrid Krause-Vilmar (ed.), *Lehrerschaft, Republik und Faschismus* (Cologne: 1978), pp. 145–210, esp. pp. 165 ff.

32 The best account is still Horst Gies, 'NSDAP und landwirtschaftliche Organisationen in der Endphase der Weimarer Republik', *Vierteljahrshefte für Zeitgeschichte*, 15, 1967, pp. 341–76.
33 Thomas Childers, 'National Socialism and the New Middle Class', in Mann (ed.), *Die Nationalsozialisten*, pp. 19–33, esp. pp. 24 ff.
34 Sandra J. Coyner, 'Class Consciousness and Consumption: The New Middle Class during the Weimar Republic', *Journal of Social History*, 10, 1977, pp. 310–31, esp. pp. 315, 325.
35 William S. Allen, *The Nazi Seizure of Power. The Experience of a Single German Town 1930–1935* (London: 1966); Jeremy Noakes, *The Nazi Party in Lower Saxony 1921–1933* (London: 1971), esp. pp. 174, 246; Geoffrey Pridham, *Hitler's Rise to Power. The Nazi Movement in Bavaria, 1923–33* (London: 1973), pp. 186 ff; Rudolf Heberle, *Landbevölkerung und Nationalsozialismus. Eine soziologische Untersuchung der politischen Willensbildung in Schleswig-Holstein 1918–1932* (Stuttgart: 1963). Also relevant are Lawrence D. Stokes, 'The Social Composition of the Nazi Party in Eutin 1925–32', *International Review of Social History*, XXIII, 1978, pp. 1–32; Rudy Koshar, 'Two "Nazisms": the Social Context of Nazi Mobilization in Marburg and Tübingen', *Social History* 7, 1982, pp. 27–42; Johnpeter H. Grill, 'The Nazi Party in Baden 1920–1945' (Doctoral dissertation, University of Michigan, 1975), esp. pp. 187 f.
36 Peter D. Stachura, 'Who Were the Nazis? A Socio-Political Analysis of the National Socialist Machtübernahme', *European Studies Review*, 11, 1981, pp. 310 ff.
37 Kater, 'Sozialer Wandel', pp. 36 ff, 51 ff; Rogowski, 'The Gauleiter', pp. 401–2.
38 Kater, 'Zum gegenseitigen Verhältnis', pp. 343, 358; Samuel A. Pratt, 'The Social Basis of Nazism and Communism in Urban Germany' (Thesis, Michigan State College, 1948), p. 117.
39 Hans-Erich Volkmann, 'Das aussenwirtschaftliche Programm der NSDAP 1930–1933', *Archiv für Sozialgeschichte*, XVII, 1977, pp. 251–74.
40 Heinrich August Winkler, 'Mittelstandsbewegung oder Volkspartei? Zur sozialen Basis der NSDAP', in Schieder (ed.), *Faschismus als soziale Bewegung*, pp. 111–12; Hans Mommsen, 'Zur Verschränkung traditioneller und faschistischer Führungsgruppen in Deutschland beim Übergang von der Bewegungs-zur Systemphase', in Schieder (ed.), *Faschismus als soziale Bewegung*, p. 164.
41 Merkl, *Making of a Stormtrooper*, pp. 153 ff; Detlef Mühlberger, 'The Sociology of the NSDAP. The Question of Working-Class Membership', *Journal of Contemporary History*, 15, 1980, pp. 500, 504; Jürgen W. Falter, 'Wählerbewegungen zur NSDAP 1924–1933', in Otto Büsch (ed.), *Wählerbewegungen in der Europäischen Geschichte* (Berlin: 1980), pp. 177 ff, 187 ff.
42 John J. Cahill, 'The NSDAP and May Day, 1923: Confrontation and Aftermath, 1923–1927, (Doctoral dissertation, University of Cincinnati, 1973), chs 1–3.
43 Max H. Kele, *Nazis and Workers. National Socialist Appeals to German Labor, 1919–1933* (Chapel Hill: 1972).
44 There are conflicting interpretations here: Detlef Mühlberger, 'The Rise of National Socialism in Westphalia 1920–1933' (Doctoral thesis, University of London, 1975), pp. 273–5 stresses the high percentage of workers in the Party. But this is flatly denied by Wilfried Böhnke, *Die NSDAP im Ruhrgebiet 1920–1933* (Bonn-Bad Godesberg: 1974), pp. 195 ff, 200 ff, 221.
45 Kater, 'Ansätze', p. 802; Albrecht Tyrell, *Führer befiehl ... Selbstzeugnisse aus der 'Kampfzeit' der NSDAP. Dokumentation und Analyse* (Düsseldorf: 1969), p. 379.
46 Henry A. Turner, 'Hitlers Einstellung zu Wirtschaft und Gesellschaft vor 1933', *Geschichte und Gesellschaft*, 2, 1971, pp. 95 ff, 105 ff.
47 Orlow, *Nazi Party*, pp. 76–127.
48 Reinhard Kühnl, *Die Nationalsozialistische Linke 1925–1930* (Meisenheim: 1966).
49 See Peter D. Stachura, 'The NSDAP and the German Working Class, 1925–1933', in Isidor Walliman and Michael Dobkowski (eds), *Towards the Holocaust. Fascism and Anti-Semitism in Weimar Germany* (New York: 1982). On the *Arbeitsgemeinschaft* the

extremely useful works by Gerhard Schildt, 'Die Arbeitsgemeinschaft Nord-West' (Doctoral dissertation, University of Freiburg i. B., 1964), and Ulrich Wörtz, 'Programmatik und Führerprinzip. Das Problem des Strasser-Kreises in der NSDAP' (Doctoral dissertation, University of Erlangen, 1966), pp. 80 ff should be consulted.

50   Peter D. Stachura, *Gregor Strasser and the Rise of Nazism* (London: 1983), chs 3 and 4.

51   Peter D. Stachura, 'Der kritische Wendepunkt? Die NSDAP und die Reichstags-wahlen vom 20. Mai 1928', *Vierteljahrshefte für Zeitgeschichte*, 26, 1978, pp. 91–2.

52   Larry E. Jones, '"The Dying Middle": Weimar Germany and the Fragmentation of Bourgeois Politics', *Central European History*, v, 1972, pp. 23–54; and his 'The Dissolution of the Bourgeois Party System in the Weimar Republic', in Bessel and Feuchtwanger (eds), *Social Change*, pp. 268–88.

53   Kühnl, *Die NS-Linke*, pp. 230–60.

54   Kele, *Nazis and Workers*, pp. 136, 141 f, 168 ff.

55   Peter D. Stachura, *Nazi Youth in the Weimar Republic* (Santa Barbara: 1975), pp. 47–57; Conan J. Fischer, 'The Occupational Background of the SA's Rank and File Membership during the Depression Years, 1929 to mid-1934', in Peter D. Stachura (ed.), *The Shaping of the Nazi State* (London: 1978), pp. 138, 152. Compare Fischer's conclusions with those of Richard Bessel, 'The SA in the Eastern Regions of Germany, 1925–1934' (Doctoral dissertation, University of Oxford, 1980), pp. 76–99. Merkl's *Making of a Stormtrooper* does not address itself directly to the vexed question of the social background of the SA's rank and file (cf. p. 94).

56   Stachura, *Gregor Strasser*, chs 5 and 6; some tentative conclusions are to be found in my article, '"Der Fall Strasser": Gregor Strasser, Hitler and National Socialism 1930–1932', in Stachura (ed.), *Nazi State*, pp. 88–130. Compare these interpretations and details with Udo Kissenkoetter, *Gregor Strasser und die NSDAP* (Stuttgart: 1978), esp. pp. 162 ff.

57   Volker Hentschel, *Weimars letzte Monate. Hitler und der Untergang der Republik* (Düsseldorf: 1978), pp. 79–101; Gerhard Schulz, *Aufstieg des Nationalsozialismus. Krise und Revolution in Deutschland* (Berlin: 1975), pp. 731 ff.

58   Mühlberger, 'Rise of National Socialism'; Rainer Hambrecht, *Der Aufstieg der NSDAP in Mittel-und Oberfranken (1925–1933)* (Nuremberg: 1976), pp. 304–8.

59   Timothy W. Mason, *Sozialpolitik im Dritten Reich. Arbeiterklasse und Volksgemein-schaft* (Opladen: 1977), ch. 2: this is available in English translation in *New German Critique*, 4, 1977, pp. 49–93.

60   Weber, 'Soziale Merkmale'; Pratt, 'Social Basis'.

61   R. I. McKibbon, 'The Myth of the Unemployed: Who Did Vote for the Nazis?', *Australian Journal of Political History*, 15, 1969, pp. 25–6; Bernt Hagtvet, 'The Theory of Mass Society and The Collapse of the Weimar Republic. A Re-Examination', Stein U. Larsen, Bernt Hagtvet and Jan Petter Myklebust (eds), *Who Were the Fascists? Social Roots of European Fascism*, (Oslo: 1980), pp. 81–5.

62   Peter H. Merkl in 'Introduction' to section on German fascism in Larsen *et al.* (eds), *Who Were the Fascists?* p. 263.

63   Heinrich A. Winkler, 'German Society, Hitler and the Illusion of Restoration 1930–33', *Journal of Contemporary History*, 11, 1976, pp. 3 ff.

64   Mason, *New German Critique*, pp. 77–8.

65   A pointer has been given by Martin Broszat's instructive but somewhat tentative article, 'National Socialism, its Social Basis and Psychological Impact', in E. J. Feuchtwanger (ed.), *Upheaval and Continuity. A Century of German History* (London: 1973), pp. 134–51, esp. pp. 145 ff.

3 National Socialism and Women before 1933

JILL STEPHENSON

While interest in National Socialism has continued unabated for half a century and more, curiosity about the contribution of German women to the Nazis' victory in 1933 has only recently revived. Contemporaries, both in and outside Germany, were indeed exercised by the apparent paradox of women supporting a party which was not only male-dominated and self-consciously male chauvinist, but also, in many of its manifestations, vulgar and violent.[1] This in itself begs questions about the extent to which women did support Hitler and the NSDAP, and about the image projected by National Socialists as they tried to attract electoral support. Once Hitler's power was consolidated, articles appeared intermittently in foreign newspapers and magazines detailing the disadvantages under which women laboured in the Third Reich, with varying degrees of accuracy.[2] Pamphlets and books were written by those on the political Left intent on investigating 'German fascism' as an integral part of the postwar political phenomenon of fascism, and these, too, included a gloomy picture of German women's fate.[3] Propaganda counter-blasts from the official German press and soothing words from the Nazis' Women's Leader, Gertrud Scholtz-Klink, to foreign guests and on visits abroad, endeavoured to evoke an idyllic image of women's life in the 'new Germany', and to portray the overwhelming response to it as favourable.[4] But the most genuinely informative account of women's life in the Third Reich came from an American sociologist, Clifford Kirkpatrick, whose study was based on a year's residence in Hitler's Germany, with judicious evaluation of the available oral and written sources and acute observation of events and people.[5] Underlying the themes of these various post-1933 publications – except the Nazi ones – was the question: why had German women brought this upon themselves?

· For almost three decades after 1945, this question remained not so much unanswered as simply unasked. Two works, of very different kinds, stand out as exceptions to the general rule of a neglect of women's role and attitudes before and during the Third Reich: those by Gabrielle Bremme, and David Schoenbaum.[6] But in the early 1970s chapters and articles on women's role and opportunities in interwar Germany began to appear,[7] to be followed by books.[8] By the early 1980s, not only is there a reasonably substantial body of literature on the subject, but also there is a widening range of scholars, in both Europe and North America, who are working on some aspect of the *Frauenfrage* (women's question) in modern German history.[9]

The reason for the almost total neglect until recently of women's role in the NSDAP and as pro-Nazi voters seems to have been twofold. First, the Nazis' insistence on excluding women from political activity suggested that from 1933 there was virtually nothing to study, in the era before the growth of interest in social history. As recently as 1978, one reviewer remarked that an essay on the Nazi women's organisations in the 1930s could 'only serve the negative purpose of demonstrating the dominance of men in Nazism'.[10] Secondly, there was widespread acceptance of broad generalisations about women's nature, attitudes and political behaviour which are scarcely more attractive than the views on these matters attributed to the National Socialists. Numerous accounts relate the hysterical idolatry with which women are alleged to have welcomed Hitler, a strong man leading an aggressively masculine movement, attributing it to simplistic psychological or psycho-sexual responses. As recently as the 1970s there has been talk of the appeal of National Socialism to 'the collective feminine subconscious',[11] and of how 'the sacrificial willingness of women to be Hitler's devotees remained politically important'.[12] One result of this approach has been the tendency to treat women – where they are mentioned – as a homogeneous group; as Claudia Koonz has said, 'Politicians, journalists, and even feminists have grouped women – like members of a religious or ethnic minority – in a single category and viewed them as a single "problem".'[13] The parallel to be drawn, of the relative neglect of women's organisational activity within the NSDAP leading to women being classed as an interest group in Strasser's 1932 reform of the Party organisation,[14] is striking. More recently, however, there have been attempts to study specific groups of women, generally on a class basis, to try to break down the stereotype of a uniform female response to National Socialism.

The revival of interest in women's contribution to the rise of National Socialism has derived from two separate developments in the 1960s and 1970s. Growing interest in social history led at first to investigation of women's role in history as something of a curiosity. The 'single category' approach, which differentiated 'Women' from 'Labour', 'Business', 'Agriculture', for example, prevailed. This developed into a trend towards including a mandatory chapter on some aspect of women's role or activities in works on a specialist theme in modern German history. But there are now also signs that reference to women's conditions, status and interests is being accepted as normal and indispensable in works which aim to shed light on the condition of society as a whole. Timothy Mason's recent work is a good example.[15] But the rise in popularity of social history did not alone account for the new emphasis on women's role. The 'new feminism' of the women's liberation movement, starting in the mid-1960s in the United States and rapidly spreading to Europe, provided additional impetus. It was not only a desire to overturn the rather insulting view of women's gullible submission to Hitler and his brown hordes – which enjoyed considerable currency – which led to intense activity, above all on the part of a rising generation of women historians. In addition, the attempt to construct what is self-consciously characterised as 'women's history' – for better or worse – led to a complete reappraisal of women's status and attitudes in general in the 1920s and early 1930s, as part of the wider context of the demise of the Weimar Republic and the triumph of National Socialism. 'Liberating women's history'[16] has, at its most constructive, developed into a process of integrating 'women's history' into the general realm of social history. The result has been that out of two rather separate developments, in social history and 'women's history', a symbiotic relationship has evolved which shows signs of becoming a true synthesis.

The new approach has been concerned chiefly with what may be called a 'condition of women' question, on the part of writers from David Schoenbaum onwards. The answer to the questions, 'Why does [the German woman] vote for a group which intends to take the ballot from her? Why does she support anti-feminism?',[17] has emerged more or less implicitly from work geared to investigating the reality of life for women in both Weimar and Nazi Germany. The paradox, as some contemporaries saw it, of women voting for 'a group which intends to take the ballot from [them]' and for 'anti-feminism', depends both on women in general regarding 'feminism' favourably (a false assumption) and on female electors being monocausally motivated (a rash assumption).

On six major points concerning the voting behaviour of women after their enfranchisement in 1918 there is general agreement.[18] First, although women electors were in a majority, their influence was modified by their tendency to vote in smaller numbers than men. This was especially marked in rural areas. Secondly, women voted far more strongly than men for clerical/conservative parties, with the accent on 'clerical'. The Catholic Centre Party and its partner, the Bavarian People's Party (BVP), benefited particularly, although the Nationalist Party (DNVP) and explicitly Evangelical interest groups also gained, in Protestant areas. Thirdly, there was correspondingly less support among women for parties of the Left. The Social Democrats (SPD) did, however, improve their standing among women voters so that by the later 1920s they were receiving almost as many women's votes as men's. But the Communist Party (KPD) failed conspicuously to attract women in substantial numbers. Fourthly, certainly until 1930, the NSDAP's support from women was very limited (but greater than the KPD's). Thereafter, there was a sharp rise in both men's and women's votes for the NSDAP, although only in a few exceptional areas did it receive half of its support from women. Whatever might have been said about 'the women's vote bringing Hitler to triumph',[19] it is clear that Hitler's electoral chances would have been even better without female suffrage. Fifthly, the 1932 presidential elections help to confirm this point: the majority of women supported Hindenburg. If women's votes alone had counted, Hitler would not have forced the contest to a second ballot. Finally, married women overwhelmingly voted in the same way as their husbands, while daughters, sisters and other female adherents often tended to vote in the same way as the head of the household.

This last point may go some way towards explaining why large numbers of women as well as men voted NSDAP in 1932. Yet it takes no account of the marked discrepancy between men's and women's support for the Party before 1932, when women were repelled by its 'campaigning methods as also its attitude towards the Churches',[20] preferring 'stability and order', the slogan used to promote Hindenburg's candidacy.[21] Similarly election results from areas where – to the disgust of feminists – women's votes were counted separately from men's show a generally high differential between men's and women's support for the Centre Party. This was particularly true in strong Catholic areas: in Bavaria, the percentage of men voting BVP (that is, Centre) in *Reichstag* elections in 1924, 1928 and 1930 was 13·5, 23·9 and 21·8 respectively, while the corresponding figures for women were 20·7, 38·1 and 35·8.[22] Clearly many women were not voting for the same party as their husband or head of household. Peterson sees the Ruhr and Upper Silesia as exceptional, with '[families divided] along lines at once of sex, religion, and politics', men voting KPD and women voting Centre.[23] But in strongly Catholic areas it would also be the case that male household members were voting differently from women in substantial numbers, given the excess of female support for the Centre. And some of these men would be voting Nazi.

The extent to which the absence of a Protestant clerical/conservative party as strong as the Catholic Centre was important in giving the NSDAP its breakthrough in the women's vote in Protestant areas is not clear. But in elections in 1931 and 1932 the Party began to make a markedly favourable impact on women, with the decline of the DNVP and, more so, the People's Party (DVP) vote, which had traditionally benefited disproportionately from the support of Protestant women. Unfortunately no one supplies data giving a breakdown by sex of the voting in the years 1930–3 in a Protestant area, but figures are available from Catholic bastions, where women's support for National Socialism was much less marked. Bremme's figures for Cologne and Helen Boak's for Bavaria show that, even if support for the NSDAP was well below the national average most of the time among both men and women in both these areas, nevertheless not only did the women's vote increase substantially in the early 1930s, but, further, the gap between men's and women's support for the NSDAP narrowed at a time when *men*'s backing for the Nazis was rising.[24]

Table 3.1 *Percentage Support for the NSDAP*

election	national[25] average	Cologne		differ- ence	Bavaria		differ- ence
		M	F		M	F	
14· 9·30	18·3	19·8	15·5	4·3	18·9	14·2	4·7
31· 7·32	37·4	26·4	22·8	3·6	—	—	—
6·11·32	33·0	21·8	19·2	2·6	27·4	24·7	2·7
5· 3·33	43·9	33·9	32·9	1·0	36·2	34·5	1·8

Richard Evans is right to stress the loyalty of Catholic women to the Centre Party, and to point out that in Cologne in July 1932 34·6 per cent of women (and 21·2 per cent of men) voted Centre.[26] This contributed to the Centre's success in the Cologne-Aachen electoral district, where even in March 1933 it could take 35·9 per cent of the total vote, compared with the NSDAP's 30·1 per cent (the lowest percentage taken by the Party anywhere in Germany then). But even in this most inhospitable area for Nazis, where some women's votes ensured that the Centre remained the dominant force, the votes of other women made the relative lack of enthusiasm on the part of women for the Nazis look less convincing. For perhaps the most interesting figure in Table 3.1 is the 2·6 per cent difference between men's and women's support for the NSDAP in Cologne in November 1932. Even at a time when the Nazis were, relatively, suffering a reverse, the gap between the sexes' support for them was continuing to narrow.

If the Centre retained its support at a time when the Nazi vote was mushrooming, so did the Left. The 3.5 million or more women who voted SPD were probably more loyal than their menfolk, who would account for most of the drift from SPD to KPD between 1928 and 1932. Bremme plausibly attributes the SPD's improved image among women by the later 1920s to its de-emphasising of its former avowed anti-clericalism and its new status as a 'party of order', particularly compared with the radicalism of the KPD.[27] Women SPD voters were unlikely to be Catholic, and came overwhelmingly from the working class.[28] Like Catholics, then, working-class women had a clear focus of loyalty. But far from all working-class women voted for the parties of the Left, or even voted at all. Mason is no doubt correct in saying that of the 3.5 million or more wage-earners and members of their families who voted Nazi in 1932 a minority were women.[29] Those working-class women who did support the NSDAP tended to be non-unionised workers in the textile industry or home workers, Protestants (or at least non-Catholics) from Saxony and Thuringia. It is possible that the energetic activities of Nazi women's groups in Leipzig and Chemnitz, particularly, contributed to this.[30] More likely, the harsh effects of the Depression on these poorer members of the working class galvanised them to vote, when they had probably tended not to do so. Since they had no commitment to a particular party, the vitality and activism of the NSDAP easily attracted them in time of desperation. It certainly seems likely that the NSDAP won a disproportionately high share of the 3 million new voters registered between May 1928 and July 1932, and of the previous non-voters. The rise in turnout coincided with a resurgence in women's voting participation, which Bremme attributes to their greater readiness to vote in time of crisis. In the Depression years, the differential between men's and women's participation rates narrowed sharply, especially in the years 1932–3.[31]

Probably 6·5 million German women voted for the NSDAP in July 1932 and 5·5 million in November 1932, many of them, no doubt, because of the influence of a husband or head of household. Even so, for the vast majority of them there was clearly a change in attitude to a party whose radicalism and anti-clericalism – or part-atheism, part-paganism – had previously been a deterrent. There was, however, potential for a Nazi appeal to women in its *völkisch* (racist–nationalist) outlook, as evidenced by the support women particularly gave to other *völkisch* groups in the 1924 elections, following the Inflation crisis. Once again in time of crisis, in the early 1930s, women in substantial numbers cast a vote for xenophobic, introverted racism, nationalism and anti-'Bolshevism', by voting for the available *völkisch* party, the NSDAP.

At the very time when the effects of the Depression made the activism and vitality of the NSDAP appealing, the Party decisively improved its electoral chances by altering its image: the rowdy, radical, anti-clerical fringe party cast itself in the role of responsible guardian of the national interest, as that was perceived by the God-fearing, clean-living, property-owning members of the middle and upper-middle classes. The appeal to non-proletarians on the whole came more naturally because the NSDAP's leaders – for all that some of them scoffed at petty bourgeois values – shared the political, economic, social and moral prejudices of the middle classes and also, conveniently, of the Christian Churches. In both camps, at any rate, attitudes were strenuously opposed to the campaigns of the KPD and radical feminists for, among other things, freely available abortion. Both the Churches and the NSDAP regarded the decline in the birth-rate and the smaller families that resulted as a sign of national decadence.[32] And the anti-democratic nature of the NSDAP was not a great source of concern to institutions whose commitment to democracy and Republicanism was at best skin-deep. The NSDAP's stated view that women's natural calling was to be wives, mothers and homemakers accorded with church leaders' sentiments, and also with those of middle-class Germans generally, including the leaders of the middle-class feminist movement.[33] Jewish feminists, too – in spite of vitriolic Nazi propaganda to the contrary – believed that the wife and mother's place was in the home.[34] And Peterson describes housework as 'the function with which [most working-class women] identified'.[35]

The Nazis' 'hostile' attitude towards women, in wishing to make the home once again their exclusive sphere of activity and influence, was in harmony with the attitudes of large numbers of Germans, especially women. For all but a very few, the 'emancipation' of the 1920s was either irrelevant or else a cruel travesty, as Renate Bridenthal has argued. 'Economic liberation' was hardly what happened to women obliged to earn a living in industry as unskilled workers on low rates of pay, or to the perennially overburdened farmer's wife. And to some, women's 'emancipation' was positively threatening: full-time wives and mothers were made to feel inadequate, while in almost all sections of society and all occupational groups employed women faced at times virulent male antagonism. This culminated in the campaign against the *'Doppelverdiener'* ('double earner', generally applied to married women) in the Depression, which, as Bridenthal says, 'made women the scapegoat for unemployment'. No group fanned the flames of discontent against employed women more effectively than the NSDAP, whose reward, according to Dörte Winkler, was an increase in votes from men and women of all classes.[36] Bremme's view that the Nazis' *'Frauenfeindlichkeit'* ('hostility towards women') was not the factor which forfeited the support of women voters before the breakthrough in the early 1930s is correct, as far as it goes.[37] The NSDAP's utterances about women's role and women's employment were an integral part of a whole propaganda package designed to appeal to large numbers of broadly conservative Germans in all sections of society, and therefore to women particularly, as the more conservative sex. Nationalism, anti-'Bolshevism', anti-modernism in culture and morality were other related parts of a package which was, in its appeal, more coherent than critics have tended to concede.

This was the platform constructed even before the NSDAP made a conscious attempt to attract women voters. Although Hitler learned from the failure of the 1923 *Putsch* that he would have to work towards political power the legal way, it was not until as late as 1932 that the Party, in the person of Strasser, accepted that the female vote as such would have to be positively wooed.[38] There can be no doubt that the NSDAP's success in casting itself in the role of a responsible party helped to erase the unfavourable image of radical anti-clericalism which had previously inhibited more than a handful of women from voting for it. Even so, the Party faced difficulties in that it was trying to appeal to the widest possible range of female opinion, and found that in doing so it was an easy target for the propaganda of other parties of all colours, which represented Nazi policies towards women in the most unfavourable light possible. The NSDAP's opponents certainly had plenty of ready-made ammunition in the crasser utterances of some Party spokesmen, but the DVP's righteous sarcasm deploring one speaker's diatribe about the demeaning effect of the franchise on women would not necessarily be echoed by the majority of the female population.[39] The middle-class feminist leader, Gertrud Bäumer, was perhaps over-pessimistic in attributing women's growing support for the NSDAP to their corresponding lack of enthusiasm for their recently won suffrage rights. But, still, members of the *NS-Frauenschaft* (NSF – Nazi Women's Group) were concerned about the unfavourable effect that the Party's public views about women's role was, in their opinion, having on the female electorate. Their pessimistic view of their own electioneering efforts compared with those of other parties' women's groups was not, however, well founded: they particularly overestimated the success of both the KPD and conservative opponents in appealing to the uncommitted above all. Measured against their ambition to achieve a clear absolute majority in the 1932 and 1933 elections, and perhaps also against the superhuman effort put in by a relatively small number of the committed, perhaps they did fail. But the speed with which the NSDAP was able to generate a virtual avalanche of support, most dramatically quickly from among female electors in 1932, was meteoric, and probably owed less to the tireless canvassing of a few individuals than to the disorientating effects of the Depression coupled with the NSDAP's growing stature in the early 1930s as a responsible party. It convinced enough Germans that it was more fitted to defend their interests against corrupting external influences than were the traditional conservative or liberal parties, whose blinkered class or sectional interests had prevented the creation of a united, national and above all anti-Marxist front.

The reasons for women's support for the NSDAP in the early 1930s are many, but they depend heavily on the circumstances of the Depression and the marked change in the Party's image. Even so, it seems more than unlikely that, overall, the Nazis were able to attract as many as half of their votes from women – the majority of the electorate – in any large-scale election. The NSDAP remained a Party that appealed more to men than to women. Part of the change in image, to enhance electoral appeal among women, included an upgrading of the *NS-Frauenschaft* in 1932, at Strasser's behest, and the deployment of leading NSF members in the 1932–3 election campaigns so that women could be seen to be arguing the Party's case for the consumption of female electors. This vital period for the NSDAP was also the one in which the NSF enjoyed its greatest prestige within the Party organisation and received more attention from Party notables than at any other time in its existence, from 1931 to 1945. It was, however, Strasser's influence above all which assured the NSF attention and some prominence in Party activities in 1932. His departure in December 1932 resulted in the NSF being consigned to insignificance and peripheral activities.[40]

In its early years, the NSDAP's character as a 'man's party' was particularly pronounced. There was no recognised women's organisation until 1928, and no unified one before the founding of the NSF in October 1931. In spite of the Party's avowed exclusion of women from political activities, women members were admitted and even welcomed; but their numbers remained consistently low. The admittedly suspect *Partei-Statistik* of 1935 shows that the NSDAP's female membership was: up to 14 September 1930, 7,625 (5·9 per cent of the total); by 30 January 1933, 64,011 (7·8 per cent); and by 1935, 136,197 (5·5 per cent).[41] Kater's figures for the pre-*Putsch* NSDAP show an even smaller proportion of women members: the 208 in his sample accounted for only 4·4 per cent of the Party's membership. But his view that 'in 1933 the share of women in the Party's membership still amounted to barely more than 4 per cent' is questionable, to say the least. First, it is based on figures in Schäfer, which derive directly from the *Partei-Statistik* which Kater himself has criticised as being unreliable. Secondly, these figures simply list 'housewives' as 4·1 per cent of the Party's 1933 membership, with no further indication of the number of women who may be included in the other categories, 'workers', 'independents', and so on.[42] The 'female membership' figures given above at least set out to be comprehensive. Kater's own figures are more refined and informative, showing that of the 208 female members registered up to 9 November 1923, in his sample, fifty-one were housewives and another seventy-two, who failed to indicate their occupation in the Party's questionnaire, were probably unemployed or non-employed members of households. In the two other largest categories, forty-three were lower-level and middling clerical workers and fourteen in domestic service; and ten were unskilled workers. The remaining eighteen belonged to a variety of categories, from artist to employer, from apprentice and student to shop assistant and higher-grade clerical worker, from artisan to lower and middling civil servant.

An interesting comparison can be made between Kater's pre-*Putsch* women NSDAP members and those described by Lawrence Stokes as belonging to the Party's local branch in Eutin, Holstein, in May 1932. There are some striking similarities between the early recruits in the largely southern-based Party and those in a small town in the far north, after eight and a half further years of 'struggle'. One in four pre-*Putsch* women members were housewives, in Eutin one in three; but in the former, 59 per cent of all women members were either housewives or likely to be household members without outside work, while in Eutin the figure was close, at 63 per cent. Similar calculations involving domestic servants yield 6·7 per cent and 6·5 per cent respectively. Stokes's other occupational categories are not sufficiently differentiated by sex to permit further comparison. But there is in both cases the clear impression that women members were, on average, older than the men.

Kater shows that 59·6 per cent of pre-*Putsch* women members were over 23, compared with 52·2 per cent of men, while Stokes calculates that in Eutin 'the average age of the membership was 34·8 years, with women generally five years older than that'. Peter Merkl's small sample of thirty-six early women Nazis gives a similar impression of the women tending to be older than the men, but, again, of members from both sexes being well represented in the younger age groups.[43] The most striking feature of Eutin's female Party membership is that it accounted for 13·9 per cent of the total, an abnormally high share, three times Kater's group's 4·4 per cent. An even greater contrast can be made with Heyen's Trier-Land-West district, where on 1 January 1935 0·4 per cent of the membership was female. In *Gau* Koblenz-Trier, to which this district belonged, the figure was 1 per cent, compared with the published Reich average of 5·5 per cent.[44]

In all these samples the numbers are very small, and it would be rash to extrapolate freely from them. Nevertheless, interesting observations can be made. The enormous difference between women's membership in Eutin and Trier falls in areas at opposite poles in terms of their inhabitants' response to Nazism. Eutin was a stronghold of the movement before 1933, whereas Trier was in a Catholic area strongly resistant to the Nazi appeal in the *Kampfzeit*. Where the NSDAP enjoyed massive support, in Eutin, women were, proportionately, even more enthusiastic than men, compared with the national average. By contrast, in inhospitable Trier, women were, again proportionately, very much less likely than men to favour the Party. The impression is that women's support was stubbornly difficult to mobilise from scratch, but that once a good start was made the bandwagon effect was proportionately greater than among men. More regional studies of the NSDAP's growth, with women given the attention they were denied in earlier ones, are needed to establish whether this impression has general validity.

The samples mentioned here suggest that among the Party's women there was a heavy preponderance of housewives and other non-employed household members, who may well have joined the Party because the husband or head of household was a member, much as women's voting patterns were influenced by their menfolk. They were more likely to be found in urban than in rural areas, to be on average slightly older than male members, and they were not admitted to any Party office, other than in the specifically women's organisation. But, as Kater points out, statistical results tell us nothing about the women who sympathised with the Party and worked for its aims without actually becoming members. It is impossible to estimate their numbers, but in 1931 one NSDAP local branch leader claimed that of the hundred women working actively for his branch only twenty were Party members. At the time of Strasser's reorganisation of the women's groups in 1931 it emerged that the NSF would be very restricted in numbers if only Party members

were included, and so he gave permission for a category of 'assist-
ants' to be added. Equally, however, while Party members may have
been especially enthusiastic, by the early 1930s there was already dead
wood in the women's ranks at least; not all paid-up members were
prepared to work as actively for the Party as Strasser expected. The
reluctance of some women sympathisers to join the Party may have
been due to its overwhelmingly masculine aspect and the conservative
outlook of people who were mostly lower-middle class – the women
themselves and also their menfolk. The official history of the women's
organisation, dating from 1937, claimed that women saw their role as
supportive, leaving 'the active political struggle' of Party members to
the men, which is really another way of saying the same thing. It is also
possible that, in what were for many depressed times, it was enough
for a family to afford a man's subscription; this was certainly claimed.[45]
What is clear is that Party membership figures do not accurately
reflect the number of women who actively supported the Nazi Party,
and that they probably are a considerable underestimate of activists'
numbers.

Although family affiliation accounted for no doubt a substantial
number of women who turned to National Socialism in the *Kampfzeit*,
other reasons brought in significant numbers in the later 1920s and early
1930s. Chief among these was the eclipse of smaller, less vital *völkisch*
groups by the NSDAP. In a sense, women who had belonged to the
Schutz-und Trutzbund, for example, became Nazis by proxy in the first
instance, through the agency of a forceful local leader who decided to
leave the dwindling group for the ascendant NSDAP. The *Frauengruppe
Leipzig* (Leipzig Women's Group) followed this pattern, and was
valuable to the NSDAP as the nucleus of the future NSF in *Gau* Saxony.
But the biggest influx of women Party members at any one time came in
1928 when Elsbeth Zander won Hitler's recognition of her *Deutscher
Frauenorden* (DFO – German Women's Order) as an accredited NSDAP
women's organisation. The bargain involved the adherence of some
4,000 more or less willing DFO members to the Nazi Party, which
probably more than doubled the Party's existing female membership.
Elsbeth Zander had drawbacks, but she personally inspired the loyalty of
a few thousand women, and they followed her into the NSDAP. Further,
the six or seven hundred recruits to the DFO each month in spring 1931
were also new members for the NSDAP. Particularly valuably, Flsbeth
Zander was said to be adept at appealing to simple, working-class
women, in the DFO's strongholds in Berlin and Chemnitz, especially,
and thus she tapped a source of support which was not otherwise inclined
to be susceptible to the Nazi message. Again, Guida Diehl, leader of the
conservative moral crusade called the Newland Movement, commanded
the support of a significant body of similarly minded women who were
drawn into the NSDAP when she became the NSF's 'cultural adviser' for

a brief period in 1931–2.[46] Even if only a fraction of the 200,000 members claimed by Newland followed her into the NSDAP, the Party clearly benefited numerically from her association with the NSF, at least in the short run.

Claudia Koonz plausibly argues that Guida Diehl's view that 'Crisis required a strong party' led Christian conservative women to swallow their instinctive aversion to the character and activities of the SA, particularly, because 'as in wartime, Germany needed warriors'.[47] No doubt it took cataclysmic economic disaster combined with the spectre of a growing Communist Party to cement the strange alliance of conformist middle-class women with groups of roughnecks. But the gravitation of die-hard reactionaries with hardline Christian moral views into the National Socialist camp is also testimony to the way in which the Party altered its image. By the early 1930s its attitude towards religion was no longer explicitly hostile. Women with *völkisch* sentiments who classed themselves as Christians could persuade themselves that the NSDAP was becoming more respectable and less lunatic as the prospect of power loomed before it. Undoubtedly decisive was the Party's implacable anti-communism: it does seem clear that, to many, 'upholding "Christian morality" in the face of the menace of "Bolshevist licence" … implied also defending Christianity itself'. The first 'Principles of the *NS-Frauenschaft*' espoused, probably genuinely, 'a German women's spirit which is rooted in GOD, nature, family, nation and homeland', in that order and with that emphasis. And leading officials of the NSF responded with 'Evangelical' or 'Catholic' when Party questionnaires enquired about religious affiliation.[48]

It is only one of the many paradoxes involved in assessing support for the NSDAP that while the Christian religion made some women proof against the Nazi appeal, particularly in Catholic strongholds, a desire to defend Christianity at all costs drove other women to support a party which was bound to be its enemy. Until more research is done into the day-to-day influence of both Churches on women's behaviour and attitudes, only very general observations of this kind can be made. Clearly, though, the change in the NSDAP's public attitude towards religion removed an obstacle which had undoubtedly deterred some who sympathised with other aspects of the Party's appeal. Combined with economic crisis, renewed strength on the left, and the eclipse of the various other *völkisch* groups by the early 1930s, it was a powerful factor in bringing Christian, conservative, middle-class women into the Party, at the same time as the effects of the Depression were attracting unemployed women from the lower-middle class and from the poorer, unorganised sections of the working class. Older women might yearn for a return to less threatening bygone days; the young, disillusioned by the false emancipation of the 1920s, were prepared to trade low-paid, monotonous factory or clerical work, or the prospect of graduate unemployment, for the husband and family Hitler had promised each of them.[49]

Yet the 'Hitler cult', which has so obsessed commentators on women's response to National Socialism, was not a major factor in the Nazi appeal. Merkl may be right in stressing its importance for his small group of early women Party members, but he also emphasises the *völkisch*, anti-Left and anti-Semitic elements of the Nazi appeal. Bremme does not regard Hitler's persona as decisive among women voters, and the results of the 1932 presidential elections reinforce her view.[50] This may simply reflect the contrast between the few who committed themselves to the Party, as members or as supporters, and the millions who were driven by fear or desperation to vote NSDAP in time of crisis. Certainly, as economic stability returned in the mid-1930s, it became apparent that the overwhelming majority of women, at least, had not been converted to National Socialism as a creed which could replace their religion and convince them of the necessity of devoting themselves to the priorities of a selfish dictatorial regime. Voters who had turned to the NSDAP, perhaps as a last resort in time of crisis, had only ever represented a minority of the electorate, even in 1933. Most of them, far less those who had not voted Nazi, were not prepared to accept the totalitarian demands of Hitler's regime as the logical consequence of their having cast a vote for the NSDAP on two or three occasions. And the religious sensibilities of women, to which the Party had eventually had to pay lip-service in the *Kampfzeit*, did not evaporate after 1933. On the contrary, the clearest examples of passive resistance to Nazi demands for conformity are to be found among groups of women with a strong attachment to their local church, Catholic or Protestant. Of all this, Party workers were well aware. For them, National Socialism might be 'a religion', and Hitler the new Messiah, but they could not detach women – and, worse, the children they were bringing up – from religion, and encountered strong resistance when they showed signs of trying to do so.[51]

Furthermore, the Party's promise to liberate women from the emancipation of the Weimar era backfired, in two important areas. Women who had welcomed National Socialism because its leaders sang the praises of non-employed wives and mothers – especially in the Depression – were not inclined to go out to work to help the German war-effort in the early 1940s. And women who looked forward to being relieved of their political responsibilities by a Party which anathematised the participation of women in politics proved thoroughly resistant to Nazi attempts to try to organise them and make them 'politically conscious'.[52] In both these cases, as with their religious allegiance, it was the women who were being consistent. The Nazi regime, by contrast, was reverting to a kind of radicalism, the conservative image adopted in the early 1930s having served its purpose. But the old radicalism was gone for ever: to this extent, the conservative phase had had a beneficial

by-product in the disappearance of the 'Nazi feminists' from prominence
by the end of 1933. The apparent paradox of their ever associating with
the NSDAP in the first place can be explained in a variety of ways. They
seem to have imagined that the Party's men could be made to change
their minds about women's role in the movement; their Nazism was
stronger than their feminism; and they were to some extent encouraged
by Strasser, who seems to have had some sympathy for them, admittedly
at a time when attracting votes from all shades of opinion mattered. But
the temporary accommodation with conservative and clerical groups in
1933 – the logical conclusion to the NSDAP's conservative appeal – was
followed by the imposition of hardline uniformity on the NSF,
producing a leadership in the Nazi women's organisations which was
hostile to 'women's rightists' and compliant in matching its activities to
the demands of the regime, whatever contortions that might involve.[53] It
is unlikely that any of this could have been predicted by Kater's
housewives, Merkl's defensive romantics, or Koonz's 'heroines' when
they joined the NSDAP in the *Kampfzeit*.

Notes

1   Letter from Gertrud Bäumer to Helene König, 1934, in E. Beckmann (ed.), *Des Lebens wie der Liebe Band: Gertrud Bäumer, Briefe* (Tübingen: 1956), p. 63; M. Beard, quoted in Helen Boak, 'Women in Weimar Germany: the "Frauenfrage" and the Female Vote', in R. Bessel and E. J. Feuchtwanger (eds), *Social Change and Political Development in Weimar Germany* (London: 1981), p. 155.

2   For example: Alice Hamilton, 'Woman's Place in Germany', *Survey Graphic*, January 1934; Judith Grunfeld, 'Women Workers in Nazi Germany', *Nation*, 13 March 1937.

3   For instance: Hilda Browning, *Women under Fascism and Communism* (London, 1934); M. Lode, 'Women under Hitler's Yoke', *The Communist International*, November 1938.

4   Gertrud Scholtz-Klink, *Die Frau im Dritten Reich* (Tübingen: 1978), pp. 519–27, for her speech to the Swedish–German Association in Stockholm, February 1937.

5   Clifford Kirkpatrick, *Nazi Germany: Its Women and Family Life* (New York: 1938).

6   Gabrielle Bremme, *Die Politische Rolle der Frau in Deutschland* (Göttingen: 1956); David Schoenbaum, *Hitler's Social Revolution: Class and Status in Nazi Germany 1933–39* (New York: 1966).

7   Jill McIntyre, 'Women and the Professions in Germany, 1930–1940', in Anthony Nicholls and Erich Matthias (eds), *German Democracy and the Triumph of Hitler* (London: 1971), pp. 175–213; Michael H. Kater, 'Krisis des Frauenstudiums in der Weimarer Republik', *Vierteljahrsschrift für Sozial-und Wirtschaftsgeschichte*, 59:2, 1972, pp. 207–50; Renate Bridenthal, 'Beyond *Kinder, Küche, Kirche*: Weimar Women at Work', *Central European History*, VI:2, 1973, pp. 148–66; Jill Stephenson, 'Girls' Higher Education in Germany in the 1930s', *Journal of Contemporary History*, 10:1, 1975, pp. 41–69.

8   Jill Stephenson, *Women in Nazi Society* (London: 1975); Richard J. Evans, *The Feminist Movement in Germany, 1894–1933* (London: 1976); Dörte Winkler, *Frauenarbeit im 'Dritten Reich'* (Hamburg: 1977); Leila Rupp, *Mobilizing Women for War. German and American Propaganda, 1939–1945* (Princeton, NJ: 1978); Stefan Bajohr, *Die Hälfte der Fabrik: Geschichte der Frauenarbeit in Deutschland 1914 bis 1945* (Marburg: 1979); Jill Stephenson, *The Nazi Organisation of Women* (London: 1981).

9   In addition to works mentioned in (7) and (8), they include: Timothy Mason, 'Women in Germany, 1925–1940: Family, Welfare and Work', *History Workshop*, 1976, no. 1, pp. 74–113, no. 2, pp. 5–32; Claudia Koonz, 'Conflicting Allegiances: Political Ideology and Women Legislators in Weimar Germany', *Signs*, I:3, 1976, pp. 663–83; Richard J. Evans, 'German Women and the Triumph of Hitler', Article Accepted for Demand Publication by the *Journal of Modern History*, 48:1, 1976, pp. 1–53; Brian Peterson, 'The Politics of Working-class Women in the Weimar Republic', *Central European History*, x:2, 1977, pp. 87–111; Claudia Koonz, 'Mothers in the Fatherland: Women in Nazi Germany', in Renate Bridenthal and Claudia Koonz (eds), *Becoming Visible. Women in European History* (Boston, Mass: 1977), pp. 445–73; Jill Stephenson, 'The Nazi Organisation of Women, 1933–39', in Peter D. Stachura (ed.), *The Shaping of the Nazi State* (London: 1978), pp. 186–209; Stefan Bajohr, 'Weiblicher Arbeitsdienst im "Dritten Reich" zwischen Ideologie und Ökonomie', *Vierteljahrshefte für Zeitgeschichte*, 1980, no. 3, pp. 331–57; Gisela Miller, 'Erziehung durch den Reichsarbeitsdienst für die weibliche Jugend (RADwJ). Ein Beitrag zur Aufklärung national-sozialistischer Erziehungideologie', in Manfred Heinemann (ed.), *Erziehung und Schulung im Dritten Reich, Teil 2: Hochschule, Erwachsenenbildung* (Stuttgart: 1980), pp. 170–93; Jill Stephenson, ' "Verantwortungsbewusstsein": Politische Schulung durch die Frauenorganisation im Dritten Reich', in Heinemann (ed.), *Erziehung*, pp. 194–205; Jill Stephenson, 'Nationalsozialistischer Dienstgedanke, bürgerliche Frauen und Frauenorganisationen im Dritten Reich', *Geschichte und Gesellschaft*, 7:1981, pp. 555–71.
10 M. S. Jones, review of Stephenson, 'Nazi Organisation', in Stachura (ed.), *Nazi State*, *New German Studies*, 6:2, 1978, p. 134.
11 Richard Grunberger, *A Social History of the Third Reich* (London: 1971), p. 254.
12 David Pryce-Jones, 'Mothers for the Reich', review of Stephenson, *Women in Nazi Society*, *Times Literary Supplement*, 2 July 1976.
13 Koonz, 'Conflicting Allegiances', p. 663.
14 Stephenson, *Nazi Organisation of Women*, p. 71.
15 Timothy W. Mason, *Sozialpolitik im Dritten Reich* (Opladen: 1977).
16 See Berenice A. Carroll (ed.), *Liberating Women's History: Theoretical and Critical Essays* (Urbana, Ilinois: 1976).
17 Quoted in Boak, 'Women in Weimar Germany', p. 155.
18 Specific sources are: Bremme, *Politische Rolle*; Evans, 'German Women'; Boak, 'Women in Weimar Germany', Peterson, 'Politics of Working-class Women'.
19 Hermann Rauschning, *Hitler Speaks. A Series of Political Conversations with Adolf Hitler on his Real Aims* (London: 1939), p. 259.
20 Bremme, *Politische Rolle*, p. 74.
21 A. Jill R. Stephenson, 'Women in German Society, 1930–40' (Ph.D. thesis, University of Edinburgh, 1974), pp. 341–2.
22 Bremme, *Politische Rolle*, p. 69.
23 Peterson, 'Politics of Working-class Women', p. 103.
24 Bremme, *Politische Rolle*, p. 74; Boak, 'Women in Weimar Germany', p. 170, n. 24.
25 Calculated from figures in *Statistisches Jahrbuch für das Deutsche Reich*, 1933, p. 539.
26 Evans, 'German Women', p. 36.
27 Bremme, *Politische Rolle*, pp. 72–3.
28 Peterson, 'Politics of Working-class Women', pp. 102, 106–8.
29 Mason, *Sozialpolitik*, pp. 63–4.
30 Stephenson, *Nazi Organisation of Women*, pp. 26, 28, 32–3, 41.
31 Bremme, *Politische Rolle*, pp. 39, 65.
32 Stephenson, *Women in Nazi Society*, pp. 38, 40, 57–61.
33 Evans, *Feminist Movement*, pp. 154–6, 236–8.
34 Marion A. Kaplan, *The Jewish Feminist Movement in Germany. The Campaigns of the Jüdischer Frauenbund, 1904–1938* (Westport, Conn: 1979), pp. 6, 13–14, 40, 70–3.
35 Peterson, 'Politics of Working-class Women', p. 100.

36 Bridenthal, 'Beyond *Kinder, Küche, Kirche*', pp. 148–66; Dörte Winkler, *Frauenarbeit im 'Dritten Reich'*, pp. 33–7.
37 Bremme, *Politische Rolle*, pp. 74–5.
38 Stephenson, *Nazi Organisation of Women*, pp. 65, 67, 68, 79–80.
39 Bundesarchiv, R45II/64, DVP Reichsgeschäftsstelle, 'Frauenrundschau', 4 March 1932, 'Nationalsozialisten und Frauen', p. 1141.
40 Stephenson, *Nazi Organisation of Women*, pp. 65–72, 75–6, 97–8, 130, 143–4.
41 Reichsorganisationsleiter (ed.), *NSDAP Partei-Statistik* (Munich: 1935), vol. I, p. 16.
42 Wolfgang Schäfer, *NSDAP. Entwicklung und Struktur der Staatspartei des Dritten Reiches* (Hanover: 1956), p. 19, Table 5, taken from *Partei-Statistik*, vol. I, p. 70; Michael Kater, 'Zur Soziographie der frühen NSDAP', *Vierteljahrshefte für Zeitgeschichte*, 19, 1971, pp. 126–7, 151–2, 155–6. The absolute numbers given are calculated from percentages given on p. 152.
43 Lawrence D. Stokes, 'The Social Composition of the Nazi Party in Eutin, 1925–32', *International Review of Social History*, XXIII, 1978, pp. 12–13, 18. The percentages are my calculation; Kater, 'Zur Soziographie', pp. 152, 156; Peter Merkl, *Political Violence under the Swastika* (Princeton, NJ: 1975), pp. 121, 136.
44 F. J. Heyen, *Nationalsozialismus im Alltag* (Boppard: 1967), p. 330.
45 Stephenson, *Nazi Organisation of Women*, pp. 25, 53 f, 67 f.
46 ibid., pp. 28–33, 36, 44, 77–81.
47 Koonz, 'Mothers in the Fatherland', p. 454.
48 Stephenson, *Nazi Organisation of Women*, pp. 35–7.
49 This is the burden of Bridenthal's argument in 'Beyond *Kinder, Küche, Kirche*', pp. 148–66.
50 Merkl, *Political Violence*, p. 136; Bremme, *Politische Rolle*, p. 75.
51 Examples of this may be found in Heyen, *Nationalsozialismus im Alltag*, pp. 179, 188–9; Edward N. Peterson, *The Limits of Hitler's Power* (Princeton, NJ: 1969), pp. 208–23, 259–63, 417–27.
52 Stephenson, *Nazi Organisation of Women*, pp. 145–6, 150, 152–6, 160–1, 180–2, 184–5.
53 ibid., pp. 35, 67, 98–102, 115–16, 124–5, 132–9, 182–4, 202–6.

4 National Socialism and the Educated Elite in the Weimar Republic

GEOFFREY J. GILES

'The National Socialist revolution in Germany is most deeply founded, has its most bigoted and best organised support in the German universities', wrote J. J. Bronowski in the Cambridge journal, *Granta*, in April 1933.[1] Historians of National Socialism would no longer accept this view, but at the time it did not seem unreasonable to many observers. The well-publicised students' bonfires of 'un-German' books, many of which were attended by professors, made it appear that the new regime had the endorsement of the German academic world. The acquiescence of the universities in the dismissals of Jewish scholars reinforced this conclusion. German professors had, as civil servants, long shown deference to the state. Their flirtations with liberalism in the first half of the nineteenth century prevented the full trust of nervous governments. Not until the creation of the German empire did academics finally place their liberal ideals behind their nationalistic aspirations. They were rewarded by the state, or more particularly by the civil service. As the latter expanded, and education became more important than birth for entry into most of its branches, the myth of the universities as bearers of culture was perpetuated by bureaucrats who were hungry for status which could be acquired regardless of social background. They conferred upon the institutions an indefinable cultural nobility which was somehow transmitted to its graduates. Professors became the undisputed leaders of the *Bildungsbürgertum* and, it must be said, relished their role. The First World War, that great crusade of the German spirit, elicited considerable enthusiasm from the professoriate. Even avowed liberals like Ernst Cassirer participated actively in the official propaganda effort, and stifled their distaste for such work.[2]

Student bodies often have a reputation for radicalism, although this characteristic is found in practice only in a small but highly visible minority. There were many examples of this in the first half of the nineteenth century, fewer under the German empire when students saw themselves more as apprentices to the status and responsibilities of the *Kulturträger*.[3] There was much rowdiness from excessive drinking, but there were few demonstrations of a political nature. All that changed during the Weimar Republic, as the size and social composition of the

German student body changed, and the expectations of university graduates were frustrated by large-scale graduate unemployment. The National Socialist Party received support from some students, as did all parties which offered an alternative to the uncertainties of Weimar Germany, but it was extremely limited. A National Socialist Students' Association (NSDStB) was founded in 1926, but did not begin to make inroads into the academic world until the onset of the Depression in 1929. An equivalent organisation for university lecturers was not set up by the Party till 1935 and will not concern us here. The Nazis did not ever entertain high hopes of winning over professors to their cause, and had some doubts about the élitist-minded student body. But students were attracted towards the Nazi movement in increasing numbers as their economic plight worsened. By 1931 even the foreign press began to notice: in July of that year, for example, the *New York Times* noted that

> most students are poor, very many abject: and what is more natural than that pinched and pinching realities should quicken the 'urge to power', – particularly in the young? Hence it comes about that many of the students turn to the vaporous but glamorous and 'strong man' gospel of Hitlerism.[4]

Radicalism might indeed be expected, but it was not so logical that students should embrace the muddled doctrine of National Socialism. Yet paradoxically the Nazis scored one of their earliest major victories in the university environment. In the summer of 1931, eighteen months before Hitler's chancellorship, the National Socialist Students' Association seized control of the national students' union. It was a sweet victory for Hitler to claim the support of educated youth at such an early date. How this had happened remained a puzzle for the observer, who was equally bewildered by the events of the spring of 1933 on German campuses.

The beatings of Jewish students, the black lists of undesirable teachers, the raids on professors' homes, the widespread dismissals, all seemed inconceivable at the very cradle of academic freedom, not least to the professors involved.[5] The faculty privately deplored the fate of their colleagues, while publicly they simply shrugged their shoulders. They gave scarcely a thought to the consideration that the universities themselves shared some responsibility for these developments. Though acknowledged as the intellectual leaders of German society, professors made very few pronouncements indicating their disapproval of the National Socialist movement. In fact many conservative professors admired the discipline which the National Socialist Student Association promised to bring to the student body. A Heidelberg professor could still naïvely say in May 1933: 'It is a strange situation but we have no fear of the results of power being given to such splendid types as young Scheel [the local Nazi student leader], with their plans for creating a type of hardworking, patriotic student.'[6]

Such contemporary writing as dealt with the relationships between education and the National Socialists up to 1945 dealt almost exclusively with the Third Reich itself.[7] The most noteworthy account was the inquiry of a Harvard sociologist, Edward Y. Hartshorne, whose book, *The German Universities and National Socialism*, appeared in 1937. It remains a useful beginning to the subject, for Hartshorne compiled an outline of the extensive administrative changes which the Nazi seizure of power had brought upon the university system. In some of this he could not know the entire story, for he relied heavily upon official decrees. The interest of Hartshorne's work, and this is what dates it, is his attempt to explore the background to the reforms and to weigh dispassionately the pros and cons of the new system. He described some of the outrages perpetrated against distinguished scholars like Fritz Haber. His investigation of the number of dismissed scholars put the proportion at 14–16 per cent of the total. And yet at the end of the book he drew up a 'balance sheet' which found as many points to praise about the new regime as he did to condemn. The faults he categorised as losses to science, the dismissals of faculty and overloading the budget with supernumerary pensions, had taken funds away from research; the annihilation on principle of free discussion, the prescription of an official dogmatic *Weltanschauung* and the politicisation of the classroom had seriously compromised scholarly creativity and excellence. The benefits he noted were not gains for science, but 'for Germany': there were no longer student riots, idlers had been eliminated, the promotion of military sports contrasted favourably with the former 'apathetic, dilettantish, over-intellectual attitude of many students'.[8] Hartshorne looked to the future of the German academic world with unwarranted optimism, speculating that the National Socialists might yet make up the deficiencies which their revolution had wrought upon the academic world and 'achieve again the distinction of a great civilization.' The book's closing lines give rise to doubts about his perceptivity: quoting Meinecke, he reiterated that

> it seems 'as though the State *must* sin' for the sake of preserving its existence. Germany has succeeded in preserving her existence amid a flux of circumstances where many a lesser nation would have collapsed. The 'Wacht am Rhein' has been re-established, and of *this* the Germans have a good right to be proud. . . . To condemn Germany alone for the 'sins' committed in the name of National Socialism is to perpetuate the fatal error of Versailles.[9]

However, this was not so different from conservative opinion in Britain at the time, and perhaps represented a more widespread view among the

British and American academics than has been subsequently admitted. Hartshorne, as a sociologist, was not much interested in the history of National Socialist involvement in the universities and discussed the pre-1933 period only briefly. He put some blame on the dispute between Carl H. Becker, the Prussian Minister of Culture, and the student body over the right to affiliate with the more openly anti-Semitic Austrian students' union, which set most German students at loggerheads with the government. Beyond this he did not attempt a detailed explanation.

In the decade after 1945 writers on higher education and National Socialism fell into two categories: apologists who sought to show how they had duped the Nazis in order to continue their scholarly activities much as before; and those who strove to understand to what degree the history of German thought and culture contained the seeds of Nazism. A typical example of the former is the self-congratulatory account of Moritz J. Bonn, a rector of the Berlin College of Commerce, which is full of anecdotes of his assertiveness:

> The papers gave me headlines and wrote me up as a hero who had single-handedly beaten down a Nazi rebellion. . . . From that time on until my resignation, I had little trouble with my Nazi students. I had spoken a language they could understand.[10]

The German historian, Gerhard Ritter, wasted no time in explaining to the public as early as December 1945 just how it had been possible for the professoriate as a whole to manifest a critical attitude towards the Nazi regime. Although new appointments led in many universities to a preponderance of National Socialists after 1933, he claims, 'happily not a single German faculty completely fell prey to the Nazis.'[11] This must have sounded strange at the time in light of the prevalent view that the totalitarian Nazi state was a monolith. Ritter was one of the first to suggest that the sheer size of the bureaucratic machinery led to considerable clumsiness and inefficiency. The fact that Ritter had helped organise the election campaign against Hitler in 1932 and had presided over a mass meeting of opponents of National Socialism had apparently been forgotten by 1937. The purpose of such essays was to reassure the non-academic world that professors had stood by their principles and beliefs under the onslaught of National Socialism, and had not completely sacrificed the integrity of the German university, as everyone outside Germany (and many in it) assumed. Nazism stood outside the mainstream of German cultural life. Ritter rejected the notion of atavistic influences in this and other writings.

Friedrich Meinecke looked back at the age of 84 and felt compelled to reach a different conclusion. In *The German Catastrophe* he briefly traced the historical influences which in his view assisted the rise of National Socialism. Among them was a failing of the education system. The rapid growth of technology in Germany at the end of the nineteenth century had increased the demand for scientific and technical specialists. Their training had become so narrow that their all-round humanistic education had been neglected: '*Homo sapiens* was supplanted by *homo faber*.'[12] The restitution of Humboldtian ideals would have removed the blinkers, according to Meinecke. Frederic Lilge also sought to identify the symptoms of decline into the 'catastrophe of German intellectual culture' which faced postwar academics. He described the inherent contradictions of Fichte's idealist conception of a university, and the strict control which the latter believed should be exercised over the minds of the students. Lilge expressed relief that Humboldt, not Fichte, had become the Prussian Secretary of Education at the critical moment of reform. He mused uncertainly on the probability of Fichte's openly supporting Hitlerian political ideals but concluded that Fichte's 'boastful nationalism . . . was already so extreme and so exclusive that action could hardly have made it more complete.' There is much of merit in Fichte's educational ideas, but the confusions in his writings 'helped to promote the political abuse of the most valuable' of these ideas. Overall, Lilge concluded, the sponsorship by Fichte of liberal education in Germany 'added less to the strength than to the insecurity and vulnerability of the very ideal of such an education.'[13] He, too, commented on the increasing specialisation of the universities and quoted some of Nietzsche's criticisms of this development. Approaching more recent times, he examined the growth of irrational thought and the weak attempts to counteract it. Lilge did not accuse any particular scholar or philosopher of being a direct precursor of Nazism. He avoided simplistic condemnations even of people like Heidegger, and instead stressed the gradual cumulative effect of whole currents of intellectual thought. He expressed more regret than censure over the failures of Weimar liberals to defend their ideals, noting merely that Becker's 'anxiousness to preserve, rather than the courage to reinterpret and re-enact, the values of a liberal education . . . was characteristic of most of the leading German educationalists of that time.'[14]

This represented virtually the extent of academic self-examination for the decade following the war. There were, in order to balance the sorry reports of *émigrés*, the stories of the successful resistance of individuals in the face of National Socialism; and there were on the other hand rather depersonalised accounts of the general failure of German thought. A more specific enquiry into the role of universities and students in the rise of Nazism was not undertaken. Academics had been made to feel uncomfortable enough by the bankruptcy of their ideals, and turned to the wider phenomenon of the National Socialism outside their walls, about which there was a host of unanswered questions.

Karl Dietrich Bracher's enormous and brilliant study of the collapse of the Weimar Republic provided many answers. He analysed the role of a number of institutions and organisations in the first part of the book, but paid scant attention to the academic world. His excursus on the radicalisation of the student body covered barely three pages and was more narrative than analytical in scope. He did note, however, that the lack of contact between academic youth and the state in which they entertained aspirations of leading positions exacerbated the atmosphere of unrest and disorder.[15] It has been subsequently noted in connection with other examples of student protest that such blockages of channels of communication invariably lead to confrontation politics on the part of the aggrieved.[16] Bracher was not able to offer a detailed explanation of the speed with which the National Socialist Students' Association turned the grievances of the students into victory for themselves.

In the following decade (1956–65) a number of German universities celebrated anniversaries with the publication of *Festschriften* on the history of the institution. The characteristic of those published in the German Democratic Republic was a preoccupation with the heroic exploits of communist student groups in the Weimar Republic and their subsequent persecution in the Third Reich. Since faculty had almost nothing to do with communist activities, the emphasis in recording their activities generally concentrated on the frequency and cordiality of academic contacts with the Soviet Union. This convention is upheld even in the latest historical treatment of universities, *Magister und Scholaren*, which offers no new analysis, preferring to eulogise the Mechterstädt martyrs, a group of labourers murdered by trigger-happy fraternity students in the unsettled period following the November Revolution.[17] This was an appalling incident but it neither epitomises nor explains the political attitudes of Weimar students. This is not to say that West German *Festschriften* were any better. Here universities were inclined to remain silent altogether. Kiel University's tercentenary volume, for example, while admitting to a nation-wide tradition of professorial anti-Semitism, attempted unconvincingly to demonstrate the positive attitude of the faculty towards the Republic. A couple of incidents involving Nazi students were described but not explained.[18]

West German universities did not make a more concerted effort to come to terms with their past until the mid-1960s. They did so then only under pressure from a newly radicalised student body, which began to ask questions about the reception of National Socialism by the academic world. Student curiosity had been sparked by such publications as Rolf Seeliger's sensationalistic pamphlets, entitled *Brown University*, which dug up embarrassing quotations by well-known professors published in the Third Reich, allegedly testifying to their authoritarianism, racism, anti-Semitism, and so on.[19] The University of Tübingen was the first to respond with a lecture series on 'German Intellectual Life and National Socialism'.[20] It was followed by similar reflections at the University of Munich and the Free University of Berlin.[21] Once more the focus of interest lay on the Third Reich itself, though there was some attempt to explain attitudes in the Weimar period. Kurt Sontheimer, who had published in 1962 an excellent book on anti-democratic thought among Weimar intellectuals, turned his attention specifically to the universities;[22] Helmut Kuhn described the atmosphere at the university on the eve of the Third Reich, prior to his emigration;[23] and Theodor Eschenburg wrote a piece about his experiences as a student before 1933.[24] If the academic establishment felt that it had thereby fulfilled its obligations towards the inquisitive socialist Left, it was mistaken. In 1967 Wolfgang Fritz Haug published a scathing attack on these lecture series. He subjected the language and thought content of all three publications (plus a fourth) to a close analysis. He recorded the frequency of such excuses given for the passivity of academics as their unpolitical nature, their blindness for what was happening, their concern to isolate pure scholarship in its own world. He felt impatient with their claims that class considerations made most academics ignore the mass movement of National Socialism. He was dissatisfied with statements such as the following one from Sontheimer because it made the universities appear like passive victims:

> The German universities fell prey to National Socialism relatively easily because their uncritical, simply patriotic and nationalistic disposition legitimated almost everything which came forward with the express claim of destroying the Weimar system of the multi-party state. The institution became the victim of its own anti-democratic prejudices.[25]

This, while certainly not denying responsibility, did not in Haug's view offer a satisfactory explanation of why these attitudes prevailed. His own answer was a polemical Marxist one, and he urged his contemporaries to break down the tight class compartmentalisation in which certainly Weimar academics had been locked and which still lingered on. The enunciation of this message seems to have been his main point in writing the book, but his criticism of the lecture series remains a thought-provoking and valid one.

Following the rigour of Haug's discussion, the books on students and professors by Hans Peter Bleuel and Ernst Klinnert were something of a disappointment.[26] Both books give a description of the currents of thought among each group in the years before the Third Reich, but they have a rather narrow base of secondary literature. While the authors did make extensive use of student newspapers and journals, they did not bother to consult the records of the German Student Union or other primary sources. One of the most valuable contributions to the field came in 1969 with the publication of Fritz Ringer's *The Decline of the German Mandarins. The German Academic Community 1890–1933*. The book was reviewed widely and at length, not always in terms of unqualified praise, though it was accepted as an important work by all. Perhaps its greatest value lay in stimulating a lively debate about the characteristics and attitudes of the German professoriate. Ringer began by describing how the professors came to their exalted position in Wilhelmine Germany. By administering state examinations, they functioned as the guardians of access into the civil service during a period when academic success was replacing qualifications of birth and family as the prerequisite for entry. The new bureaucratic élite sought to enhance their position by declaring their teachers (and by implication themselves) to be 'bearers of culture' – members of a select club, acceptance in which was attested by the possession of a university degree. Ringer explained that the elevated position of the professoriate and the rest of the educated élite was feasible only because German society was in a period of transition, where social and political development lagged well behind the country's economic advances. The gradual transformation of an essentially feudal state into a heavily bureaucratic monarchy favoured the development of this strong and self-conscious mandarin élite.[27] Yet after 1918 other measures of social value and esteem competed vigorously with the university degree, as they do in all democratised and highly industrial societies. All professors felt unquestionably threatened, and reacted in two distinct ways.

His examination of the Weimar academic world was limited largely to the social sciences. Given the difficulties of generalising from the work of some highly individual scholars, Ringer painted a convincing picture of the values which almost all professors shared. The Weimar Republic showed the renowned neutrality of the German professor to be a myth. The majority of them were adamantly opposed to the concept of a republican government. Ringer labelled them the 'orthodox' professors and showed how they reverted more and more to emotional and irrational pleas for their favourite causes. Even the *Vernunftrepublikaner* who stood behind the Republic as a political reality and at least temporary necessity, the 'modernists' as Ringer called them, were far from avid in their support. They would have preferred another form of government and thus did little to rally to the defence of the current one beyond a dry, intellectual endorsement. The more violent manifestations of national insecurity were repugnant to them, but very few modernists spoke out against anti-Semitic disturbances, for example. The few who did comment made no attempt to disguise their own, more moderate predisposition against the Jews.[28] In fact, anti-Semitism had long been a common though tacit sentiment on German university campuses. Academic freedom really existed, as Max Weber observed, only 'within the limits of officially accepted political and religious views'.[29] This history of ideas, or rather the aversion to them, had been studied before; what Ringer did was to add a sociological perspective to the question. Almost every German professor felt too much haughty disdain for a supposed party of the masses to support the National Socialists before 1933. This is not to say that there was outright rejection of the movement. As late as 1932 Eduard Spranger, in what Ringer described correctly as a classic mandarin response to National Socialism, argued against a professorial motion of censure regarding Nazi student violence, believing that this 'national movement among the students [was] still genuine at the core, only undisciplined in its form.'[30] Similar examples may be found elsewhere. As a model for the whole of the professoriate, Ringer's study was persuasive. There is, however, still a need for investigations of other branches of scholarship which Ringer neglected. Something like Beyerchen's study of physicists in the Third Reich, extending back through the Weimar Republic would be instructive.[31] Of even greater interest would be an examination of the political and intellectual attitudes of scholars in some of the areas which suffered from considerable ideological contamination after 1933, such as geography and anthropology, where the focus has hitherto been largely on the Third Reich.

Herbert Döring studied a particular group of Ringer's 'modernists', who grouped themselves loosely in the so-called 'Weimar Circle'. Even these few professors who remained ostensibly loyal to the Weimar Republic were more concerned with the maintenance of their own social and intellectual leadership than in any intrinsic merits of the democratic government. Döring denied, as have other critics of Ringer, that the professors were ever members of the *ruling* class, and saw them more as the spokesmen of the real rulers.[32] Situated thus on the periphery, they felt particularly vulnerable to the shifts in the structure of society, as political mass parties and interest groups were increasingly able to make their views count through their own spokesmen. The German professor in the Weimar Republic no longer spoke for the whole of society, as he had once felt was the case.

If we are faced in the case of the professoriate with 'the paradox of an intelligentsia which appears to conform rather than rebel', in what ways did the student body differ?[33] The student protest movement of the late 1960s sparked interest in the behaviour of students in earlier times. Jürgen Schwarz took a thorough look at the attitudes of German students towards the foundation of the Weimar Republic and its early years up to 1923. The general enmity of students towards the Republic was an accepted commonplace, but Schwarz showed that initially there was a considerable effort on the part of students to accept and adapt to the new form of government. Only after the signing of the Versailles Treaty did the guardedly positive attitude give way to the entrenched *völkisch* nationalism which in 1923 took on a revolutionary air.[34] Specialised monographs of this nature in the 1970s began to correct certain details of the earlier, broadly conceived articles by Nipperdey and Zorn on Weimar student politics.[35]

It remained uncertain precisely how the National Socialist Students' Association had succeeded in seizing power so quickly and so decisively in 1931 in the hitherto solidly fraternity-dominated German Students' Union. The rightist orientation of the students was well documented but this, as in the case of the professors, did not turn the average student automatically into a Nazi. The development of the National Socialist Students' Association during the Weimar years was expertly unravelled by Anselm Faust. Ursula Dibner, in an earlier unpublished dissertation, had provided a useful introduction but was hampered by too-limited sources to give more than a fragmentary description of the events of those years.[36] Faust immersed himself in the recently available archives of the Nazi student organisation, and set out his analysis with admirable clarity. He investigated the students' *mentalité*, and the effect of his dwindling expectations in light of the economic situation. The material welfare of the average student was reflected in a number of ways. For example, the number of students who took a job during the vacation rose from 10 per cent in 1921, to 50 per cent in 1922 and 90 per cent in 1923.[37] The overall position improved during the middle years of the Weimar Republic but worsened sharply after 1929, and the more so for students, for whom jobs became far less available at that time than in the earlier part of the decade.

Faust's focus rests upon the National Socialist Students' Association (NSDStB) but he steps well beyond the confines of a narrow institutional history when he describes the interrelationships between the organisation and other sectors of the student body. Particularly useful is his examination of the fraternity world and its attraction to National Socialism. Simply by dint of being such well-organised groups comprising more than half the students, the fraternities represented a rich prize to the Nazi student leaders as a fertile ground for the dissemination of their ideology. In the first two years of the NSDStB's existence after 1926, little was done to exploit this opportunity, for the first national NSDStB leader, Wilhelm Tempel, adopted an increasingly antagonistic stance towards the supposed élitism of the fraternities. He veered off on a course of a social revolutionary rhetoric which was alien to the thinking of most students (who wanted protection not socialism), and of the Nazi Party itself. Michael Kater pointed out in a well-defined article on Tempel's leadership of the early NSDStB that while there was indeed some feeling among the rank and file of the Party that students were being élitist by having their own specialist Nazi organisation at all, the NSDStB was just too small and insignificant at this time for the Party leadership to concern itself with the minutiae of Tempel's policies.[38] It was only when the NSDStB began to show some promise after a few student election successes in 1928 that dissatisfaction with Tempel's direction mounted and assured his dismissal. He had never been all that popular with the local groups, and this early period of the NSDStB was characterised by Faust as 'an uninterrupted succession of internal crises'.[39] There was also considerable local opposition throughout the leadership of Tempel's successor, the high-handed Baldur von Schirach. Despite his unpopularity, Schirach changed the direction of the NSDStB towards a policy of winning over the fraternities, and masterminded the campaigns which eventually led to the extraordinary seizure of power of the German Students' Union in the summer of 1931. Faust describes convincingly how Schirach was able to bring about this surprising coup. The activism of the local groups was backed by the ruthless politicking of the national leadership. The NSDStB did more and, with its much-touted youthful idealism, appeared to care more about student concerns than the cautious, often seemingly ossified fraternity leadership, which was composed of many men whose youth lay far behind them. There were several *causes célèbres* in the universities of Weimar Germany, most of them created and all of them exploited by the Nazi student leadership. Although the issues of pacifism, anti-Semitism, student fees, and university overcrowding were general concerns, the fraternity leadership supported the agitation by the Nazis in a lukewarm manner. An important reason for this was the desire to win governmental favour towards the release of frozen student fees in order to finance the German Students' Union. Such tactical considerations were not understood by the students at large and the fraternity leadership seemed to be hedging on questions of principle where the NSDStB was taking a firm stand. It was the shrewd Baldur von Schirach, distrusted and disliked by almost everyone in turn, who constantly insisted that the NSDStB make a nuisance of itself, so that it gradually became known as the champion of popular grievances against the petty obstructions of the callous and insincere authority.

Faust reconstructed the political history of the NSDStB from extensive archival research more thoroughly than any of his predecessors. He also related changes in the ideological outlook of the students to their socio-economic tribulations. But still the majority of the students did not become members of the NSDStB, which numbered only some 8,000 members at the beginning of 1933. One naturally wonders just who they were, what type of student was particularly drawn into membership of the organisation. In a skilful compilation of the scanty statistical information from this early period, Faust suggested in a series of tables that the average NSDStB members were not very different from the rest of the student body:[40] they were not drawn consistently from any particular discipline. There was no predominance either of the 'permanent student' type or of the inexperienced freshman: rather they came from all semesters of study. Nazi student leaders devoted a tremendous amount of time to NSDStB activities, but they were not drop-outs who neglected their studies totally: the available evidence shows that they were successful in their examinations. Nor can one claim conclusively that there was a smaller or greater proportion of fraternity students in the NSDStB than in the student body at large. Individual universities behaved in different ways, as can also be seen in Faust's comparative data from four towns which shows to which fraternities NSDStB members belonged. Once more, the evidence is lacking that particular types of fraternity were peculiarly susceptible to National Socialism. What Faust succeeded in proving, and what many interested Germans wish still to deny, was the general appeal of National Socialism to the student body.

This theme was also pursued in Michael Kater's masterly book, *Studentenschaft und Rechtsradikalismus in Deutschland 1918–1933*. As one would expect from one of the leading social historians in the field today, Kater offered sophisticated interpretations of a mass of quantitative data. He provided more extensive material than Faust on the profile of NSDStB members by discipline, which reinforced Faust's findings. He also showed that the social background of NSDStB members (using figures from the University of Würzburg) was not much different from the distribution of the upper-middle, lower-middle and working classes among the student body as a whole.[41] The socio-economic condition of the students interested Kater most of all, and he documented the utmost seriousness of the actualities of student life and prospects with a wealth of fascinating detail. This is indeed social history at its best (more's the pity that no English translation of the book has been published!). Others had written that Weimar student life was often grim: Kater set out to discover how grim, for how long, for what proportion of the students, and just how and where this tied in with the rise of Right–radicalism. He found as many as two-thirds of the student population in difficulties which were exacerbated by government cuts in student aid and an increase in tuition fees. But at least the students could eat cheaply and well in the university refectories. Not so, said Kater, and presented figures on the calorific content of refectory meals to show that dependence upon them would have resulted in malnutrition. In order to underline the seriousness of this, he then went on to examine the incidence of tuberculosis as an example of the increasing susceptibility of students to disease during the period, burrowing out figures from diverse sources on the students of Breslau, Leipzig, Munich, Dresden, Tübingen, Stuttgart and Königsberg.[42] The book is replete with such examples of meticulous enquiry. Kater demonstrated that students were worse off, and more consistently so, than any other group in German society. Even the more stable middle years of the Republic brought little hope to them. They suffered, in Kater's words, under a 'permanent economic state of emergency'.[43] Many contemporary comments were merely impressionistic, and a remark on the alarming increase in suicides in 1932 seems to fall into this category. It set Kater searching as always for concrete quantitative data, and he found that students were three times more likely to commit suicide than the population at large even in the years before the economic depression.[44] It is Kater's contention that the fraternities began to lose ground in student politics as soon as they neglected their initial emphasis on student welfare, and turned instead to questions of academic politics. The NSDStB, despite its primary concern with politics, did on the other hand play an active role in trying to provide for its members, for example with job referrals. The evidence is sketchy here, but in most other things it becomes clear that the NSDStB was much better organised than the fraternities. To the debates on defence questions or anti-Semitism the NSDStB brought little that was new. Most of the arguments had already been made by other student groups. The NSDStB, however, became identified in the public mind with these, due to the fact that their campaigns were 'more precisely motivated, more forcefully articulated and in the end better organized as well' than those of the fraternities.[45] A number of studies turned in the early 1970s to a closer examination of the organisation at the local level.

A start had been made in 1965 in the German Democratic Republic with a dissertation on the University of Rostock. The emphasis lay on the Nazification of the university after 1933, but some attention was given to the student elections from 1928 onwards. The NSDStB faced considerable opposition from other student groups as it tried to amend the students' union constitution to introduce the 'leader principle', in order to perpetuate its own control, and failed to achieve this until after January 1933. Much of this study consisted of finger-pointing at professors who were advocates of 'fascist German imperialism' in the Third Reich, but the author did excuse the faculty prior to 1933 for not rallying to combat the rise of National Socialism. The education and background of most of them had not led them into contact with the science of Marxism–Leninism. Therefore the author believed that they could not be in a position to recognise behind the slogans the true intentions of the economically dominant classes.[46] Clearly this conciliatory explanation will not do. Simple knowledge of Marxism–Leninism does not necessarily presuppose acceptance of it, although East German writers assume that this could not be otherwise.

In 1972 Paul Kluke published a lengthy history of the University of Frankfurt am Main from 1914 to 1932. It was a semi-official history, more concerned with development, achievements and the overcoming of material difficulties than with the ideological orientation of the university in the face of the rise of National Socialism. A chapter on the rectorate and its problems dealt not with the radicalisation of the student body but with such matters as the shortage of classroom and office space.[47] It is a pity that Kluke, with access to the university archives, did not cast his net more widely. He did introduce some interesting material, for example, on the sorry treatment of the *Privatdozenten* by the full professors and the resulting politicisation of these untenured lecturers.[48]

But as regards National Socialist influences, he contented himself with a summary treatment of student politics in this period, concentrating on the noisier NSDStB demonstrations. Kluke doled out some rather veiled criticism to the rector in the academic year 1929–30 for not curbing vigorously enough the 'rowdy propaganda' of the Nazi group, but did not discuss the reasons for the rector's cautious preference for silence rather than confrontation.[49] Kluke wrote that after 1933 Frankfurt 'shared the fate' of other universities in the Third Reich, as though destiny had spared her in the previous years, and the history of the university during the Weimar Republic had almost nothing to do with the rise of Nazism.[50]

Partly as a result of the availability of archives, a number of individual studies of universities have concentrated on the student body. Manfred Franze's dissertation on the students at Erlangen was the earliest to attempt to cover the whole period from 1918 to 1945.[51] The first part of the book, in which he analysed the reasons for the students' susceptibility to National Socialism, is particularly interesting and included some discussion of sociological factors. Bracher's thorough election analyses showed that confessional factors were of considerable importance for the incidence of resistance to National Socialism and Franze attributed Erlangen's early fall to the NSDStB partly to its role as the centre of Franconian protestantism. He placed rather more of the blame on the student fraternities, which encompassed over half the students. It was they who politicised student affairs in the mid-1920s, and by imposing their brand of *völkisch* nationalism upon the student body as a whole, prepared the way for the acceptance of National Socialism. Franze also documented in detail the political manoeuvres to which the NSDStB resorted in the course of their student government campaigns.

One of the methodologically most rigorous studies to appear was Wolfgang Kreutzberger's work on the Freiburg students in the Weimar Republic. He was especially interested in their social background, reasoning that their view of society and political orientation was formed in outline before they arrived at the university, under family and educational influences. He examined the expected attitudes and 'political potential' of students from civil service, *Mittelstand*, free professional, and working-class homes, as they might develop anywhere in the country. Applying the local data to this model, he found that Freiburg should have been rather susceptible to National Socialism. The fact that it was not – and the NSDStB generally won no more than 25 per cent of the student vote – can be explained, in Kreutzberger's view, largely by the unusually solid and stable element of the Catholic fraternities (and Youth Movement groups) in the student elections.[52] Confessional factors, then, played a decisive role in pre-1933 resistance to Hitler in the student world. Just as the Centre Party generally acted as a bulwark against National Socialist electoral success in Catholic areas, so too the

Catholic fraternities in Freiburg formed a solid voting block which over the whole period 1922–31 regularly won about 35 per cent of the poll. Peter Spitznagel used Kreutzberger's premiss in his dissertation on the student body at the University of Würzburg. He too emphasised the role of the Catholic fraternities, who gained approximately 42 per cent of the votes in student elections at Würzburg from 1922–31. The contrast between the universities of Erlangen and Würzburg, both of them in Franconia, is an especially illuminating one, and seems to reinforce the importance of confessional and regional background. Spitznagel asserted, with a tinge of regional prejudice himself, that an influx of Protestant students from Prussia gave the Nazis the electoral success that had previously eluded them. The size of the indigenous Catholic contingent remained stable but at the end of the Weimar Republic the rise of support for the NSDStB was accompanied by an increase in the size of the student body drawn more heavily from the Protestant middle class.[53]

Arye Carmon's dissertation on the University of Heidelberg attributed much of the Nazis' success in the university to the sensationalistic campaigns mounted by them, for example, against the pacifist Professor Emil Gumbel.[54] The NSDStB were able to make much political capital out of this and had the support of the faculty to boot. The dissertation by Geoffrey Giles on the University of Hamburg, the only institution for which the local NSDStB files survive intact, also stressed the activism and dedication of the local group.[55] The cautious sympathy of many professors there for the Nazi students, together with their active hostility towards pacifist and socialist student groups, meant that little official action was taken to curb more than the worst excesses of the Nazi student group. Neither the progressive atmosphere of this young postwar university, nor the socialist traditions of the city of Hamburg had a noticeable effect on the outcome of the student elections. Unlike Freiburg's or Würzburg's Catholic students, the socialists and republicans among Hamburg's students were simply not well organised. Student politics tended here as elsewhere to be dominated by the fraternities, and masterly political intriguers though they were, they were outmanoeuvred by the NSDStB. The fraternities' underestimation of the NSDStB is examined in another recent essay by the same author.[56] The dissertation by Giles covers the whole period of the NSDStB's existence up to 1945, and it is to the Third Reich itself that the emphasis of research now seems to be shifting, with the increasing availability of archival material. Uwe Adam explored the topic 'University and National Socialism' in the case of Tübingen in terms of the Third Reich only. He frankly admitted, however, that he had no interest in 'defining causes or results, but only in the description of circumstances',[57] which is a pity. The investigation of the causes of National Socialist susceptibilities at Tübingen was left to Walter Jens' splendid *roman vrai* on the history of the university, which is wonderfully vivid, but anecdotal and ultimately unsatisfactory in providing more than an impressionistic explanation.[58]

The research of the last decade in particular, then, has led to the emergence of a reasonably clear picture of the influence of National Socialism upon students and professors before 1933. The opposition of the latter to the Republic, their ostensible unwillingness to become involved in political affairs but their open distaste for anything that smacked of democracy and especially socialism, their toleration even of violence provided it was directed against such targets, all contributed to their failure to dissociate themselves vigorously from National Socialism. Instead they struggled to look for its positive aspects. The students, crippled economically and psychologically, rising to the traditional social aspirations of their estate, frustrated by the worsening job market, appalled by the inability of the democratic government to remedy the situation, looked for a strong, youthful, radical leadership. While only a minority of the student body ever voted for the Nazis, their votes were enough to install the NSDStB at the head of student government in the earliest 'seizure of power' which the Nazi movement enjoyed. We have a good idea of how they did it. One or two grey areas do, however, remain. The individual universities so far studied have all been remarkable for one reason or another: Heidelberg was the centre of a national scandal, Erlangen one of the main strongholds of National Socialist student support, Freiburg and Würzburg were very Catholic, Hamburg very 'Red'. We still do not have a reliable sense of the typical university in the Weimar Republic. It would be useful to have one or two more local studies of average-sized universities in places where the political and confessional profile approximated that of the Reich in general. Studies of the political thought of the professors have been thorough and illuminating. It is among the students that some further work needs to be done. Much of the history of the fraternities has been written by their own members and is drily antiquarian in nature. Fraternity associations are still often reluctant to open their archives to outsiders, but independent investigations of these important student groups need to be undertaken in order to present a more differentiated picture. The socialist and communist student groups have received rather perfunctory examination to date. They are usually dismissed as being small and insignificant, but they were the main political rivals of the NSDStB. It would be fascinating to subject these groups to the same sort of analysis as has lately been given to the NSDStB, to build up a social and confessional profile of their membership, to examine the appeal of their activities, the specific orientation of their propaganda, their awareness of political realities and the causes of their ineffectuality. Such questions are dealt with only briefly by most authors. It would be much more difficult to find the answers for these groups. Fewer records remain, yet some material does still exist in university archives which could throw light on this. Rigorously critical oral history could help to fill some gaps, but the opportunities for locating survivors are diminishing all the time, and should be quickly grasped. Studies of this nature would enhance our overall understanding of the phenomenon of National Socialism among the educated élite.

Notes

1   'The Nazi Movement and the Universities', *Granta*, 19 April 1933, reprinted in Jim Philip, John Simpson and Nicholas Snowman (eds), *The Best of Granta 1889–1966* (London: 1967), p. 85.
2   David R. Lipton, *Ernst Cassirer: The Dilemma of a Liberal Intellectual in Germany, 1914–1933* (Toronto: 1978), p. 50.
3   See for example Konrad H. Jarausch, 'The Source of German Student Unrest', in Lawrence Stone (ed.), *The University in Society* (Princeton, NJ: 1974), vol. II, pp. 533–67.
4   'Students of Reich Turning to Fascism', *New York Times*, 12 July 1931.
5   Geoffrey J. Giles, 'University Government in Nazi Germany: Hamburg', *Minerva*, xvi, 2, Summer 1978, pp. 196–221.
6   'Nazi Discipline Claims Students', *New York Times*, 3 May 1933.
7   See for example Abraham Wolf, *Higher Education in Nazi Germany, or Education for World Conquest* (London: 1944), or Gregor Ziemer, *Education for Death. The Making of a Nazi* (London: 1942).
8   Edward Y. Hartshorne, *The German Universities and National Socialism* (London: 1937), p. 168.
9   ibid., pp. 173 f.
10   Moritz J. Bonn, *Wandering Scholar* (New York: 1948), p. 335.
11   Gerhard Ritter, 'The German Professor in the Third Reich', *Review of Politics*, 8, 2, April 1946, p. 248 (originally published in *Die Gegenwart*, December 1945).
12   Friedrich Meinecke, *The German Catastrophe. Reflections and Recollections* (Cambridge, Mass: 1950), p. 38.
13   Frederic Lilge, *The Abuse of Learning. The Failure of the German University* (New York: 1948), p. 55.
14   ibid., p. 148.
15   Karl Dietrich Bracher, *Die Auflösung der Weimarer Republik. Eine Studie zum Problem des Machtverfalls in der Demokratie* (Villingen: 1971, 5th edn), pp. 132–4.
16   Seymour Martin Lipset, 'Students and Politics in Comparative Studies', in Seymour Martin Lipset and Philip G. Altbach, *Students in Revolt* (Boston, Mass: 1970), p. xxx.
17   See the chapter, 'Im Widerstreit zwischen Fortschritt und Reaktion. Universitäten und Hochschulen in der Weimarer Republik', in Günter Steiger and Werner Fläschendräger (eds), *Magister und Scholaren. Professoren und Studenten. Geschichte deutscher Universitäten und Hochschulen im Überblick* (Leipzig/Jena/Berlin: 1981), pp. 145–72.
18   *Geschichte der Christian-Albrechts-Universität Kiel 1665–1965* (Kiel: 1965), Vol. I, pt 2, pp. 50–81.
19   Rolf Seeliger, *Braune Universität. Dokumentation mit Stellungnahmen*, 6 vols, (Munich: 1964–8).
20   Andreas Flitner (ed.), *Deutsches Geistesleben und Nationalsozialismus. Eine Vortragsreihe der Universität Tübingen* (Tübingen: 1965).
21   *Die deutsche Universität im Dritten Reich. Eine Vortragsreihe der Universität München* (Munich: 1966), and *Nationalsozialismus und die deutsche Universität. Universitätstage 1966* (Berlin: 1966).

22 Kurt Sontheimer, 'Die Haltung der deutschen Universitäten zur Weimarer Republik', in *Nationalsozialismus und die deutsche Universität*, pp. 24–42. See also Sontheimer, *Antidemokratisches Denken in der Weimarer Republik. Die politischen Ideen des deutschen Nationalismus zwischen 1918 und 1933* (Munich: 1962).

23 Helmut Kuhn, 'Die deutsche Universität am Vorabend der Machtergreifung', in *Die deutsche Universität im Dritten Reich*, pp. 15–43.

24 Theodor Eschenburg, 'Aus dem Universitätsleben vor 1933', in Flitner (ed.), *Deutsches Geistesleben und Nationalsozialismus*, pp. 24–46.

25 Quoted in Wolfgang Fritz Haug, *Der hilflose Antifaschismus. Zur Kritik der Vorlesungs-reihen über Wissenschaft und NS an deutschen Universitäten* (Frankfurt: 1970, 3rd edn), p. 56.

26 Hans Bleuel and Ernst Klinnert, *Deutsche Studenten auf dem Weg ins Dritte Reich. Ideologien-Programme-Atkionen, 1918–1945*, (Gütersloh: 1967); Hans Peter Bleuel, *Deutschlands Bekenner. Professoren zwischen Kaiserreich und Diktatur* (Berne/Munich/Vienna: 1968).

27 Fritz K. Ringer, *The Decline of the German Mandarins. The German Academic Community, 1890–1933* (Cambridge, Mass: 1969), p. 7.

28 ibid., p. 239.

29 ibid., p. 143.

30 ibid., p. 439.

31 Alan D. Beyerchen, *Scientists Under Hitler. Politics and the Physics Community in the Third Reich* (New Haven, Conn: 1977).

32 Herbert Döring, *Der Weimarer Kreis. Studien zum politischen Bewusstsein verfassungs-treuer Hochschullehrer in der Weimarer Republik* (Meisenheim: 1975), pp. 249 f.

33 See Kenneth D. Barkin's review article on Ringer's book, *Journal of Modern History*, 43, 2, June 1971, here p. 284.

34 Jürgen Schwarz, *Studenten in der Weimarer Republik. Die deutsche Studentenschaft in der Zeit von 1918 bis 1923 und ihre Stellung zur Politik* (Berlin: 1971).

35 Thomas Nipperdey, 'Die deutsche Studentenschaft in den ersten Jahren der Weimarer Republik', in Adolf Grimme (ed.), *Kulturverwaltung der zwanziger Jahre. Alte Dokumente und neue Beiträge* (Stuttgart: 1961), pp. 18–48; Wolfgang Zorn, 'Die politische Entwicklung des deutschen Studententums 1924–31', in *Ein Leben aus freier Mitte. Festschrift für Ulrich Noack* (Göttingen: 1961), pp. 296–325.

36 Ursula Dibner, 'The History of the National Socialist German Student League', (Ph.D. thesis, University of Michigan, 1969).

37 Anselm Faust, *Der Nationalsozialistische Deutsche Studentenbund. Studenten und Nationalsozialismus in der Weimarer Republik* (Düsseldorf: 1973), Vol. 1, p. 115.

38 Michael H. Kater, 'Der NS-Studentenbund von 1926 bis 1928. Randgruppe zwischen Hitler und Strasser', *Vierteljahrshefte für Zeitgeschichte*, 22, 2, April 1974, pp. 148–90.

39 Faust, *Der Nationalsozialistische Deutsche Studentenbund*, Vol. 1, p. 61.

40 See the appendices in ibid., Vol. 2, pp. 140–50.

41 Michael H. Kater, *Studentenschaft und Rechtsradikalismus in Deutschland, 1918–1933. Eine sozialgeschichtliche Studie zur Bildungskrise in der Weimarer Republik* (Hamburg: 1975), p. 217.

42 ibid., pp. 50–6.

43 ibid., p. 43.

44 ibid., p. 108.

45 ibid., p. 162.

46 Ruth Carlsen, 'Zum Prozess der Faschisierung und zu den Auswirkungen der faschistischen Diktatur auf die Universität Rostock', (Diss. Phil., University of Rostock, 1965).

47 Paul Kluke, *Die Stiftungsuniversität Frankfurt am Main 1914–1932* (Frankfurt-on-Main: 1972), pp. 523–32.

48 ibid., pp. 292 ff. and 552 ff.

49 ibid., p. 577. For some discussion of this problem, see Geoffrey J. Giles, 'The National Socialist Students' Association in Hamburg, 1926–1945' (Ph.D. thesis, University of Cambridge, 1975), pp. 96 ff.
50 Kluke, *Die Stiftungsuniversität*, p. 587.
51 Manfred Franze, *Die Erlanger Studentenschaft 1918–1945* (Würzburg: 1972).
52 Wolfgang Kreutzberger, *Studenten und Politik 1918–1933. Der Fall Freiburg im Breisgau* (Göttingen: 1972), pp. 71 f.
53 Peter Spitznagel, 'Studentenschaft und Nationalsozialismus in Würzburg 1927–1933', (Diss. Phil., University of Würzburg, 1974), pp. 177–81.
54 Arye Z. Carmon, 'The University of Heidelberg and National Socialism, 1930–1935', (Ph.D. thesis, University of Wisconsin, 1974), pp. 151 and 170.
55 See n. 49.
56 Geoffrey J. Giles, 'Die Verbändepolitik des Nationalsozialistischen Deutschen Studentenbundes', in Christian Probst (ed.), *Darstellungen und Quellen zur Geschichte der deutschen Einheitsbewegung im neunzehnten und zwanzigsten Jahrhundert*, Vol. XI (Heidelberg: 1981), pp. 95–155.
57 Uwe Dietrich Adam, *Hochschule und Nationalsozialismus. Die Universität Tübingen im Dritten Reich* (Tübingen: 1977), p. 4.
58 See esp. ch. 12, 'Den Vorhang zu und alle Fragen offen', in Walter Jens, *Eine deutsche Universität. 500 Jahre Tübinger Gelehrtenrepublik* (Munich: 1977).

5   German Youth, the Youth Movement and National Socialism in the Weimar Republic

PETER D. STACHURA

Greater attention than ever before is now being given by scholars to the contribution made by the Youth Movement, and the younger generation as a whole, to the shaping of German society and politics during the interwar period. Most of this academic focus has centred on the independent sector of the Youth Movement, which was represented before the First World War by the *Wandervogel* and after 1918 until the *Machtergreifung* by Free German Youth (1918–23) and, more importantly, *Bündische* Youth. The independent Youth Movement was both the authentic core and pacemaker for the wider German Youth Movement, which during the 1920s attracted around 5 million members organised in a multifarious variety of confessional, sports, vocational, paramilitary and political associations. But many of these were influenced to one degree or another, despite their different interests, programmes and ideals, by the example of the *Wandervogel* and its successors of the autonomous youth tradition.

The *Wandervogel*'s appearance around the turn of the century was intimately related to deep concerns and uncertainties in German middle-class life at that time as the Wilhelmine Reich became increasingly unstable as a result of pressures engendered by the failure or unwillingness of an anachronistic social and political system to come to terms with modern urban-industrial society. The *Wandervogel* constituted an important manifestation of a bourgeois malaise in Germany; it was a vehicle of youthful protest against an adult world whose stuffy, materialistic values were no longer acceptable, and from which the younger generation of the middle classes felt profoundly alienated.[1] The *Wandervogel* asserted the right of youth for self-expression and self-fulfilment independent of the constricting influence of parents, teachers and church authorities. Youth wanted the opportunity at last to act as a separate social entity and to formulate their own standards in a society which they believed had become not only anonymous and depersonalised, but also largely meaningless. This concept of the autonomy of youth was later articulated in most dramatic form during a convention of *Wandervogel* groups and assorted allies at the Hohe Meissner mountain near Kassel in October 1913 when the so-called Meissner

Formula was laid down as the basis of the movement's *raison d'être*. Although lacking concrete objectives, and heavily influenced by a romantic–idealistic and irrational view of life, expressed by its love of Nature and nostalgia for mediaeval times, the *Wandervogel* had attracted some 25,000 followers by 1914. It was not overtly political, but was undoubtedly caught up in the nationalist ethos of the established classes. Almost all of its membership came from a solid middle-class and Protestant background, in particular, the educated, propertied bourgeoisie.[2]

The First World War radically transformed the *Wandervogel*. The movement, which had been notoriously susceptible to secessions and splits before 1914, was now hopelessly divided and disorganised as political differences among members came to the fore and as the leadership cadres were decimated by the exigencies of war. A fresh beginning had to be made after 1918, but during the early 1920s all semblance of unity, coherence and leadership was lost amidst the turmoil afflicting Germany in general. Not until 1923 was a certain degree of order restored in the shape of the next phase of the independent Youth Movement's development, *Bündische* Youth.[3] Despite maintaining an overwhelmingly middle-class character and consciously nurturing a sense of élitism, *Bündische* Youth was never a united movement: it embraced under the conveniently descriptive term *Bündische*[4] a veritable galaxy of different kinds of groups, all of which, however, acknowledged and continued the spirit and tradition initiated by the *Wandervogel* until 1933 when they were disbanded by the National Socialist regime. Before then, *Bündische* Youth had been drawn inevitably, if unwillingly for the most part, into the intense political controversies of the Weimar era.

Every historian of the Youth Movement sooner or later comes up against the vexed question of its relationship to National Socialism. In specific terms, attention has been concentrated on the problem of the Youth Movement as a precursor of the Hitler Youth (HJ) and NSDAP, and how far it may be said to have contributed, directly or indirectly, consciously or unconsciously, to the successful rise of Hitler. These questions have produced a proliferation of opinion and a wide spectrum of sometimes acrimonious disagreement. That so much interest should be directed towards this particular feature of the Youth Movement's evolution is not entirely unexpected in view of the intensive scholarly examination of the reasons for the collapse of the Weimar Republic and of the important historical phenomenon of interwar fascism. A clear consensus on the problem is not in prospect despite the debate having already passed through several distinctive stages of development.

For many contemporary observers, the special attraction National Socialism seemed to have for youth demanded an investigation of the Youth Movement's role in the anti-republican and authoritarian

'National Opposition', of which, of course, the NSDAP became the dominant element in the early 1930s. Vociferously claiming to be a party of youth under such slogans as 'National Socialism is the organised will of Youth' (*Nationalsozialismus ist organisierter Jugendwille*), 'Make way, you old ones, your time is up!' (Gregor Strasser), and 'Who has Youth has the future, who has the future has Youth', the NSDAP's exhortations for ultra-nationalism, heroic idealism, commitment and militancy struck a deep responsive chord among the younger generation, particularly middle-class youth. The Party went to considerable lengths to stress that it epitomised the revolt of young Germany against the Weimar geron-tocracy, and its carefully cultivated image of dynamism paid handsome dividends. The NSDAP's exploding electoral constituency from 1930 onwards and its dramatic expansion in organised followers embraced a substantial proportion of the 20–30-year-old age bracket. This fact was also reflected in the Party's comparatively young *Reichstag* representa-tion and in its leadership, including *Gauleiters*. By conveying a sense of hope, expectation and excitement to youth, the NSDAP seemed to breathe life into the widely discussed concept in Weimar of the 'mission of youth' (*Sendung der jungen Nation*).[5] The Party, of course, did not become successful in this respect through its propaganda efforts alone; rather, its propaganda exploited a deep-seated resentment among youth which had become bitterly disillusioned by the performance of the Republic. The political outlook of youth progressively radicalised as a result of their depressing material situation, in which an above-average rate of unemployment was a crucial factor,[6] and their frustration at the sheer inability of the parliamentary system of government and the political parties to help them. Also of critical importance were the socio-psychological influences on youth stemming from the destruction of traditional family and institutional values in consequence of the First World War, hyperinflation and Depression. This was a generation which rapidly came to believe that personal as well as political problems were best dealt with through violent means rather than through reasoned argument: might was right, appeared to be the message.[7] The NSDAP (and to a much lesser extent, the KPD) capitalised on the bitterness of youth.

Some members of the independent Youth Movement immediately sought, in reaction to the NSDAP campaign, to identify with Hitler, and this attitude was supported by historians like Will Vesper and Luise Fick, both of whom asserted that *Bündische* Youth was the direct predecessor of the HJ. About the same time, Hermann Rauschning, writing from a different perspective, saw in the *Wandervogel* the genesis of a revolutionary dynamism among youth which culminated in National Socialism.[8] For its part, however, the HJ rejected any basic line of continuity with the independent Youth Movement, with *Reichsjugend-führer* Baldur von Schirach being especially scathing in his condemnation of the *Bündische* sector.[9] The official outlook of the HJ until the end of the war was that though it had adopted a number of external forms and ideas from the *Wandervogel* and its successors, the National Socialist youth organisation represented a unique type of movement which had no authentic precursors.[10]

After 1945 the historiography of the Youth Movement–National Socialist relationship underwent further changes of emphasis and argument. In the immediate postwar period there appeared many publications from former members of the Youth Movement whose aim was to exonerate it from all significant complicity in the débâcle of the Third Reich, and moreover, to underline the contribution made by the Youth Movement to the anti-Hitler resistance.[11] This school of thought was uncritical and frequently degenerated into righteous self-justification in defending the role and character of the Youth Movement. Such heavy apologetics stemmed, of course, from current trends in West German society during the late 1940s and 1950s which desired to isolate National Socialism from the mainstream of 'traditional' German political and cultural values. It was claimed that in essence Hitler was an evil aberration, while the mass of ordinary Germans had been simply passive onlookers, so to speak. The Youth Movement, like many other institutions and organisations of pre-1933 Germany, was consequently absolved of any serious responsibility for National Socialism.

Independent scholarly interest in the Youth Movement, beginning in the late 1950s, brought a welcome degree of objectivity to bear on the problem. None the less, opinion continued to remain as sharply divided as ever. In the 1960s it became fashionable in many quarters to accept that the *Wandervogel–Bündische* tradition was intrinsically pre-fascist and hence that the autonomous sector was indeed a forerunner of the HJ.[12] This disposition reflected once again certain trends in the wider historiography of modern Germany, especially as the nature of fascism and National Socialism began to be studied within the context of their connections with organised capitalism and the bourgeoisie. Ideological and political perceptions thus intruded into the discussion, though by no means dominated it, as a series of well-researched and carefully presented scholarly studies on the Youth Movement showed.[13]

A formidable body of thought maintained that the Youth Movement did make a noteworthy contribution to the rise of Hitler. George L. Mosse stressed the importance of the *völkisch* link between the Youth Movement and the NSDAP, though conceded that 'most members of the [independent] Youth Movement were openly hostile towards National Socialism'.[14] This critical view had already been expressed in a more general and less erudite way some years previously by Howard Becker.[15] Further support was forthcoming from Harry Pross, who believed that in demanding the totality of the *Gemeinschaft* the Youth Movement was

fully unprepared to resist the NSDAP's totalitarianism,[16] from Robert
Waite, who stressed the influence of certain *Wandervogel* ideals on the
generation which populated the *Freikorps* and later Hitler's movement,[17]
from Wilhelm Roessler, who argued that the Youth Movement abandoned the use of reason in favour of mystical–romantic idealism,[18] and
from Joachim Fest, who claimed that *Bündische* Youth's alleged lack of
political and social maturity as well as fondness for things romantic and
military, had catastrophic consequences for the younger generation.[19]
More recently the critics of the Youth Movement have been joined by
Hubertus Kunert[20] and Michael H. Kater, whose stimulating study has
added a new qualitative dimension to the debate and also to wider
discussion about the element of continuity in modern German history as
a whole.[21] He contends that large sections of *Bündische* Youth were
fascistoid before 1933 and that the Third Reich was compatible with the
fundamental ideas and character of the movement, thus making it
relatively easy for the HJ to integrate middle-class youth into the
totalitarian state. This outcome, Kater argues further, was inevitably
brought about by underlying currents in the Youth Movement since the
time of the *Wandervogel*.

A more moderately inclined stance is represented by an equally
respectable and scholarly group. First in the field was Michael Jovy who
emphasised the anti-authoritarian and even democratic components of
Bündische ideology, as well as a decline in anti-Semitism in the movement
during the early 1930s.[22] That *Bündische* Youth was a forerunner of the
HJ is explicitly denied by Karl Paetel, Fritz Borinski and Werner Milch,
Karl Seidelmann, Gerhard Ziemer, Raabe and Laqueur.[23] On the other
hand, Laqueur admits that the Youth Movement must bear the same
degree of responsibility for Hitler as all other German organisations of
the Weimar era – with a few exceptions – and specifically pinpoints the
Youth Movement's intellectual rather than moral culpability. Raabe, in
criticising the negative attitude displayed by *Bündische* Youth to politics
in general and to the Weimar Republic in particular, concludes that the
movement was 'indirectly co-responsible' for the rise of the NSDAP – a
view subscribed to by Werner Klose and Adam Wandruszka.[24] Joseph
Held prefers the charge of co-responsibility from the standpoint of the
Youth Movement's alleged failure to provide a strong moral basis by
which its members could have resisted National Socialism.[25] In his
excellent monograph, Jakob Müller, in extending in some ways the
earlier thesis of Armin Mohler that the Youth Movement was a
neo-conservative reform body – in effect, part of the so-called 'Conservative Revolution' – repudiates the whole notion of there being substantive
similarity between the movement and the NSDAP. The ethos of the
Youth Movement, he claims, was incompatible with the coarse,
fanatical, political *Weltanschauung* of Hitler.[26] Peter Loewenberg seems
to shift responsibility for the younger generation's susceptibility to

National Socialism away from the particular situation of *Bündische* Youth by accentuating the psychological conditioning of German youth in childhood through the traumatic experiences of the First World War and its highly unstable aftermath.[27]

Works dealing specifically with the HJ are by no means unanimous in their assessment of that organisation's relationship with *Bündische* Youth. While outright apologists for the HJ such as Blohm and Griesmayr/Würschinger – all former members of it, incidentally – do not address themselves in any detail to this particular question, they suggest that the HJ represented the fulfilment of the *Wandervogel* tradition – hence reverting to the stance adopted almost half a century previously by Vesper and Fick. Another former HJ member, Koch, argues in his careless, discursive and popular study that the HJ was a 'distorted form' of the Youth Movement. It is clear, however, that Koch, true to form, has completely misunderstood the German Romantic tradition, so that his point is as worthless as the other conclusions in his book. Klönne, Brandenburg and Klose, on the other hand, offer more sober if basically inconclusive assessments of the question, whereas Stachura is more forthright in denying that there was a fundamental compatibility between the two organisations.[28]

In view of these widely differing interpretations of the autonomous Youth Movement's role *vis-à-vis* National Socialism, it might be appropriate to establish, first of all, some perceptives on the problem which, it is hoped, will help to clarify the context within which the debate may be taken further. In particular, such an exercise might eliminate the major scourge of this issue, namely an over-readiness on the part of historians to make sweeping generalisations which are, from a purely intellectual angle, invariably unacceptable.

In the first instance, we are dealing only with the independent Youth Movement. Exempt from consideration are those millions of youths, bourgeois and proletarian, who were organised in the non-independent sector, the so-called youth tutelage groups, and some of whom may even have been influenced to an extent by the basic principles of *Bündische* Youth. No one has charged Catholic youth, for example, with major or even minor responsibility for National Socialism's success. Catholic youth shared the general immunity to NSDAP blandishments displayed by the older generations of Catholics before 1933 because they possessed in their own organisational, social and political life revolving around the Church and the Centre Party a secure basis of support, underpinned by a certain defensive introspectiveness resulting from decades of discrimination and persecution during and after the *Kulturkampf*. The small minority of Catholic youths who felt the need to break out from this ghetto situation in the search for a more satisfying meaning to life usually did so by synthesising *Bündische* and Christian ideals in groups like *Quickborn*, and not by approximating to Hitler. This is not to forget, of course, that by the late 1920s anti-liberal and nationalist attitudes were increasingly apparent in Catholic youth circles.[29]

By the same token, it need hardly be said that the gulf between socialist/communist youth and National Socialism was much greater. None of their groups aided the rise of Hitler, except it should be noted that they all showed a distinct lack of political maturity in defending democracy, as exemplified by the *Sozialistische Arbeiterjugend*, and in opposing National Socialism, as indicated by the *Kommunistischer Jugendverband Deutschlands*.[30] It may be proper, on the other hand, to include a relatively large percentage of Protestant youth, who shared on the whole the anti-democratic, nationalist and authoritarian attitudes of their parents and elders. The Protestant small-town and rural-based lower *Mittelstand* provided, of course, the backbone of Hitler's support among both the electorate and organised followers. Groups such as the *Bibelkreise* had strong and barely concealed pro-Nazi sympathies before 1933.[31] Protestant youth was, therefore, a component of the broader political and cultural ethos, dating from the time of the Wilhelmine Reich, which signally assisted Hitler to power, but it would be impracticable to examine them side by side with a distinctive and single organisational entity that was the independent Youth Movement. The number of youths or sections of the broader German Youth Movement which can be legitimately examined in terms of their relationship with, or alleged affinity to, National Socialism constitutes a very small fraction of organised youth during the Weimar period. In 1919, for example, Free German Youth accounted for a mere 0·7 per cent of the total, while in 1927 *Bündische* Youth embraced only 1·3 per cent, or 56,350 at a time when 4,338,850 youths were affiliated to the *Reichsausschuss der deutschen Jugendverbände* (National Committee of German Youth Groups).[32] Complementing this numerical élitism was the sociological composition of *Bündische* Youth for its members were drawn almost exclusively from the Protestant upper *Mittelstand*.[33] Thus, any conclusions on this question must relate only to this small minority and not to the German Youth Movement in general or to the younger generation of the Weimar era.

Supporting this particular qualification are a few ancillary points. It must not be forgotten that under discussion is a movement of youth whose rank-and-file membership was usually under 18 years of age. The immaturity for which *Bündische* Youth has been so often upbraided is attributable in good measure to this undeniable biological fact. It may be necessary to distinguish between the leadership, who were older and sometimes conspicuously middle-aged adults, and the youngsters who followed them. In any event, the leaders are considered by most observers to have been more susceptible to National Socialism than the youths. Under-18-year-olds cannot be castigated too harshly for political events which they were not capable of influencing. In addition,

Bündische Youth was by choice an apolitical body, and it seems unfair, therefore, to criticise it for not being more actively engaged in politics. The movement was essentially social and educational. Its main concern was to create through educational means the 'new man', on the basis of comradeship, trust and constructive endeavour.[34] Although everyday politics came in for wider debate in *Bündische* circles towards the end of the 1920s and a greater number of *Bündische* personnel became politically involved than before, the pursuit of social, educational, cultural and personal ideals remained the *raison d'être* of the movement. In this respect, the political record of *Bündische* Youth pales into relative insignificance when its considerable and widely acclaimed achievements in the spheres of social welfare, popular and adult education, voluntary labour camps, hostelling, teacher-training, experimental schools and others are taken into due account. Its contribution to the liberalisation of Weimar school education consisted not only of the support it gave to progressive reforms and its promotion of education as a humanitarian discipline, but also of its success in having school-pupils recognised as a group whose preferences, needs and desires had to be taken fully into account in the formulation of educational policy. *Bündische* Youth's cultural influence was most strikingly illustrated in music (with which the Boberhaus in Silesia and Georg Götsch's *Musikheim* in Frankfurt-on-Oder will always be associated), architecture and drama. In all these different and variegated spheres, *Bündische* Youth exercised a forward-looking and vibrant influence, proving that it could take its place in the vanguard of emancipatory tendencies in Weimar society.[35] It may be considered a gross distortion, therefore, to condemn the movement for what it had no desire to be, a political entity. *Bündische* Youth, it can be validly argued, ought to be judged according to the standards, criteria and priorities it set itself. Political assessments of it are not to be accepted as absolute and all-embracing, that is, pertaining to its general character, whose core and substance were intentionally non-political. To do otherwise is to misrepresent the historical role of *Bündische* Youth.

Another point is that it must not be overlooked that *Bündische* Youth was from both an organisational and ideological viewpoint, a profoundly diffuse phenomenon. It is difficult to generalise about almost any particular feature of the movement's activity given the bewildering variety and complexity of groups, leaders, ideas and relationships within it.

Following on from the view that too much significance should not be attached to the specifically political nature of *Bündische* Youth, an additional corrective may be indicated when it is acknowledged that the course of Weimar politics, including the collapse of democracy and the success of National Socialism, was determined by institutions and interest groups other than the independent Youth Movement. It cannot be our purpose in this paper to expose and analyse the weaknesses of the democratic parties, the defects of the constitutional and judicial structure of the state, the economic upheavals or the absence of positive political leadership. Yet it is incontrovertibly in these areas that the fundamental causes of the Republic's demise are to be found. Measured against the diverse range of factors present in the situation which produced Hitler, *Bündische* Youth was politically inconsequential and impotent.

Critics have frequently cited post-1933 developments in support of their contention that *Bündische* Youth was inherently inclined towards National Socialism. The fact that many *Bündische* members, encouraged by the early example of the *Deutsche Freischar* leadership,[36] were able to reach an accommodation with the Third Reich fairly quickly, whether out of sheer opportunism or genuine conviction, is understood to be illustrative of their latent fascist proclivities. Also, the fragmented and ineffectual opposition offered to the regime by scattered, local *Bündische* groups is usually quoted as further evidence of these propensities. Such arguments are simplistic for they totally ignore the complexities of the resistance phenomenon.[37] It is equally unacceptable to use the repeated Gestapo prohibitions of *Bündische* activity in the 1930s as proof of the widespread nature of opposition.[38] There is a strong case, however, for not considering any post-1933 *Bündische* behaviour in relation to the question of the movement's standing towards the NSDAP.[39]

In 1933 an entirely different set of circumstances was introduced into German political life in which long-established attitudes were questioned, compromised or discarded in all kinds of organisations and sections of society. In the face of a ruthless policy of *Gleichschaltung*, backed up by terror tactics on a wide scale, such a situation was hardly unexpected. Reactions of individuals and groups to the *Machtergreifung* were not always authentic or logical extensions or expressions of previously cherished opinions. For instance, the Catholic Church, which had frequently and vehemently denounced the NSDAP before 1933, suddenly discovered that there were indeed common bonds between Catholicism and National Socialism which could be built upon to provide lasting co-operation between the Church and the regime.[40] The Concordat of July 1933 was the most practical and dramatic result of the metamorphosis in Catholic thinking. Similarly, many former socialist, democratic–liberal, and even communist supporters joined the band-wagon either through voting for the NSDAP in the March 1933 elections, and subsequently in plebiscites, or through joining a Party organisation. Are these people to be charged with harbouring pro-fascist ideas before 1933? It is highly unlikely. But by the same token, the spirit of accommodation evident in many *Bündische* ranks in 1933 may be interpreted, not as the inevitable consequence of earlier pro-Nazi sentiments, but more accurately as the result of the movement's adaptation in radically changed surroundings to the National Socialist revolution. In this regard, lines of continuity between the Weimar Republic and Hitler's Germany are not applicable. The problem of the *Bündische*–NSDAP relationship must be assessed within the confines of developments *before* 1933.

From this perspective arises the very real problem of defining what exactly is meant by terms such as 'pre-fascist', 'proto-fascist', or 'fascistoid'. Kater uses the latter to indicate in a rather general way some sort of affinity to National Socialism, while Meier-Cronemeyer complicates matters by stating that 'occasionally' *Bündische* groups were 'fascistoid' but not 'fascist' without making clear the distinction.[41] As long as these descriptive expressions are used loosely there can be no meaningful clarification of the basic problem at hand.

The final and perhaps most critical perspective emanates from the question of source material. The overwhelming bulk of views concerning the Youth Movement's position *vis-à-vis* Hitler are subjective, or at best, based on fragmentary evidence. Until much more intensive and detailed research into primary sources is undertaken, the whole problem will continue to be debated at a relatively tentative and unsatisfactory level.[42] Scholarly studies are required, for example, of at least the most prominent *Bündische* groups, including local and regional variations within them. The *Deutsche Freischar* is an obvious candidate. Towards this end, the archives of the German Youth Movement at Burg Ludwigstein provide an indispensable starting-point, to be supplemented by the *Bundesarchiv* in Koblenz and major regional archives. Only as a consequence of such a primary-based, scholarly approach will a proper balance be given to the field of Youth Movement studies, thus to offset further the influence of personal recollections, prejudices and apologetics, and to spotlight further the fallacious idea that the Youth Movement can be understood only by those who experienced it. The paucity of the empirical evidence which has been adduced hitherto in support of the conflicting points of view in this debate underlines the need for research along the lines mentioned above.

The evidence so far falls into two principal categories: politico-ideological and organisational–personal. Critics maintain that essential elements of the *Bündische* ideology were the same, or virtually the same, as corresponding parts of the National Socialist *Weltanschauung*. It is pointed out that *Bündische* Youth was, in general, nationalistic, anti-liberal, romantic, anti-Semitic, *völkisch*, authoritarian, anti-urban and irrational, thus an indisputable section of the wider restorative, anti-modernist forces in Weimar society. It is also argued that recognisable National Socialist concepts like the Reich, *Führerschaft und Gefolgschaft*, *Volksgemeinschaft*, the *Führerprinzip*, a Greater Germany, and so on, were all deeply embedded in the *Bündische* ethos. Some of the movement's activities, notably its work among German ethnic minorities in eastern and south-eastern Europe, have been interpreted as helping to lay the foundations of later National Socialist practices, such as the quest for *Lebensraum*.[43] Apologists deny that there was any real ideological affinity between the two movements, that any apparent resemblances are fortuitous and limited only to externals, and in essence more of a semantic than an intrinsic nature.[44] The programme, objectives, and operational methods of *Bündische* Youth and National Socialist were quite different, it is affirmed.

There is in both interpretations a tendency towards overstatement, even towards exaggeration in some respects. For instance, to equate *Bündische* anti-Semitism with the NSDAP brand is untenable.[45] The whole *völkisch* orientation of *Bündische* Youth lacked that violent and politically overbearing, biological–racial quality which characterised the Hitlerian outlook. Anti-Semitism was never taken as seriously by *Bündische* youths as the National Socialists because there were many other issues regarded as being of far greater significance to the socio-cultural and educational development of their movement. The 'Jewish question' never attained the paramountcy it did in Nazi circles.[46] At the same time it is probably doubtful whether anti-Semitism was actually declining still further as an influence in *Bündische* Youth by the late 1920s. As indicated previously in this paper, the politico-ideological ideas of *Bündische* Youth were not wholly representative of its character. Alongside the notions about Reich, *Führerprinzip* and so on, must be placed the movement's deep humanity, philanthropy, comradeship, loyalty, goodwill, wholesome sense of duty (*Pflichtbewusstsein*) and concept of altruistic service – qualities not immediately associated with the NSDAP.

Additionally the *Bündische* political–ideological ideas lacked definition and precision: they were nebulous, emotional, and expressive of Utopian idealism rather than of a concrete political creed. It cannot be seriously thought that the *Bündische* Reich concept envisaged anything like the nightmare that was the National Socialist Third Reich because it was little more than a vague expression of a neo-romantic yearning for a future authoritarian, élitist state of the kind hinted at by two of the most important intellectual influences on the German Youth Movement, Moeller van den Bruck and Ernst Jünger. Karl Paetel tried to convey the meaning of the *Bündische* perception of the Reich concept in saying: 'The New Reich was neither Luther's realm of God nor a political German Reich, though it contained elements of both; rather it was primarily the symbol of the new attitude of a new generation'.[47] Similarly the *Bündische* comprehension of a *Volksgemeinschaft* had not a great deal in common with the socially all-embracing, mass and racial-politically rooted National Socialist version.[48] There was, moreover, a clear absence of common ground with regard to the idea of charismatic leadership. The *Bündische* version was educational, while in the NSDAP it had an abrasively political–cultist connotation based on the person of one leader, Hitler. Finally the Nazi glorification of war and militarism as the apotheosis of human experience and achievement was quite different in character and ethical content from the somewhat naïvely romantic vision of knights and good deeds in the service of humanitarianism and honour which was expressed by *Bündische* Youth. There can be no denying that the political–ideological ideas of *Bündische* Youth and National Socialism were both derived, broadly speaking, from the German idealist–romanticist experience, but it would be erroneous to conclude on this basis that German romanticism was inherently fascistic. As a neo-conservative phenomenon *Bündische* Youth did have ideological points of contact with National Socialism but they were of a decidedly limited nature.[49]

On a purely political level, the evidence against *Bündische* Youth is even more sparse and unconvincing. It was hardly alone during the Weimar era in being generally anti-republican though all shades of political opinion – with the exception of the radical and communist Left – could be found among its ranks, including, notably, democratic elements.[50] The movement did not have a single, unified view on any subject, political or otherwise, and had little inclination for party politics or the realities of the state and governmental systems. For this reason, *Bündische* Youth has been rather harshly criticised for not evolving a broad political consensus which would have allowed it to perceive the dangers of totalitarianism and perhaps to have offered resistance when the moment for action arrived in the early 1930s.[51] Despite the intense discussion of political issues in its ranks it never developed anything approaching a programme of action. Only on a few rare occasions did *Bündische* Youth descend from its lofty, intellectual appreciation of politics to become actively involved in the harsh realities of everyday political rough and tumble. In 1930 several groups led by the *Deutsche Freischar* helped establish the German State Party and the same year the *Jungnationale Bund* actively helped the newly founded Conservative People's Party (KVP). Both undertakings proved abortive, as did Dr Kleo Pleyer's attempt in 1932 to organise a new style of political party based on *Bündische* principles, the *Bündische Reichsschaft*. A final contribution was made at the end of 1932 when a few *Bündische* elements supported the endeavour of Chancellor Kurt von Schleicher to create a broadly based conservative–nationalist front as the backbone of his government. Otherwise, a sense of individual political responsibility was not widely prevalent among members. But then, and again it has to be emphasised, politics was only a peripheral function of the movement and the failings of which it was guilty were rampant throughout other Weimar organisations. *Bündische* Youth clearly did not actively promote Hitler's cause, and if it did so passively, it was merely by default.

It is now accepted that two well-known contemporary assessments exaggerated the extent of *Bündische* support for National Socialism.[52]

The vast majority of these youths kept their distance rather disdainfully from the NSDAP whose fanaticism, political commitment, violent methods and populism were anathema to the élitist-conscious *Bündische* tradition. There were occasions, of course, especially in the early 1930s, when certain *Bündische* members did join Hitler's movement. The *Jungnationale Bund* lost a relatively high number of its followers in 1929/30, and the more right-wing organisations like the *Freischar junger Nation* and *Grossdeutsche Jugendbund* suffered losses right up to 1933. Yet the total number of *Bündische* members involved was, overall, insignificant. The HJ held little attraction even for those *Bündische* youths who counted themselves pro-Nazi. Not only did the HJ's penchant for violence and political engagement repel them but also its social revolutionary radicalism and demands for a socialist, egalitarian *Volksgemeinschaft* were positively distasteful to the bourgeois *Bündische* youths. The not entirely unsympathetic Heinz Däubler of the *Jungwandervogel* expressed this outlook to some degree when he remarked:

> We recognise the Hitler Youth in so far as it represents, as a mass movement, a useful instrument in the hands of the NSDAP in the fight against Marxism and its youth associations. However, we repudiate the Hitler Youth as long as it attempts to mix its tasks with the aims of the *Wandervogel*. The spirit of the *Wandervogel* is not that of a militarily organised mass movement.[53]

For its part, the HJ ceaselessly denounced *Bündische* Youth in uncompromising language. In any case, the HJ was not a youth organisation in the authentic Youth Movement tradition: it was an overtly political and propaganda troupe of fanatical young National Socialists. It is unrealistic, therefore, to attempt a meaningful comparison between the two movements, for their *raison d'être* was fundamentally different, despite superficial similarities in respect of some of their ideological perceptions.

The only section of *Bündische* Youth which offered clear and constant support for National Socialism was, of course, the *völkisch* groups, notably the *Geusen, Schilljugend, Adler und Falken, Freischar Schill* and the *Artamanen*, 'The shock troops of the National Socialist Movement in the countryside'.[54] These groups had a combined membership of no more than ten or eleven thousand in the early 1930s. But although publicly committed to the NSDAP they were all determined to maintain their organisational integrity and independence, and failed to come to terms for this reason with the HJ over the question of setting up a broadly based National Socialist youth movement in 1929.[55] The groups' élitism and rejection of party political involvement ensured that their identification with National Socialism was not total.

The available evidence suggests that *Bündische* Youth was a political failure, but also that it cannot be rightly considered a precursor of National Socialism or a major contributor to Hitler's success. *Bündische* Youth's lack of political awareness as well as its espousal of a nationalistic, anti-democratic ideology certainly did little to enhance the intellectual and cultural climate in which the Weimar Republic was asked to achieve stability. Its failure to propagate the ideals of democratic freedom indirectly performed a service for Hitler in that its members were more vulnerable when the time came to confront totalitarianism. *Bündische* Youth was not a bulwark against National Socialism, yet its role and impact in the broader field of Weimar politics was unimportant. Even within the younger generation, the movement's capacity to influence politically was, because of its exclusive social and ethical character, patently circumscribed. Compared with the ineptitude of many other organisations before 1933, the sins of omission of *Bündische* Youth hardly merit the passionate criticism levelled at it from some observers. It was part of the wider neo-conservative movement in Weimar Germany, and cannot be legitimately considered to have been either Nazi or proto-Nazi. *Bündische* Youth did not create or significantly exacerbate the chaos in Weimar politics of which the NSDAP was the most conspicuous beneficiary. But this must be treated as an interim judgement which further research may confirm, modify, or even drastically change. Until such time, however, the solid and constructive achievements of *Bündische* Youth in many non-political spheres must overshadow its political faults. The historical record of the movement, assessed from these varied perspectives, was as good as any and better than most in the Weimar era. Spengler's oft-quoted view of the independent Youth Movement as 'honest, but nothing else' fails to do it justice.[56]

Notes

This is a revised version of my article, 'Deutsche Jugendbewegung und Nationalsozialismus. Interpretationen und Perspektiven', *Jahrbuch des Archivs der deutschen Jugendbewegung*, 12, 1980, pp. 35–52.

1   The earliest general account of the movement, and still considered to be something of a classic is Hans Blüher, *Wandervogel. Geschichte einer Bewegung*, 2 vols (Jena 1912).
2   Ulrich Aufmuth, *Die deutsche Wandervogelbewegung unter soziologischem Aspekt* (Göttingen: 1979), pp. 86 ff, 236.
3   cf. Hermann Siefert, *Die Bündische Aufbruch 1919–1923* (Bad Godesberg: 1963); Gerhard Ziemer and Hans Wolf: *Wandervogel und Freideutsche Jugend* (Bad Godesberg: 1961); Knud Ahlborn, *Kurze Chronik der Freideutschen Jugendbewegung 1913 bis 1953* (Bad Godesberg: 1953).
4   The term *Bündische* is derived from the *Bund* (group), the concept and practise of which was the essential element of the movement's ethos.
5   On the theme of the youth–fascism symbiosis see the judicious remarks of Juan J. Linz, 'Some Notes Toward a Comparative Study of Fascism in Sociological Historical Perspective', in Walter Laqueur (ed.), *Fascism. A Reader's Guide* (London: 1976), pp. 33 ff, 43 ff.

6   Joachim Bartz and Dagmar Mor, 'Der Weg in die Jugendzwangsarbeit-Massnahmen gegen Jugendarbeitslosigkeit zwischen 1925 and 1935', in Gero Lenhardt (ed.), *Der hilflose Sozialstaat. Jugendarbeitslosigkeit und Politik* (Frankfurt: 1979), pp. 28–94.

7   Irmtraud Götz von Olenhusen, 'Die Krise der jungen Generation und der Aufstieg des Nationalsozialismus', *Jahrbuch des Archivs der deutschen Jugendbewegung*, 12, 1980, pp. 53–82, esp. pp. 61 ff.

8   Will Vesper (ed.), *Deutsche Jugend. 30 Jahre Geschichte einer Bewegung* (Berlin: 1934), pp. ix f; Luise Fick, *Die Deutsche Jugendbewegung* (Jena: 1939); Hermann Rauschning, *The Revolution of Nihilism* (New York: 1939), pp. 64 f.

9   Baldur von Schirach, *Die Hitler-Jugend. Idee und Gestalt* (Leipzig: 1934), pp. 13 ff., 22.

10   Friedrich Wilhelm Hymmen in *Wille und Macht, Führerorgan der Nationalsozialistischen Jugend*, no. 22, 1934, p. 16.

11   An example is furnished by Hans Ebeling, *The German Youth Movement. Its Past and Future* (London: 1945), pp. 7 ff., 20 ff.

12   Felix Messerschmid, 'Dokumentation der deutschen Jugendbewegung', *Geschichte in Wissenschaft und Unterricht*, 26, 1975, p. 499.

13   Two examples, published at the beginning of the decade, will suffice: Walter Z. Laqueur, *Young Germany. A History of the German Youth Movement* (London: 1962); Felix Raabe, *Die Bündische Jugend. Ein Beitrag zur Geschichte der Weimarer Republik* (Stuttgart: 1961).

14   George L. Mosse, *The Crisis of German Ideology. Intellectual Origins of the Third Reich* (New York: 1971), pp. 188, 310.

15   Howard Becker, *German Youth. Bond or Free* (London: 1946), Conclusion.

16   Harry E. Pross (ed.), *Die Zerstörung der deutschen Politik. Dokumente 1871–1933* (Frankfurt: 1959), p. 155; also in his *Jugend. Eros. Politik. Die Geschichte der deutschen Jugendverbände* (Berne: 1964).

17   Robert G. L. Waite, *Vanguard of Nazism. The Free Corps Movement in Postwar Germany 1918–1923* (New York: 1969 edn), pp. 17 ff.

18   Wilhelm Roessler, *Jugend im Erziehungsfeld. Haltung und Verhalten der deutschen Jugend in der 1. Hälfte des 20. Jahrhunderts* (Düsseldorf: 1957), p. 231.

19   Joachim C. Fest, *The Face of the Third Reich* (London: 1970), pp. 222, 225 f.

20   Hubertus Kunert, *Deutsche Reformpädagogik und Faschismus* (Hanover: 1973), pp. 73, 89 f.

21   Michael H. Kater, 'Bürgerliche Jugendbewegung und Hitlerjugend in Deutschland von 1926 bis 1939', *Archiv für Sozialgeschichte*, XVII, 1977, pp. 127–74, see esp. pp. 165, 174.

22   Michael E. Jovy, 'Deutsche Jugendbewegung und Nationalsozialismus. Versuch einer Klärung ihrer Zusammenhänge und Gegensätze' (Doctoral dissertation, University of Cologne, 1952), pp. 131, 225.

23   Karl O. Paetel: *Jugend in der Entscheidung 1913–1933–1945* (Bad Godesberg: 1963), p. 5; Fritz Borinski and Werner Milch: *Jugendbewegung. The Story of German Youth 1896–1933* (London: 1945), p. 43; Karl Seidelmann, 'War die Jugendbewegung präfaschistisch?', *Jahrbuch des Archivs der deutschen Jugendbewegung*, 7, 1975, p. 74; Gerhard Ziemer, 'Die Deutsche Jugendbewegung und der Staat', *Jahrbuch des Archivs der deutschen Jugendbewegung*, 5, 1973, pp. 46–8; Raabe, *Bündische Jugend*, pp. 160 f.; Laqueur, *Young Germany*, p. 234.

24   Laqueur, *Young Germany*, pp. 197, 217; Raabe, *Bündische Jugend*, pp. 200 f.; Werner Klose, *Generation im Gleichschritt. Eine Dokumentation* (Oldenburg: 1964), p. 38; Adam Wandruszka, 'Die Deutsche Jugendbewegung als Historisches Phänomen', *Quellen und Forschungen aus italienischen Archiven und Bibliotheken*, 51, 1972, p. 537.

25   Joseph Held, 'Embattled Youth. The Independent German Youth Movements in the Twentieth Century' (Doctoral dissertation, Rutgers State University, 1968), Conclusion.

26   Armin Mohler, *Die konservative Revolution in Deutschland 1918–1932* (Stuttgart:

1950), Preface; Jakob Müller, *Die Jugendbewegung als deutsche Hauptrichtung neukonservativer Reform* (Zurich: 1971), pp. 290 ff.

27 Peter Loewenberg, 'The Psychological Origins of the Nazi Youth Cohort', *American Historical Review*, 76, 1971, pp. 1457–1502.

28 Erich Blohm, *Hitler-Jugend. Soziale Tatgemeinschaft* (Witten: 1977); Gottfried Griesmayr and Otto Würschinger, *Idee und Gestalt der Hitlerjugend* (Leoni am Starnberger See: 1979); Hansjoachim W. Koch, *The Hitler Youth. Origins and Development 1922–45* (London: 1975); Arno Klönne, *Hitlerjugend. Die Jugend und Ihre Organisation im Dritten Reich* (Hanover: 1956); Hans-Christian Brandenburg, *Die Geschichte der HJ. Wege und Irrwege einer Generation* (Cologne: 1968); Klose, *Generation im Gleichschritt*; Peter D. Stachura, *Nazi Youth in the Weimar Republic* (Santa Barbara and Oxford: 1975).

29 The best account of the Catholic Youth Movement to date is Barbara Schellenberger, *Katholische Jugend und Drittes Reich* (Mainz: 1975).

30 cf. Wolfgang Uellenberg, *Die Auseinandersetzungen sozialdemokratischer Jugendorganisationen mit dem Nationalsozialismus* (Bonn: 1981); Erich Ebert, *Arbeiterjugend 1904–1945. Sozialistische Erziehungsgemeinschaft-Politische Organisation* (Frankfurt: 1980); Peter D. Stachura, *The German Youth Movement 1900–1945. An Interpretative and Documentary History* (London: 1981), pp. 94 ff.

31 Manfred Priepke, *Die Evangelische Jugend im Dritten Reich 1933–1936* (Hanover: 1960), pp. 17 f.

32 Karl O. Paetel, 'Die deutsche Jugendbewegung als politisches Phänomen', *Politische Studien*, 8, 1957, p. 3; Raabe, *Bündische Jugend*, p. 66 puts the figure at 2·1 per cent or 91,210 – still representing an exiguous percentage of the whole.

33 Walter Jantzen, 'Die soziologische Herkunft der Führerschicht in der deutschen Jugendbewegung. 1900 bis 1933', in *Jahrbuch der Ranke-Gesellschaft*, 3, 1957, pp. 127–35; Helmut Grau, 'Bündische Jugend – Spielweise der 'Bourgeoisie'? Aspekte des Wandels der Sozialstruktur bündischer Gruppen vor und nach dem II. Weltkrieg', *Jahrbuch des Archivs der deutschen Jugendbewegung*, 4, 1972, pp. 63–74.

34 Karl Seidelmann, 'Der "neue Mensch"', in Elizabeth Korn, Otto Suppert and Karl Vogt (eds): *Die Jugendbewegung. Welt und Wirkung* (Düsseldorf: 1963), pp. 15 ff.

35 Heinz S. Rosenbusch, *Die deutsche Jugendbewegung in Ihren pädagogische Formen und Wirkungen* (Frankfurt: 1973), *passim*; Hans Bohnenkamp, 'Jugendbewegung und Schulreform', in Korn *et al.* (eds), *Die Jugendbewegung*, pp. 39 ff.; Hans-Michael Elzer, 'Reformpädagogik und Jugendbewegung', *Jahrbuch des Archivs der deutschen Jugendbewegung*, 7, 1975, pp. 6–15; Stachura, *German Youth Movement*, pp. 53 ff.; Erich Bitterhof (ed.), *Das Musikheim Frankfurt/Oder 1929–41* (Burg Ludwigstein: 1980); Dorothea Kolland, *Die Jugendmusikbewegung* (Stuttgart: 1979).

36 Public declaration to the NSDAP of 8 March 1933, quoted in Paetel, *Jugend in der Entscheidung*, p. 142.

37 This point is poignantly revealed in respect of Köbel's d.j. 1.11. group by Winfried Mogge, 'Bündische Jugend und Nationalsozialismus. Probleme der Forschung, illustriert am Beispiel Eberhard Koebels und der Deutschen Jungenschaft', paper presented to conference of the Historischen Kommission der Deutschen Gesellschaft für Erziehungswissenschaft, Bielefeld 1978, and published in abbreviated form in *Informationen zur Erziehung-und Bildungshistorischen Forschung*, no. 14, 1980, pp. 137–53. The most informative studies of youth resistance to Hitler have been published recently. They include Dieter Hehr and Wolfgang Hippe, *Navajos und Edelweisspiraten. Berichte vom Jugendwiderstand im Dritten Reich* (Frankfurt: 1980); Arno Klönne, 'Jugendprotest und Jugendopposition. Von der HJ-Erziehung zum Cliquenwesen der Kriegszeit', in Martin Broszat, Elke Fröhlich and Anton Grossman (eds), *Bayern in der NS-Zeit*, Vol. IV: *Herrschaft und Gesellschaft im Konflikt* (Munich: 1981), pp. 527–620; Detlev Peukert, *Arbeiterjugend gegen HJ und Gestapo* (Cologne: 1980); Lothar Gruchmann, 'Jugendopposition und Justiz im Dritten Reich', in Wolfgang Benz (ed.), *Miscellanea. Festschrift für Helmut Krausnick* (Stuttgart: 1980), pp. 103–30.

38   As done, for example, by Ger van Roon, 'Wirkungen der Jugendbewegung im Deutschen Widerstand', *Jahrbuch des Archivs der deutschen Jugendbewegung*, 6, 1974, pp. 31–7.

39   The resistance theme constitutes an integral part of Kater's hypothesis in 'Bürgerliche Jugendbewegung', pp. 160 ff.

40   See, for example, Joseph Lortz, *Zugang zum Nationalsozialismus kirchengeschichtlich gesehen* (Münster: 1933); and M. Schmaus, *Begegnung zwischen katholischem Christentum und nationalsozialistischer Weltanschauung* (Münster: 1933).

41   Kater, 'Bürgerliche Jugendbewegung', pp. 165, 174; Hermann Meier-Cronemeyer, 'Gemeinschaft und Glaube. Reflexionen über die Deutsche Jugendbewegung', *Jahrbuch des Instituts für Deutsche Geschichte*, VI, 1977, p. 452.

42   cf. Winfried Mogge, '"Dämme wider die Vergesslichkeit". Neue Aufgaben des Archivs der deutschen Jugendbewegung', *Ludwigsteiner Blätter*, 116, 1977 (September), pp. 3 ff.; Mogge, '"Der gespannte Bogen". Jugendbewegung und Nationalsozialismus', *Jahrbuch des Archivs der deutschen Jugendbewegung*, 13, 1981, pp. 11–34, esp. pp. 24 ff.

43   Kater, 'Bürgerliche Jugendbewegung', p. 136. See also Peter Nasarski (ed.), *Deutsche Jugendbewegung in Europa. Versuch einer Bilanz* (Cologne: 1967), and the *Jahrbuch des Archivs der deutschen Jugendbewegung*, 9, 1977, *passim*.

44   Raabe, *Bündische Jugend*, pp. 97 ff., 106 ff., 120 ff.; and Ulrike Schmidt, 'Über das Verhältnis von Jugendbewegung und Hitlerjugend', *Geschichte in Wissenschaft und Unterricht*, XVI, 1965, pp. 19–37, esp. pp. 25 ff.

45   As attempted, for example, by W. Mehrmann, *Der Antisemitismus in der bürgerlichen Jugendbewegung und an den Universitäten* (East Berlin: 1972).

46   Walter Z. Laqueur, 'The German Youth Movement and the "Jewish Question". A Preliminary Survey', *Yearbook of the Leo Baeck Institute*, VI, 1961, pp. 200 f.

47   Karl O. Paetel, *Das Bild vom Menschen in der deutschen Jugendführung* (Bad Godesberg: 1954), p. 44.

48   Joseph Held, 'Die Volksgemeinschaftsidee in der Deutschen Jugendbewegung: Tätigkeit und Weltanschauung einiger Jugendvereine zur Zeit der Weimarer Republik', *Jahrbuch des Instituts für Deutsche Geschichte*, 6, 1977, pp. 460 ff.

49   The point has been recently stressed by, among others, Arno Klönne, 'Jugendbewegung und Faschismus', *Jahrbuch des Archivs der deutschen Jugendbewegung*, 12, 1980, pp. 23–34, esp. pp. 26 f.

50   The Leuchtenburg Circle was one of the few *Bündische* groups to have been consistently committed to democracy. See Fritz Borinski, Horst Grimm, Edgar Winkler and Erich Wolf (eds): *Jugend im politischen Protest. Der Leuchtenburgkreis 1923–1933–1977* (Frankfurt: 1977), pp. 9 ff.

51   Ludwig Liebs, 'Bündische Jugend und Politische Parteien-Verbot und Auflösung der Bünde im Jahre 1933', in Rudolf Kneip *et al.* (eds), *Jugend zwischen den Kriegen. Eine Sammlung von Aussagen und Dokumenten über den Sachsenkreis im Freideutschen Konvent* (Heidenheim: 1967), p. 159.

52   Werner Kindt, '"Bund oder Partei"? in der Jugendbewegung', *Das Junge Deutschland*, 26, 1932, no. 12 (December), p. 397; Josepha Fischer, 'Entwicklungen und Wandlungen in den Jugendverbänden im Jahre 1930', *Das Junge Deutschland*, 25, 1931, no. 2 (February), pp. 49–58, esp. p. 56.

53   *Die Kommenden*, July–August, 1932, quoted in Werner Kindt (ed.), *Die deutsche Jugendbewegung, 1920 bis 1933. Die Bündische Zeit. Quellenschriften* (Düsseldorf: 1974), p. 166.

54   Günter Kaufmann, in *Das Junge Deutschland*, 28, 1934, no. 9 (September), p. 280. See also Michael H. Kater's excellent 'Die Artamanen – Völkische Jugend in der Weimarer Republik', *Historische Zeitschrift*, 213, 1971, pp. 577–638.

55   Stachura, *Nazi Youth*, pp. 97 f.

56   Oswald Spengler, *Politische Pflichten der deutschen Jugend* (Munich: 1924), p. 28.

6 The Industrial Elite and the Nazis in the Weimar Republic

DICK GEARY

That some integral link existed between capitalism and the rise of fascism in interwar Europe was an article of faith for the theorists of the German Communist Party (KPD) and the Third Communist International, although the debates of the Comintern in the mid-1920s reveal a refreshing absence of dogmatism.[1] In the late 1920s, however, international communism and especially its Moscow mentors in this so-called 'third period' came to believe that fascism was a last-ditch attempt on the part of big business to shore up the structures of capitalism in the world Depression, which in turn was now identified as *the* final crisis of that mode of production by all but the most perspicacious of Comintern theorists.[2] Such beliefs were strengthened by widespread contemporary knowledge that some industrialists such as Fritz Thyssen undoubtedly made contributions to the treasury of the NSDAP and by the subsequent benefits that accrued to the business empires of Krupp, IG Farben and others after Hitler assumed the chancellor's mantle in 1933. The connection between industry and Hitler has been restated by many recent historians, especially but not exclusively in the DDR. However, the overwhelming majority of these latter-day commentators are no longer prepared to argue that Nazism triumphed as a result of the machinations of an undifferentiated interest that can be termed 'big business' or 'monopoly capital'.

Kuczynski, in his analysis of the fate of the Weimar Republic,[3] makes a clear-cut distinction between two factions of big business, between coal, iron and steel – the most reactionary group – on the one hand, and a marginally less reactionary alliance of the chemical and electrical industries on the other. According to this account, the politics of the period between 1918 and 1932 were dominated by an uncomfortable alliance between the more progressive faction and right-wing trade union and SPD leaders. With the onset of the Depression, however, heavy industry, which was in any case more seriously injured by the economic crisis, increasingly tried to create a mass basis of support for its interests in the NSDAP and thus played a major role in bringing Hitler to power.

A somewhat different analysis of conflicts within the business élite appears in the work of Gossweiler, who recognises that Kuczyński's work fails to discuss the role of banking interests – an especially serious omission, given the close interconnections between finance and industrial capital in Germany – and who himself distinguishes between two competing financial empires, one exclusively German and the other linked to American capital.[4] Gossweiler's distinction overlaps partially, but only partially, with that between coal, iron and steel on the one hand, and the electrical and chemical industries on the other, and claims that both groups gave money to the Nazis to secure the representation of their particular interests within the Party.

These analyses by no means exhaust the various ways in which the fragmentation of the industrial lobby can be described. Hallgarten, for example, focuses on a supposed conflict between 'family enterprises' on the one hand, and 'joint stock concerns' on the other, the former fearing totalitarian rule, unlike the latter; a point reiterated by Treue.[5] Yet another line of differentiation within the industrial camp is identified by the East German historian Czichon, which this time separates those who supported the Nazi concept of an autarchic German economy, isolated from the international market, and a group of 'Keynsians'. The triumph of National Socialism is then attributed to the splitting of the Keynsian camp under the chancellorship of General Schleicher in late 1932. According to this theory, the 'Left Keynsians' backed Schleicher's attempts to regenerate German economic activity in co-operation with some sections of organised labour and the so-called 'Left Nazis' around Gregor Strasser, whilst the 'Right Keynsians' now supported Hitler's candidature for the chancellorship together with the autarchists. Once again some overlap is claimed between the proponents of autarchy and heavy industry on the one hand, and Keynsian attitudes and the interests of the export, electrical and chemical interests together with finance on the other.[6]

The variety of these expositions of internal division within the industrial camp should not blind us to certain common themes. All the above accounts attribute a major role in Hitler's rise to power to the machinations of industrial capital and all assume an intimate relationship between at least some sections of the business community and the NSDAP. They also attempt to relate the political behaviour of industrialists to specific economic interests; and in particular, they identify differences of interest between a declining heavy industrial sector, suffering a real crisis of profitability and expending a large percentage of its total outlay on wages, and a more dynamic, export-oriented, capital-intensive and less-Nazi sector, incorporating the chemical and electrical industries, at least in part.

The most brutal critique of such arguments is to be found in the work of the American historian Henry Ashby Turner.[7] His criticisms are of both a methodological and substantive kind. First, Turner doubts that

industry played such a decisive role in the political events that
undermined the fabric of Weimar democracy. It would seem that the
opposition of agrarian interests and of President Hindenburg to certain
aspects of Brüning's agricultural policy was more instrumental in
removing the Chancellor than business pressure;[8] whilst other recent
research suggests that von Papen's decision to incorporate Hitler into his
plans in early 1933 was personal, rather than dictated by particular
industrialists such as Springorum, head of both the so-called *Langnamverein* (a pressure group of heavy industry) and the Association of
Northwest German Iron and Steel Industrialists after 1930.[9] Secondly,
Turner claims that East German scholarship has based its arguments on
an insufficiently broad base of sources, even in the case of Czichon. Thus
a great deal of Turner's argument turns on detailed empirical refutation
of particular aspects of DDR historiography. Thus he disputes Gossweiler's claim that Gregor Strasser was an agent for the giant chemicals
group, IG Farben; and points out that far too much has been made of
Emil Kirdorf's *temporary* membership of the Nazi Party in 1927/8: for
Kirdorf, the director of the Rhenish-Westphalian Coal Syndicate,
resigned from the NSDAP in 1928, supported the DNVP for most of the
next five years and rejoined the fascist ranks only in 1934. The central
point which Turner wishes to make through the deployment of a mass of
data, however, is that no simple alignment existed between concrete
economic interests on the one hand and the complex and variegated
political behaviour of individual industrialists on the other. Thus he
points out that although Carl Bosch and Carl Duisberg of IG Farben
(chemicals) were certainly hostile to the Nazis in 1932, the same firm
none the less gave some money to the Party for reasons to be examined
later. Thus the electrical industry was no more united or single-minded:
for Hermann Bücher of AEG was distributing funds to some sections of
the NSDAP, in particular, an opponent of Goebbels, in early 1931. And
thus, although Fritz Thyssen and Emil Kirdorf from heavy industry
could be genuinely described as sympathetic to the Nazis, the same could
not be said of Paul Reusch, managing director of the *Gutehoffnungshütte*,
or Ernst Poensgen of the *Vereinigte Stahlwerke*, who remained 'reserved'
towards and 'mistrustful' of Hitler and his cronies. It was even less true
of Gustav Krupp, Peter Klöckner and Otto Wolff, who disliked – not
surprisingly – the anti-capitalist facets of Nazi propaganda, especially in
the Ruhr. Equally an attempt to associate light industry with Keynsian
attitudes becomes problematic, as Czichon places a host of the representatives of heavy industry in this category: Flick, Klöckner, Reusch,
Silverberg, Springorum. Krupp, Wilmowsky and Wolff are even
accounted as 'Left Keynsians'; which, according to Turner, further
demonstrates the impossibility and illogicality of reducing political
differences to differences of economic interest. Turner prefers to
stress the divisions of political affiliation, even within the

infamous informal group of leading Ruhr industrialists, the *Ruhrlade*. Krupp, Silverberg and Vögler belonged to the German People's Party (DVP), Springorum and Thyssen were members of the German Nationalist Party (DNVP) and Klöckner supported the Catholic Centre Party in 1928. Of these several subsequently switched political allegiance and other members of the *Ruhrlade* remained politically unaffiliated.

A further point which figures prominently in Turner's analysis is that, even where industrialists manifestly did contribute to Nazi Party funds, they did so with reservations, often in order to win the Party over to 'sound' economic policies and to counter the influence of the 'Nazi Left'. Furthermore, their contributions to the Nazi Party were less substantial than those made by the same industrialists to the other non-socialist parties. Thus, although it is true that some of IG Farben's political fund found its way to the NSDAP in 1932, most of it was offered to the other 'more respectable' bourgeois parties, such as the DVP and the DNVP. The same was also true of Friedrich Flick, one of Germany's greatest steel tycoons, who contributed to every political party except the Communists as a form of insurance. From such detailed analysis Turner concludes that Fritz Thyssen was something of a maverick; and that it is impossible to talk of big business as a whole, or even specific factions of capital, actually supporting the Nazis. He also contends that small rather than big business was much more likely to have been enthused by the Nazi message; and this contention finds considerable validation in those studies of NSDAP membership and electoral support that have stressed the *lower*-middle class constituency of the Party.[10]

Such detailed findings obviously render crass generalisation danger-ous but they are by no means the last word. It can be claimed that Turner's work is as blind to some evidence as that of the DDR historians is to other material. Thus a major critique of Turner's conclusions is to be found in the writings of Dirk Stegmann as well as of his East German contemporaries. It can first be contended that although industrial contributions to NSDAP funds may have been made with reservations or to limit the influence of Nazi radicals, they were contributions none the less and thus enabled Hitler to wage his massive electoral campaigns. Without such financial contributions, the existence of which even Turner does not care to deny, Nazi party organisation might well have collapsed. Furthermore, Stegmann does list a substantial number of industrialists as funders or supporters of the Nazis.[11] This of course raises the crucial question: which body of data is more representative of industry as a whole? As Stegmann points out, it simply will not do to identify individual businessmen from, say, chemicals, who did not baulk at the prospect of Hitler as Chancellor, or from iron and steel who proved relatively 'liberal', and claim on this basis that all generalisations about political behaviour and economic interests are unfounded. Some kind of quantification would be necessary for any such conclusion to be drawn; and neither side in the debate has really engaged in such a difficult undertaking. Equally, such a conclusion would require a far more detailed examination of the specific economic interests of different firms and sectors than is provided, as far as I can see, in any of Turner's work. Nor can any attempt to assess the political identity of different industrial interests be abstracted from the chronology of political developments in Weimar: industrialists, like everyone else, adjusted to changes of circumstance, could be hostile to the Weimar Republic at one moment and at least temporarily more sympathetic at another. In this sense Stegmann, Neebe,[12] Grübler[13] and Abraham[14] seem to me to have a superior grasp of the *development* of industrial attitudes after 1918 and especially in the Depression years. Perhaps most importantly of all, the vital question is not so much who gave money to the Nazis but rather the more general issue of the relationship of the industrial élite to the Weimar Republic: for it can be argued that even if most leading businessmen were not supporters or even funders of the NSDAP, they none the less were prepared to tolerate a coalition government that included Hitler and above all had come to the conclusion that the political system of Weimar could no longer be sustained. Clearly, therefore, we must attempt to analyse the relationship of industry towards the institutions of the Weimar Republic from the revolution of 1918 onwards.

As well as pointing to the very different political allegiances of individual industrialists, Turner has claimed that they were in the main indifferent to specific constitutional forms, that is, neither 'republican' nor 'anti-republican'.[15] Certainly at the time of the abortive Kapp *Putsch* in 1920, industry as a whole did not desert the Republic but did reveal considerable apathy or confusion on the issue of its survival.[16] The early years of the Weimar Republic were also characterised by an unprecedented degree of co-operation between the representatives of organised labour, especially the Free Trade Union leaders, and industry, typified by the Stinnes–Legien agreement of November 1918 and the subsequent co-operative venture known as the *Zentralarbeitsgemeinschaft* (ZAG). In a sense, the establishment of a working democratic order in postwar Germany was predicated upon this agreement between capital and labour. David Abraham goes even further and claims that as long as those industries which were prepared to co-operate with organised labour and thus the institutional system of Weimar held sway or at least remained influential, parliamentary democracy was secure, secure upon the foundations of an alliance between organised labour and what he chooses to characterise as export-oriented, capital-intensive, dynamic industries, especially those producing chemicals and electrical goods. Thus he makes great play of the famous speech of Paul Silverberg, head of the national industrial pressure group, the *Reichsverband der Deutschen Industrie*, at Dresden in 1926, in which Silverberg stated the necessity of working with the Social Democrats on the basis of the Weimar Republic. Abraham does recognise, however, that the declining heavy industries with high labour costs and a domestic-market strategy were never so enamoured of co-operation and that they played a major role in the overthrow of Weimar during the Depression.

Even this view of industry's relationship with the Weimar Republic seems to me to be unduly optimistic. It must first of all be stressed that not only was the co-operation of capital and labour in the ZAG short-lived but also such co-operation was the product of a singular set of circumstances at the end of the First World War. In a sense, the revolutionary upheavals of the period between 1918 and 1923 and what appeared to be the very real threat of socialisation of at least some industrial sectors forced co-operation upon the likes of Stinnes as a lesser evil. Comments of individual industrialists make this crystal clear. Stinnes himself described the ZAG as providing a 'breathing space', whilst Jakob Wilhelm Reichert, director of the Association of German Iron and Steel Industrialists, saw that the question of the hour was, 'How can we save industry?'[17] The point is made even clearer in a programme for the future drawn up by the *Reichsverband* as early as 1922, which looked forward to a significant reduction in taxes, social security provision and wages, and above all to an abolition of the statutory eight-hour working day.[18] Significantly Paul Silverberg played a major role in the formulation of this programme, which further suggests that his speech of 1926 must be treated with caution. Neebe's recent study argues that Silverberg's career and speeches were invariably character-ised by a tactical opportunism. Designed to ensure the recognition of industrial interests through some degree of popular support, he could advocate co-operation with the SPD in 1926 and without the SPD but with the Nazis in late 1932! Furthermore, as both Schneider[19] and Weisbrod[20] point out, the speech of 1926 is less conciliatory than sometimes imagined. The acceptance of Social Democrats and the Free Trade Unions as partners depended upon their willingness to abandon the language of class warfare and above all to leave the running of the economy to 'to those who knew best', namely, the industrialists themselves. This last point is crucial to Schneider's whole account of the tortured relationship between industry and democratic structures in the Weimar Republic: industry was not prepared to accept the rights of any other institution or social group to interfere with 'the economy'. If equal rights were to be admitted at all, then only in the political sphere. But in postwar Germany such a distinction between politics and economics was clearly illusory. Democracy did mean that labour too made claims on the state for social welfare and the representation of its interests; and such demands of necessity impinged upon taxation and labour relations, which in turn and of necessity affected issues of profitability and the organisation of industry. These consequences of genuine pluralism were never accepted by German industry. Again, co-operation with labour in the ZAG was also dictated by the need to combat the retention of state economic controls after demobilisation;[21] whilst the relative tolerance of unions and willingness to compromise on wage claims on the part of industrialists between 1919 and 1922 was made possible by the utterly exceptional boom conditions generated by the devaluation of the mark on international currency markets and by the inflation. Prices and profits outstripped wages – paid in a devalued currency – and thus employers could afford to buy industrial peace. As early as the 1922 programme of a special committee of the *Reichsverband der Deutschen Industrie* (RDI), mentioned above, it was clear that industry did not expect these unusual conditions to last and that it was already determined to reverse many of the gains of labour. After 1923 the stabilisation crisis followed by a perpetual crisis of overcapacity and profitability in heavy industry – relieved only partially during the British strikes of 1926 – made that determination all the stronger.

Most commentators are agreed that it is difficult to generalise about the attitude of 'industry' to the Weimar Republic. The Kapp *Putsch*, as we have already seen, was a testimony to division and confusion. However, these commentators rarely dissent from the view that *in general* some sectors of industry – chemicals, the electrical industry, some sections of the processing and finishing industries in engineering – were more tolerant of the political institutions of the Weimar Republic and more prepared to co-operate with the representatives of organised labour than others.[22] Thus the German Democratic Party, *the* German liberal party committed to the new Republic, initially received considerable funding from the electrical giant Siemens. Carl Duisberg of IG Farben can with some degree of accuracy be described as a loyal supporter of Weimar and the democratic system, and one who further called for the abandonment of prewar hostility towards the unions; whilst Hermann Bücher of AEG advocated compromise between capital and labour and gave explicit support to state arbitration in industrial disputes.[23] In 1926 Silverberg's controversial Dresden speech found difficulty in generating general enthusiasm among the ranks of the RDI, but among his supporters were to be numbered the leading figures of the electrical industry – Siemens, Duisberg, von Raumer – chemicals and machine-building,[24] though, as Weisbrod points out, these people were also hesitant to provide outspoken support in public.[25] These same groups attempted to revive the ZAG in 1930, especially through the initiative of Hermann Bücher, Hans von Raumer and Siemens (electricals), Carl Bosch (chemicals), Abraham Frohwein (textiles) and Hans Kraemer (paper and printing).[26] The initiative was sabotaged, however, by the opposition of Thyssen, Ernst von Borsig and other members of a lobby that was in no way prepared to co-operate with organised labour. Even in 1931 the former industrial sectors continued to support the chancellorship of Brüning when heavy industrial support shifted away and demanded a stronger line against collective wage agreements and arbitration;[27] whilst in the same year Bosch of IG Farben attempted to come to a voluntary agreement with the unions over a reduction in the length of the working day, an attempt for which he was reprimanded by heavy industry.[28] Such support for Brüning survived his failure to adopt a tougher line on labour relations. On the other hand, the progressive industrial faction was less enamoured of Papen's assault on wage agreements and in particular the agrarian tariffs he introduced.[29] In fact throughout the Weimar Republic the representatives of the more progressive industrial camp were less prepared to co-operate with the representatives of agrarian interests, especially the *Reichslandbund*, than some sections of heavy industry. The electro-technical, chemical, machine-building and textile industries were generally committed to a strategy of low prices for basic materials and international reconciliation to guarantee export markets. Hence, of course, their support for Stresemann in the internal political squabbles of the DVP.[30] Such industrialists were naturally hostile to agricultural protection, favoured trade treaties which implied agricultural imports as well as foreign markets for the export of manufactures and thus were at odds with the autarchic aims of the agrarian lobby.[31]

The key to the relatively conciliatory position of such industries both internationally – in terms of their willingness to seek compromise on the question of reparations – and domestically – their readiness to deal with the representatives of organised labour and tolerate mandatory arbitration and collective wage agreements – is to be found, not surprisingly, in the relative prosperity of these sectors in the ailing Weimar economy. Whereas heavy industry was in difficulties from the mid-1920s onwards, that is, even before the onset of the world economic Depression, the machine industry and especially chemicals and electrics proved exceptionally buoyant, at least until 1931. Indeed, to the middle of that year export markets were still crucial to this sector, which obviously explains its stance on tariffs and international co-operation. Furthermore, the greater profitability of these firms meant that they could afford to meet union demands on the question of hours and wages more easily than their counterparts in coal, iron and steel. This was especially true as labour costs constituted a substantially less significant proportion of total costs than was the case in most branches of heavy industry. Thus whereas mining had only a 4 per cent profit rate in 1927 according to an RDI survey and that of iron and steel was even lower, electro-technology produced one of 7 per cent and textiles one of 10 per cent, precisely because wages were low in textiles and an insubstantial part of total costs in electro-technology. Conversely mining's labour costs represented over 50 per cent of total costs, easily the highest proportion of all major industries. In chemicals the figure dropped to a mere 15 per cent.[32]

There can be no doubt, therefore, that there did exist within German industry a relatively progressive sector whose attitude towards the Weimar Republic was at least one of tolerance. The question remains, however: how influential was this sector and how typical was it of industry as a whole?

There is substantial evidence that the representation of industrial interests between at least 1925 and 1930 did lie in the hands of the progressive faction of capital to some extent. An all-out attack upon the social and labour legislation of the Weimar Republic was not mounted by the RDI before the Depression. Furthermore, many positions of influence within this organisation, the main national pressure group of German industry, were held by representatives of chemicals, the electrical industry and machine-building: in 1925 Carl Duisberg of IG Farben was elected head of the *Reichsverband* against the competition of Albert Vögler, a representative of steel interests, and Ernst von Borsig, the locomotive manufacturer and leader of the uncompromising employers' association, the *Arbeitgeberverband*. The RDI leadership also included Hermann Bücher of the electrical industry and the various advisory committees fell from the hands of heavy industry into those of a sectorally and regionally diverse group. Not surprisingly, therefore, Ruhr industrialists began to despair of an organisation that was now dominated by 'Berlin political types'.[33] It would be false to conclude from this, however, as Abraham seems to in the main, that heavy industrial interests were severely circumscribed in their exercise of influence between 1925 and 1930. Indeed Weisbrod claims that even in this period the powerful coal, iron and steel lobbies of the Ruhr possessed something not short of the power of veto over various economic issues. Thus the processing, electrical and chemical industries were never able to destroy the cartelised price structures of German heavy industry but rather reached agreement in 1925 in the AVI accords, in which in return for the maintenance of cartelised prices the primary producers agreed to refund to exporters of finished goods the difference between the domestic and world price of their products for those quantities that were later exported. Silverberg's advocacy of reconciliation with the Social Democrats in 1926, although supported by more progressive elements, met with widespread resistance within the RDI; and although the *Langnamverein* (Association for Furthering the Joint Economic Interests of the Rhineland and Westphalia) played a major role in co-ordinating that resistance, it also came from industrial organisations in Saxony, Hanover, Oldenburg, Bavaria, the Halle lignite industry, North German woollen manufacturers and Heidelberg cement interests, amongst others.[34] The revival of the *Zentralarbeitsgemeinschaft* in 1930 was also sabotaged by the opposition of heavy industry, which in mid-1931 also reminded Carl Bosch and the government that what was at issue was not simply the reduction in working hours but the dismantling of the whole system of mandatory collective wage agreements and arbitration. The ability of heavy industry, especially in the Ruhr, to exercise such influence was partly a consequence of its geographical concentration and high level of both formal and informal organisation;[35] and certainly such influence remained strong, even between 1925 and 1930. In the Depression it again became paramount. Although Krupp must be numbered amongst the more conciliatory representatives of heavy industry, Abraham sees his election as head of the RDI and the replacement of Duisberg in September 1931 as the culmination of a process that had begun in the previous year, whereby organisational changes in the *Reichsverband* increased the representation of heavy industrial interests, a point made equally forcefully by Weisbrod.[36]

Thus the power of the progressive faction should not be exaggerated, even in the mid-1920s. It is also true that some money from the chemical and electrical industries made its way to the Nazis, as we have seen. Most important of all, the deepening of the recession and the onset of economic crisis amongst the formerly dynamic industries led even them to question some aspects of republican government in the 1930s and made them less conciliatory. As early as January 1930 even Carl Duisberg claimed that 'capital is being destroyed through the unproductive use of public funds. . . . Only an immediate and radical reversal in state policies can help,' thus criticising Weimar's progressive social welfare legislation.[37] Although, moreover, some sections of the electrical and chemical industries were not opposed to some degree of reflation in late 1932 as a way out of the economic crisis, they remained most suspicious of Schleicher's dealings with the Free Trade Unions and the 'Left Nazis'.[38]

The attitudes of the more dynamic industrial sectors described above cannot be taken as symptomatic of German industry as a whole. Although Fritz Thyssen, the steel tycoon, and Emil Kirdorf were unusual in their political affiliation to radical nationalism for most of the 1920s, it is certainly true that heavy industry as a whole disliked particular aspects of the Weimar Republic from the start and played a large part in frustrating various liberal initiatives. We have already seen that opposition from heavy industry undermined Silverberg's attempts at a reconciliation with labour and subsequent efforts to revive the ZAG in 1930. It also led to the overthrow of parliamentary government in Germany in 1928/30, in so far as the possibility of compromise between the SPD and DVP on the issue of unemployment insurance was sabotaged not only by the pressure of Free Trade Unions and radical Social Democrats but also by the heavy industrial faction within the DVP.[39] It was heavy industry – together with smaller businesses in Saxony – that broke with Chancellor Brüning on the grounds that mandatory arbitration, statutory wages legislation and a fixed working day were not abolished[40] and who were most horrified by Schleicher's commitment to some form of reflationary collaboration with labour subsequently.[41] Heavy industry provided the troops who mobilised against the Young Plan[42] and many of the non-agrarian supporters of the Harzburg Front, though the precise political affiliation of this support was most varied.

The reasons for such hostility to compromise are not hard to find. Ever since the mid-1920s coal, iron and steel had suffered from a crisis of profitability, compounded by the fact that in some cases at least labour costs constituted a relatively high percentage of total costs. Confronted with increased international competition and a decreased base of raw materials and market as a result of losses in the peace settlement of 1919, these industries came to rely upon a protected and cartelised price structure. Hence their disinterest and often active opposition to international reconciliation and trade treaties. Even in the best years of Weimar firms in these sectors worked at well below their capacity: German steel works produced at only just over 60 per cent capacity in 1925, 77 per cent in the peak year of 1927 and 55 per cent in 1930.[43] This problem was in turn a consequence not simply of a restricted market but also of a massive increase in productive potential as a result of rationalisation – amalgamation, concentration, the use of new technology – in the mid-1920s.[44] Such overcapacity became fatal in the years of Depression after 1929. A consequence of these problems was that coal, iron and steel could not afford to buy industrial peace, unlike AEG or IG Farben. It also meant that they were exceptionally sensitive to increased costs, either in the shape of wage settlements, insurance contributions or taxation.

Herein lies the key to employer hostility to the Weimar Republic: for the Weimar Republic, however imperfect it may have been, was a social welfare state which introduced a vast expansion of social welfare provision and in particular a system of unemployment insurance, all of which had to be paid for through taxation. Furthermore the Weimar years saw the introduction of statutory collective wage agreements and compulsory and binding arbitration, which until 1930 normally favoured labour in industrial disputes.[45] Those industries with problems of profitability claimed that such measures destroyed their competitiveness and left them bankrupt; and they associated such measures with the political structures of Weimar, in which industry had to compete with the SPD and the trade unions for influence – a situation quite unlike that before the First World War. This was why they described state economic policy as 'cold socialism' and the state itself as a 'trade union state'.[46] Business tolerance of democratic politics did not extend to interference in the running of the economy; and if the political system did interfere, as in its imposition of wage norms and a minimum working day, then loyalty was forfeit. This became quite clear in the industrial dispute in the Ruhr iron industry in 1928, which subsequently became known as the *Ruhreisenstreit* and in which no fewer than a quarter of a million workers were locked out.[47] What Ruhr industry, or at least some sections of it, were now prepared to do was not simply challenge a particular wages settlement but the whole system of state arbitration and collective agreements, the so-called *Zwangstarif*, as Max Schlenker of the *Langnamverein* and others confessed.[48] In various disputes Paul Reusch made plain that what concerned him was not the actual length of the working day but its statutory regulation;[49] and in so far as such constraints were linked to the democratic institutions of the Weimar Republic, so industrial support was always problematic. As early as December 1925, for example, Jacob Reichert of the iron and steel industry called for rule by presidential decree rather than by parliamentary majority, and in this he was supported by Ernst von Borsig, the arch-nationalist press baron Hugenberg, Thyssen and Groebler, again of the iron industry.[50]

Now it would be false to claim that all heavy industrialists shared these views throughout the torrid history of Weimar, or that such views were typical of German industry as a whole. They were clearly different to those of a more progressive alliance, as we have seen, and were not shared, for example, by Krupp, who was unhappy about the 1928 lock-out and was in any case the head of a massive vertical empire that included locomotive and sewing machine production as well as primary production of coal, iron and steel, and had significant and complicating export interests, by Otto Wolff from steel and coal, who wanted co-operation with the unions, and by Paul Silverberg whose perpetual aim was some form of mass support for industrial policies (initially via the SPD in 1926 and later through Schleicher and Strasser) who had interests in lignite, Ruhr coal *and* large-scale electricity generation and who acted as a mediator between heavy industry and the finishing industries. What does seem to be true, however, is that as time went on the less progressive groups came to reassert their dominance and that their attitudes towards the Weimar Republic and especially its labour legislation became more critical and more widespread.

In this evolution the Young Plan, the electoral success of the SPD and its participation in government once again in 1928, a series of arbitration decisions that were seen as favouring labour, and the fact that financial support was given by the government to the workers locked out in the *Ruhreisenstreit*, all created a crisis of political confidence and seemed to validate criticism of the Republic as a tool of trade union interests. Against this background only a few industrialists such as Kirdorf and Thyssen actually turned to the Nazis or gave them substantial financial support. However, many others now despaired of the fragmentation of bourgeois politics into innumerable political factions and called for an end to 'socialist' – by which they meant SPD and Free Trade Union rather than communist – influence. The deepening of the recession made compromise even less possible, although Brüning's first term of office, which dismantled some previous labour legislation and lowered wages, met with broad approval from the business community. This accord did not survive. The growth of Nazism as a mass political movement increasingly rendered illusory hopes of an anti-socialist *Sammlung* of bourgeois groups without the NSDAP, whilst the further ravages of the Depression and the fact that statutory wage levels and arbitration were not removed by Brüning, indeed the fact that his survival depended upon at least the tacit consent of the SPD, soon led to disaffection amongst the ranks of coal, iron and steel and of Saxon industrial interests. The RDI, Silverberg and those who were relatively moderate had increasing difficulty in holding the industrial camp together and some deserted to the ultra-nationalist Harzburg Front (Reusch, Springorum, Vögler, Poensgen), where Thyssen and his kind were already to be found. However, confusion and hesitancy were now the order of the day and the politics of the Harzburg Front, founded to combat the reparations settlement, were far from united. In general it is fair to say that anti-Brüning attitudes became more widespread and that ideas of a bourgeois bloc now to include the Nazis, albeit as junior partners, became more common. Thus in March 1932 Fritz Springorum of Hoesch iron and steel and treasurer of heavy industry's political fund stated 'a rightist government is only possible with the co-operation of the NSDAP' and went on to argue for giving the Nazis financial support.[51] This was also the time, of course, when Hitler and other leading Nazis were making a deliberate attempt to win over industry through the good offices of Thyssen, Keppler and Schacht, former President of the *Reichsbank*, and by guaranteeing that the NSDAP would respect the right of management to manage.

It would still be wrong to conclude that at this juncture 'industry' had opted decisively for an alliance that would include the Nazis. Reusch, Springorum and Poensgen were still suspicious of the NSDAP, and the more liberal faction continued to support Brüning. Brüning's fall, to a large extent the result of agrarian pressure, and his replacement by Papen and a more aggressive anti-labour stand, reflected in severe wage reductions amongst other things, was also sufficient to generate some satisfaction in industrial circles. What disturbed this picture of relative harmony was not so much Papen's introduction of import controls for agricultural products, which, contrary to Abraham's contention, led none the less to a severe rift between even heavy industry, which by now had lost its export markets entirely, and agriculture, but rather the dangerous strategy of Schleicher, Papen's successor as Chancellor. Schleicher was prepared to reintroduce labour legislation, abolished by the previous administration, to court the support of both the Free Trade Unions and the 'left-wing' of the NSDAP around Gregor Strasser, and to engage in an ambitious reflationary programme of job-creation. Reichert, director of the Association of German Iron and Steel Industrialists, now found that he no longer had direct access to the Chancellor and there were even rumours that iron and steel would be nationalised. Such policies rehabilitated Papen in industrial circles: Schleicher could rely upon the support of only a small group of somewhat wayward industrialists – Wolff, Silverberg and not many others. Such policies revived schemes of a united bourgeois bloc, though again not necessarily with Hitler initially. Papen could not generate parliamentary support, however, without the NSDAP after the results of the *Reichstag* elections of 1932. Indeed, the NSDAP controlled more support than all the other bourgeois parties combined. Furthermore the prospect of Nazi inclusion in government was now less daunting, given the decline in electoral support for NSDAP in the second *Reichstag* elections of 1932: Hitler would be more malleable, they fondly imagined, especially as the influence of Strasser and the radicals within the Party had now been curbed. Thus a point had been reached where the stabilisation of industry, the dismantling of the welfare and labour legislation of Weimar and the assumption of power by a coalition including the Nazis could be envisaged. According to Stegmann, Papen did discusss the inclusion of Hitler in a future Cabinet with Reusch, Krupp, Springorum and Vögler on 7 January 1933; and thus industry, or at least the *Ruhrlade*, was not taken by surprise. As Neebe reminds us, this does not imply that the move was *prompted* by industrial interests; but it does suggest that it was a move they were prepared to tolerate.

This, it seems, and not who actually financed the Nazis and how much they gave, is the crucial point about the industrial élite in the Weimar Republic. Though they had differing opinions amongst themselves, they were never that keen on the institutions of collective wages and compulsory arbitration, which some opposed from the start. The economic crisis of the early 1930s, the loss of markets, the disappearance of profits, which were exclusively – and arguably unjustly[52] – attributed to the power of organised labour meant that struggles were no longer about the distribution of the national product but the ability of the capitalist system to reproduce itself within the political framework of Weimar. Large numbers of industrialists thought not and so wanted rid of the Republic. Whether Hitler was the man for the job was not certain; but the realities of political support in 1932/3 meant that he could not be ignored. He might be unreliable; but he was useful.

Notes

1   *Protokolle der Kongresse der Kommunistischen Internationale. Verhandlungen in Moskau 1921–5* (Hamburg: 1921–5).

2   For an account of Comintern attitudes see Nicos Poulantzas, *Fascisme et Dictature* (Paris: 1970). For the more subtle evaluation of Eugen Varga see Laszlo M. Tikos, 'Waiting for the World Revolution: Soviet reactions to the Great Depression', in *Journal of Contemporary History*, vol. 4, no. 4, 1969.

3 Jürgen Kuczynski, *Klassen und Klassenkämpfe im imperialistischen Deutschland und in der BRD* (Frankfurt-on-Main: 1972), pp. 418–74 *passim*.

4 Kurt Gossweiler, *Grossbanken, Industriemonopole, Staat* (East Berlin: 1971).

5 G. W. F. Hallgarten, *Hitler, Reichswehr und Industrie* (Frankfurt: 1962); Wilhelm Treue, 'Die Einstellung einiger deutscher Grossindustrieller zu Hitlers Aussenpolitik', in *Geschichte in Wissenschaft und Unterricht*, 17, 1966, p. 496.

6 Eberhard Czichon, *Wer verhalf Hitler zur Macht* (Cologne: 1967).

7 H. A. Turner, 'Big Business and the Rise of Hitler', *American Historical Review*, LXXV, no. I, 1969, pp. 56–70; 'The Ruhrlade' in *Central European History*, 3, 1970, pp. 195–228; *Faschismus und Kapitalismus in Deutschland* (Göttingen: 1972); 'Das Verhältnis des Grossunternehmertums zur NSDAP', in Hans Mommsen, Dietmar Petzina and Bernd Weisbrod (eds), *Industrielles System und politische Entwicklung in der Weimarer Republik* (Düsseldorf: 1974), pp. 919–31; 'Grossunternehmer und Nationalsozialismus', *Historische Zeitschrift*, vol. 221, 1975, pp. 18–68.

8 David Abraham, *The Collapse of the Weimar Republic* (Princeton, NJ: 1981), pp. 85–115.

9 Reinhard Neebe, *Grossindustrie, Staat und NSDAP 1930–1933* (Göttingen: 1981).

10 For a recent summary of work in this area see Peter D. Stachura, 'Who were the Nazis? A Socio-Political Analysis of the National Socialist Machtübernahme', *European Studies Review*, II, no. 3, 1981, pp. 293–324.

11 Dirk Stegmann, 'Zum Verhältnis von Grossindustrie und Nationalsozialismus 1930–33', *Archiv für Sozialgeschichte*, 13, 1973, pp. 399–482; 'Kapitalismus und Faschismus in Deutschland 1929–1934', in *Gesellschaft*, 6 (Frankfurt-on-Main: 1976), pp. 19–91; 'Antiquierte Personalisierung oder sozialökonomische Faschismus-Analyse?', *Archiv Für Sozialgeschichte*, 17, 1977, pp. 275–96.

12 Neebe, *Grossindustrie*.

13 Michael Grübler, *Die Spitzenverbände der Wirtschaft und das erste Kabinett Brüning* (Düsseldorf: 1982).

14 Abraham, *Weimar Republic*.

15 Turner, 'Big Business', p. 57.

16 Hans H. Biegert, 'Gewerkschaftspolitik in der Phase des Kapp-Lüttwitz-Putsches' in Mommsen *et al.*, *Industrielles System* p. 198; Gerald D. Feldman, 'Big Business and the Kapp Putsch', *Central European History*, IV, no. 2, 1971, pp. 99–130.

17 Quotations in Michael Schneider, *Unternehmer und Demokratie* (Bonn: 1975), pp. 42 and 37 f.

18 Gerald D. Feldman, *Iron and Steel in the German Inflation* (Princeton, NJ: 1977), pp. 319–45.

19 Schneider, *Unternehmer*, pp. 55–9.

20 Bernd Weisbrod, *Schwerindustrie in der Krise* (Wuppertal: 1978), pp. 246–72; see also Dirk Stegmann, 'Die Silverberg-Kontroverse', in Hans-Ulrich Wehler, *Sozialgeschichte Heute* (Göttingen: 1974), pp. 594–610.

21 Feldman, *Iron*, ch. 3.

22 This is central to Abraham's account and is further borne out by Schneider, *Unternehmer*, p. 106; Stegmann, 'Verhältnis', pp. 421 f and 435 f; Neebe, *Grossindustrie*; and Grübler, *Die Spitzenverbände der Wirtschaft*.

23 Abraham, *Weimar Republic*, pp. 135 f.

24 Stegmann, 'Verhältnis', p. 409.

25 Weisbrod, *Schwerindustrie*, pp. 256 f.

26 ibid., pp. 492 f; Abraham, *Weimar Republic*, pp. 165 ff.

27 Stegmann, 'Verhältnis', pp. 421 f.

28 Grübler, *Die Spitzenverbände der Wirtschaft*, *passim*.

29 Abraham, *Weimar Republic*, pp. 171 f and 216 ff.

30 Lothar Döhn, *Politik und Interesse* (Meisenheim an Glan: 1970).

31 Abraham, *Weimar Republic*, pp. 86–9.

32 Reichsverband der deutschen Industrie, *Besteuerung, Ertrag und Arbeitslohn im Jahre 1927* (Berlin: 1929).
33 Abraham, *Weimar Republic*, pp. 132 ff; Weisbrod, *Schwerindustrie*, p. 220.
34 Weisbrod, *Schwerindustrie*, pp. 256 f.
35 ibid., pp. 23 f.
36 ibid., p. 484; Abraham, *Weimar Republic*, pp. 24 and 156 f.
37 Quoted in Abraham, *Weimar Republic*, p. 263.
38 Stegmann, 'Verhältnis', pp. 435 f.
39 Abraham, *Weimar Republic*, p. 47; Döhn, *Politik und Interesse, passim.*
40 Grübler, *Die Spitzenverbände der Wirtschaft*; Neebe, *Grossindustrie.*
41 Stegmann, 'Verhältnis', pp. 435 f.
42 Abraham, *Weimar Republic*, p. 48.
43 Weisbrod, *Schwerindustrie*, pp. 48 ff.
44 ibid., pp. 52–60.
45 On the social welfare legislation of Weimar see Ludwig Preller, *Sozialpolitik in der Weimarer Republik* (Stuttgart: 1949). On hours, wages and arbitration legislation see Hans-Hermann Hartwich, *Arbeitsmarkt, Verbände und Staat* (Berlin: 1967) and Otto Kahn-Freund, *Labour Law and Politics in the Weimar Republic* (ed. and introd. by Roy Lewis and Jon Clark, Oxford: 1981).
46 Schneider, *Unternehmer*, pp. 156 f.
47 Weisbrod, *Schwerindustrie*, pp. 415–56; Michael Schneider, *Auf dem Weg in die Krise* (Wentorf: 1974); Ursula Hüllbüsch, 'Der Ruhreisenstreit', in Mommsen *et al.*, *Industrielles System* pp. 271–89.
48 Schneider, *Unternehmer*, pp. 82 f.
49 ibid., p. 65.
50 Stegmann, 'Verhältnis', pp. 408 f.
51 Quoted in Abraham, *Weimar Republic*, p. 321. This whole account, both preceding and following the quotation, is largely drawn from Abraham, Stegmann, Grübler, Neebe and Weisbrod.
52 Weisbrod, *Schwerindustrie*, provides an interesting critique of industry's complaints about the burden of wages and taxation, pointing out that some firms spent more on private welfare provision than the state system, that labour costs were not that different from prewar levels but that raw material costs rose much more substantially. The fundamental problem, however, was the massive overcapacity generated by an – in a sense – unwarranted process of rationalisation and technological modernisation at a time when markets were shrinking. This problem was further compounded by high cartelised prices. (See ch. 3.)

7 Etudes in Political History: Reichswehr, NSDAP, and the Seizure of Power*

MICHAEL GEYER

Having struggled in vain to bring some order into the diverse literature on the relationship between the National Socialist movement and the *Reichswehr*, it seems best for me to make this issue itself the main theme of the essay. What, after all, do Nazis and the military have in common? To be sure, they were thrown together time and again in the most diverse, sometimes bizarre and mysterious, but ultimately fatal events. From the perspective of a general survey it may even look as though they were predestined for each other. They shared a desire for rearmament and the violent aggrandisement of Germany and most certainly remained glued together after 1933 despite frictions and tensions. However, their unequal and unbalanced relationship can scarcely be subsumed under one heading. For the relationship, which dates back to the prehistory of the radicalisation of the army and the middle classes during war and revolution, began properly with Hitler's temporary employment as a fiery propaganda speaker for the Territorial Command VII (Bavaria) and his Beer Hall coup directed in part against the *Reichswehr* itself; it continued with allegations about Nazi infiltration of the officer corps and more innocent friendships across the lines, with repeated negotiations between the army and the National Socialist leadership, and the banning of the SA; it culminated, finally, in General Schleicher's concept of a *Querfront*, his utter failure, his dismissal as Chancellor, fear of a military *coup d'état* to save a non-existent Republic, the immediate rearrangement of the two protagonists, and in the extraordinary finale in which the new National Socialist Chancellor sought to convince leading army and navy officers of *his* sincerity. The dynamics of their relationship derived from so vastly different sources that attempts to fold them into *one* coherent and continuous story – the one of the *Reichswehr* and the National Socialist party which led up to the seizure of power and to the defeat of both in 1945 – would distort far more than depict reality.

What is it that makes this reality so elusive despite ample evidence and despite countless studies? It is not the lack of knowledge of one or the other aspect of the story. One might rather venture the thesis that it is the loss of the firm anchor in that common inversion of Whiggish history which says that Germany moved from small disasters to even bigger ones, the prime movers being the aristocratic army and an emaciated bourgeoisie. The Third Reich and the war which it unleashed with the help of the military was a catastrophe for Germany and Europe, but the lineages of that disaster do no longer seem to be that clearly drawn. Hence, much of the work, which only 25–30 years ago focused on the concept of a German 'nemesis of power', today is no more than a string of episodes.[1]

Nevertheless, a more coherent linkage between the two protagonists is implicit in different sets of episodes such as top-level negotiations, ideological bonds, rearmament, foreign policy. They have been explored by a variety of scholars. They have led to a number of assumptions about the character of the relationship between Nazis and the *Reichswehr*. These need clarification first.

The Weimar military had been considered to be unreliable long before 1933. A great number of contemporaries had distrusted the *Reichswehr*. They focused their attention on individuals, primarily Seeckt or Schleicher, on the formation of both *Reichswehr* and the Nazi Party in the revolutionary period between 1918 and 1923, on particular practices of the *Reichswehr* such as the secret rearmament and training of recruits, or on the behaviour and mentalities of parts of the officer corps, whether the monarchical sentiment of the older generation or National Socialistic tendencies among the younger ones.

Such suspicion was well founded. Neither Seeckt nor Schleicher were steadfast pillars of the Weimar Republic, secret rearmament was not just a fantasy of some Left–liberal minds, and there is strong evidence of both National Socialist and monarchical sentiment in the officer corps. Moreover, while the suggestion was exaggerated that the officer corps actively and continuously conspired to overthrow the Republic, there is still convincing and overwhelming support for the argument that the Weimar military's meddling in politics did contribute to the downfall of the Republic and that the *Reichswehr*, though not actively bringing the Nazis to power, nevertheless had a great interest in harnessing the strength of the National Socialist movement. The *Reichswehr* was one of the big winners of 1933.[2]

There have always been fuzzy edges to this argument. Thus, it has been argued since the 1930s[3] that the officer corps as a whole was much too conservative to give credit to the unruly Nazi movement. While the behaviour and the attitudes of the officer corps have never been fully explored, this plausible assumption has provoked the counter-argument that Nazis and officers, while worlds apart, still shared a 'partial identity of goals'.[4] Even when the frictions between Party and the military after 1933 made quite clear that the National Socialists and the traditional military outlook could not be easily squared, this partial identity of goals – defined as the shared goal of waging war for military hegemony in Europe – chained the two protagonists together.

Currently this seems to be the prevalent thesis among some of the foremost military historians in the interwar years. It is quickly replacing an older view, held particularly by American historians, who have always been somewhat more taken with the marvels of the German war machine and its professionals.[5] They argued for a much more aloof relationship between the military and the National Socialists and emphasised military resistance against the Nazi mobilisation and the Nazi regime. Similarly the concept of a 'partial identity of goals' differs substantially from the one that stresses the adoption of National Socialist and racist practices during the war and a wholesale carry-over of National Socialist ideas into the military organisation.[6] This recent argument has caused quite a stir, but so far has not been generalised into a comprehensive new assessment of the German armed forces in the interwar years. It could very well prove to be fruitful considering the tradition of imperialist, counter-revolutionary and 'total' people's wars of the German army,[7] but still suffers from the lack of a more thorough and detailed study of the actual events on a formally political plane.

Each of these interpretations makes important new contributions, but none to date suffices to overthrow the standard works of the late 1950s and early 1960s which concentrated on the analysis of the political events leading up to 1933.[8] They were written during the controversies over German rearmament after the Second World War and partly responded to that most idiosyncratic history of the German army by Wheeler-Bennett. His altogether intemperate trouncing of Schleicher as the *bête noire* of German military history has led to an especially careful analysis of what actually happened.[9] The fruits of this labour consisted in the so-called *Zähmungskonzept* (the concept of 'taming' or integrating the Nazis) which made sense of the stop-go politics of Schleicher in relation to the National Socialist party. Schleicher – one might add, Hitler as well – wanted to prevent another all-out struggle between the two protagonists. The result was two and a half years of jockeying, engagements and disengagements, shady deals and backroom politics, which were additionally complicated by Hindenburg being elected by the 'wrong majority' and by his thorough dislike of Hitler. Underlying all these overtures was Schleicher's rationale, that the army wanted to share the nationalist masses with Hitler without properly sharing power in the political arena. Once this proved to be impossible, Schleicher was ousted: power had to be shared.

The description of the *Zähmungskonzept* and its evolution still fits the documentary evidence very well. However, the underlying assumptions of this concept have come under fire. Originally it was very much seen as a last and desperate holding operation to stave off the Hitler regime to come. Classical parallels were readily drawn. Even though Schleicher was quite an unlikely candidate, the drama of the period and the dire consequences of his fall made him into a veracious Roman dictator (or a late Hegelian representative of the state) who stood poised to save the *res publica*. Alas, Schleicher proved to be a *cunctator*, the plebeian revolution took its course, and the beleaguered *civitas* was run over.[10] This assumption is benevolent fiction.[11] One might usefully want to debate whether there was anything left of a liberal and pluralistic Republic in 1932 or whether we observe the decomposition of an authoritarian regime that only two years before was hailed as the saviour from the woes of parliamentarism. But there is just very little room for debate whether the *Reichswehr* and its leadership in 1932 wanted to save a republic. They did not. 'Taming' the Nazis did not mean to make them ready for democracy. It never occurred to anybody to think or talk in these terms, so dead were the notions of liberty and equality.

While Western Marxists have so far concentrated rather on the 'ideological' than on the 'repressive' apparatuses,[12] military historians of the German Democratic Republic have produced a great deal of research on the *Reichswehr* which proposes an interesting contrast to the above. Marxist scholars generally emphasise that the *Reichswehr* had a stake in the Third Reich, which it helped to bring about, but was dependent on more fundamental economic forces. The generalists and the most economically inclined point to one or the other formation of monopoly capitalism and interpret the procession from Groener to Schleicher to Blomberg/Hitler as an outgrowth of contradictions in the reactionary capitalist camp.[13] But Marxist *military* historians, who form a quite separate and distinct club, have rather downgraded the *Reichswehr*-as-agent assumption. They fall in step with an interpretation that stresses the identity of reactionary goals of industry, *Reichswehr*, and the Nazi party, but they have also begun to emphasise the radicalisation of the military under the impact of the growing threat to the dominant order by the working class under the leadership of the Communist Party. Rather than simply seeing the military as another manifestation of a simple capitalist conspiracy, they tended to stress the agonistic character of the Weimar Republic.[14]

It is difficult to comprehend why, given the available documentary evidence, an approach along these lines has never been fully explored. For the conceptual limitation of the prevailing non-Marxist interpretations is precisely its failure to focus on one of the most evident reasons for Nazi–military co-operation, namely, the commonly perceived revolutionary threat. Indeed, the period between 1918 and 1923 is the common point of reference for both. Without looking back to that period the political climate of the 1930s hardly makes sense.[15] Communist historians (and the KPD) may have never quite trusted the revolutionary fervour of the 'masses', but *Reichswehr* officers and the National Socialist leadership readily took for granted the workers' ability to organise another revolution[16] and replayed in their minds the events of 1918 to 1923 again and again. While the more careful liberal and conservative view has never completely ignored this phenomenon,[17] they could and should have featured it more prominently.

Without setting aside the above approaches, let us consider a slightly different, and not yet fully developed line of interpretation that focuses Nazi–military relations through the lens of rearmament. This vantage point provides a new angle, but not a built-in bias – it is not yet entirely clear which way the argument will go.[18] The rearmament issue may help to bridge the gap between the military on the one hand and politics on the other. The prevailing view considers these to be separate spheres in which the former ideally is subjugated to the latter, unless extraordinary factors reverse the order. These factors are normally sought outside the realm of the military, either in individual malice (as in the case of Wheeler-Bennett's Schleicher) or more consistently in the anti-liberal tradition of the Prussian–German army or in the anti-democratic orientation of monopoly capitalism. The actual work of the military as a source of its behaviour is normally excluded as being merely instrumental. Thus, military politics easily becomes a mere curious appendix to what is otherwise 'normal' and 'professional',[19] the latter being the domain of more technically and professionally inclined 'military' historians as opposed to 'political' and 'social' historians. Officers who happen to venture into politics are conspicuous for this very fact. Reading that General Schleicher was dandyish, womanising, emotional, unstable, untrustworthy and crooked – crooked as only politicians are in folklore – we really wonder whether we get to know something about Schleicher or about the prejudices of officers in politics. These are common stereotypes shared by the military and civilians alike.

However, the organisation of violence by the state is neither normal nor simply instrumental and professional, but it is a social, political, and economic activity of the state which is performed by specialists in the military institution. Hence, it should be possible to analyse the social and political nature of everyday military work, even if it is not conducted with a particular political intent. Moreover, it should be possible to link military work with military policies. From here we might find our way back to the relation between the *Reichswehr* and National Socialists. It is a complicated path, but it seems to be the one that is adequate for an increasingly bureaucratised world and in a segmented, fragmented and specialised and professionalised political arena.

This approach has yielded some first results. It has been convincingly shown that the struggles over the allocation of resources and military concerns about recruitment shaped military attitudes towards the late Weimar Republic. Certainly these struggles account for the increasing alienation of the army from the moderate Left and Centre. Moreover, they played a role in the *PreuBenschlag* in 1932, and last but not least in the actual seizure of power in 1933.[20] The direction of the military machine proved to be detrimental to the few remaining vestiges of a republican system.

This approach has been repeatedly criticised. Indeed, it is rather mechanistic to assume that there was a direct link between military work and military politics in which the former explains the latter.[21] Why, it is asked, should the *Reichswehr* have turned to the Right rather than to the Left and the republican *Reichsbanner*? In more general terms: why should the German army have turned against the republican political system, while other armies which were caught in similar quandaries have not? In the last instance, this is a comparative question. Why did the German army go one way, while armies in other advanced industrial nations went in the opposite direction? Despite occasional scares and revelations, they are not normally known to conspire against parliamentarism just to push through their demands.

This critique, unfortunately, implies a ready answer which we have heard already: ultimately the course of the German army was shaped by peculiar Prussian–German traditions and attitudes. German military politics could be explained only with reference to these and similar external factors, because there is no such thing as military politics except in extraordinary circumstances. The Prussian *Sonderweg* was one such example. It was a reflex of the peculiar Prussian political and social system which fortunately has vanished. We are back at square one; the dangers of rearmament and militarism are those of a distant past.[22]

Mentalities and ideologies, of course, did play a most important role. Their emphasis is more than justifiable. But the reference to a peculiar German mind-set has replaced the more careful construction of a framework for the process of military politics and, for that matter, of any politics for too long. The process of politics, even under extraordinary circumstances which may have prevailed in the centre of Europe, is not so amorphous as to allow mentalities to work their way to decisions in a pure form (and, hence, cannot explain them sufficiently) nor is it so mechanistic as to allow military work to turn into military politics instantly. Rather, these are two facets in a structured and dynamic process. At the current stage of historiography we need more than anything else a clearer understanding of the process of politics – rather than the procession of events – in order to untangle how these and similar elements and factors are intertwined.

Two more general points seem to be warranted in this context. One cannot help but recognise that much of the recent study of politics – and especially of German politics – has been displaced by the description of events which are strung together by reference to some ulterior cause. This is not 'neo-historicism', but 'magic realism' in which historians move from realism to surrealism rather than from reality to its sources. Events take on a multitude of shades, colours and meaning. The raw material of history, reality as it can be observed in the prism of documents of all kinds, is repackaged and processed in a seemingly endless number of ways – except the one which has been traditionally at the centre of the German study of politics: namely that the realism of events is the outcome of struggles over power both in the national and international arena.

These struggles over power – and in the realm of the state this is the struggle over the extraction of resources *by* the state and the struggle over their distribution and redistribution *in* the state – is replaced by a fusion of events and ideologies (goals or world-views), actions and concepts. The danger of the older 'German' approach to politics has always been an undue literalism. It should be kept in mind, however, that the struggle over power as a structured process never appears in its raw form and rarely leads to the extreme of the use of violence. It is always embedded in and conducted as a discourse over the necessities and benefits of distribution and redistribution. This is the proper place for the study of mentalities and ideologies. Without the notion of struggle, though, politics becomes an enchanted world of words and a procession of obliquely focused events.

The study of power is further compromised by the tendency to telescope the realism of events into magic formulae that create a 'plastic', and readily exchangeable point of reference. As a result, there seems to be no end and no rule except the continuity of struggle which can be grasped only in individual bits. These discrete bits of events are strung together by reference to surreal categories (like the balance of power as the magic element that holds the myriad of actions together). However, there are pegs which hold *Politik*. It is not arbitrary. There is reason in how and why *Politik* moves (that being the over-arching issue) and there is reason in how and why the military acts. *Militärpolitik* echoes and reflects national and international struggles over power at every twist and turn, but military politics twist and turn according to its own logic of development. This is the development of the means of destruction. It holds an iron rule over the military organisations and their professionals. Military men might try to escape it – the French military in the interwar years is as good an example as the American army in Vietnam. They ultimately pay a price for escapism, because the struggle over power and even more its extreme form, the use of violence, does not leave much room for baroque constructions and self-deception, even if these exist for good reasons.[23]

In the interwar years the organisation of violence had become a comprehensive and nation-wide undertaking that encompassed both the actual preparations of the army and of the nation as a whole for war. Without particular malice the military became directly involved in the inequalities and tensions of society.[24] They were forced to deal with them much to the chagrin of more class-conscious, traditional and conservative officers,[25] because the comprehensive organisation of violence made obsolete previous forms of social relations between the officer corps and civil society. It foreclosed the option of 'staying out of politics' by allying with the social élite of a given country and by concentrating on a well-established professional routine within the confines of the state and the family ties to the upper classes.[26] A new division of labour between civil authorities and the military needed to be created, but most of all, the military needed a society of civil and military employees in the pursuit of the preparation (and conduct) of war.[27] The expansion of the *Herrschaftsbetrieb* of the military obliterated deeply rooted social ties that had previously given the military stature and prestige. This is the painful conversion from the professional caste of the officer corps of the nineteenth century to the military managers of the twentieth. The latter gained their prestige from the organisation of violence alone which, in turn, depended on their ability to employ society and economy for their purpose.[28] The military was in search for a 'service-society' which had its own gradation to the extreme – the militant *Volksgemeinschaft*.

In this search the military is both subject and object of political affairs. This dialectic has thrown off more than one scholar, because traditional theories of militarism encourage a linear approach. They all argue that the cause for the military moving into a pivotal position in the political arena or in society and economy must be sought after either in the military or in society but never in the tense interaction between them. This interrelation is difficult to grasp in any portrayal of the military. We cannot cover it in the same breath. In order to get at it we have to switch from a study of the military to a study of overall politics, in which the military is but a part and is allotted a special place, except if we want to assume that the military pushes its way into the forefront solely due to the quality of its martial capabilities. This idea, however, has been discredited even for the more entrenched military dictatorships of today's world. It has been convincingly shown that even those iron-fisted regimes reflect the national and international struggle over power very gingerly and that even under severest martial law they come and go with the development of *Politik*. They cannot stop the *national* struggle over power, which shapes them more than they shape it. Neither can the military stop the development of destructive forces without falling behind in the *international* struggle over power: these are the parameters in which the military acts.

The intent of this excursion may become evident now: we do know a great deal about the German military and we know even more about German politics. But all the approaches so far have shown a peculiar lack of interest in establishing a political framework to accommodate the dialectic of the military as subject and object at the interface of domestic and international affairs. This is no small task, but it is an important one, because we know one thing from the study of events leading up to the seizure of power in 1933: the military played an ever more prominent, though, as it turns out, ultimately not decisive part.[29] What better example for the above dialectic can there be?

Let us, therefore, try to sketch briefly the outlines of the fields of tension and their inner movements by working our way from the *Reichswehr*'s own situation to the shaping of the *Reichswehr*'s role in state and society; for this is the dialectic that moved the German military, and this is the only way in which military work, military politics and military ideology can be fruitfully linked.

The *Reichswehr*'s main pursuit and the essence of its policy was rearmament.[30] It was less an army than an army in being which was striving to gain what the General Staff (*Truppenamt*) defined as a defensive capability, that is, the wherewithal to defend German sovereignty and territorial integrity by means of military force and force alone, and, subsequently, an offensive capability. While the latter was never an actual working basis of the *Reichswehr* after 1923 it was, nevertheless, its long-term vision. Rearmament implied a notion of a national order geared to what the military defined as their minimal needs – which neither excluded nor included an explicit stance on the system of government of the Weimar Republic – and an international order that was built on military force. The latter most definitely implied a restructuring of the rudimentary international order of the interwar years. This was not simply because the *Reichswehr* strove to become a military factor in Europe, and a dominant one at that, but because it systematically and categorically negated the establishment of even a semblance of international order on the basis of diplomatic arrangements and compromise or on alternative forms of power relations. Once again, during most of the phase of relative stabilisation of the Weimar Republic the military accommodated and began to use the mechanics of existing international order (some of the leading officers felt they had no other choice given the weakness of German military force), but while there was no great concern for the Weimar Republic as republic, there was considerable concern over international order not being built on force and force alone.[31]

After initial havoc in which the *Reichswehr* leadership more than once lost control over their own subordinates on a regional and local level who drifted in and out of the internecine social war between 1918 and 1923, the 'primacy of long range planning' was finally established in 1924. With it the first stage of interrelations with the young Nazi Party came to an end as well. This early relationship was shaped by the domestic civil strife and the *Reichswehr*'s radical and even brutal stance against the Left, in particular against the grassroots mobilisation of workers. The very inequality between the army and the upstart party served the *Reichswehr*'s claim to prime authority as representative of the German state and, ultimately, brought the tense relationship with the Nazis and other Right-radical groups to an abrupt end.[32]

Rearmament was rationalised and bureaucratised in the military institution and legitimised by subsequent Weimar governments. Thus, rearmament, recruitment, and secret training were laid out in detailed plans which could be accelerated and which ultimately were to lead up to the 'grand army' that was capable of waging European war.[33]

The first trap we might fall into opens here. We might be inclined to assume that there was a straight line from the institutionalisation of these goals and plans to the breakdown of the Republic, the seizure of power, and the subsequent unilateral rearmament.[34] We might also assume that National Socialists, heavy industrialists and others joined the bandwagon of rearmament under the impact of the Depression, thus putting more and more pressure on the Weimar Republic until it collapsed. However, as important as these goals and the social interactions which they inspired may have been, the dynamics leading up to 1933 did not unfold in a straight line. They rather developed out of stresses and strains which were implicit in the process of rearmament itself. The goal of rearmament was important because it gave direction to the many choices to be made. The propulsion of the development, however, came from the frictions that arose from the seemingly routinised and politically legitimised implementation of rearmament in the Weimar Republic. It is there that the Nazi movement enters the scene once again. In other words, the decisive role of the Nazi movement did not consist in demanding more armaments, but in acting as a catalyst in the formation of a dominant alliance around the issue of armaments. The Nazi leaders did so by resolving some of the basic contradictions of the process of rearmament through force. But let us approach this process of Nazi involvement in rearmament step by step because the Nazis got engaged only at the tail-end of the process of rearmament.

One of the fields of tensions were the armed forces themselves. One level of these tensions is well known: the armaments plans developed out of a series of internal compromises about what is feasible and what is most important. This satisfied nobody, but left some more dissatisfied than others. Thus, the navy and several army programmes felt that they had been shortchanged. This, of course, did not push them into the arms of the Nazis, but it did mean that there was pressure building for a change, which the National Socialists were potentially able to accommodate.[35] Nobody else promised massive rearmament louder than the National Socialists. It is at such pressure points that rather innocent friendship networks between leading officers and former officers who had joined the Nazi Party did or could become quite important. The significance of these networks consisted in their very existence and in their reach to the very managerial core of the *Reichswehr*.[36]

Much more important was the issue of rearmament for the German officer corps at large, because the mystique of rearmament formed the ideological link which held this corps together. Had it only demonstrated a little more aristocratic self-confidence and had it only been a little more part of the German social élite![37] Had it only relied a little more on the old soldierly virtues as their British and French counterparts![38] But it did neither. After the great cleaning out of the older generation of officers between 1928 and 1930, which itself was a reflection of rearmament, (no fewer than twenty-nine generals were retired in 1929/30) the *Reichswehr* officer corps was remarkably young, remarkably bourgeois, and upwardly mobile.[39] It had always been intellectual (49 per cent with *Abitur*, 8·6 per cent with fewer than six semesters and 12·3 with more than six semesters of university studies) and overly urban in origin (85·2 per cent originated from 'towns').[40] The *Reichswehr* officer corps no longer resembled that self-contained caste which would naturally assume that it *is* the German élite.[41]

The *Reichswehr* officer corps on the eve of the Third Reich was rather composed of men who *wanted to become* the German élite through the resurrection of the German army which, in turn, meant rearmament. This was their 'weakness' which Nazi propaganda consciously or unconsciously attacked with great tenacity and not without success,[42] because the one outstanding element in a trial against three 'National Socialist' officers in the *Reichswehr* was exactly the identification of rearmament, German grandeur and National Socialist political goals.[43] Very few officers were committed National Socialists, but the very identity of the profession, their status, and their daily work centred around an issue which the National Socialists considered a top priority as well. Even material considerations, and class- and generation-bound elements played a role in this: the older aristocratic officers were concentrated in the upper ranks, while the multitude of junior officers saw little chance for promotion in the 100,000-man army permitted by the Versailles Treaty.

These circumstances are mentioned at such length not because they brought the Nazis into power, but rather to counteract a still pervasive, and quite wrongheaded idea about the nature and the impact of National Socialist ideology.[44] One did not need to be irrational, romantic or radical, one did not even need to be a 'Nazi' to be in favour of that movement and its goals. One just needed to be an ordinary, ambitious young officer in the German armed forces with no particular philosophy at all. Indeed, one had to be a very committed and dedicated anti-National Socialist with very strong convictions in order *not* to fit into that movement. However, as pointed out, the young officers of the *Reichswehr* did not normally come from social backgrounds (be they aristocratic, socialist, rural Catholic) with that kind of dedication.

Other and altogether more important pressure points of rearmament are better known, though they also have not been analysed in sufficient detail. One of the better-known ones is the problem of recruitment and secret training. It has always been alleged that the *Reichswehr* had a distinct penchant for Right–radical or monarchical, at any rate anti-democratic young men for its 'not so secret' training programmes. The *Reichswehr* always emphatically denied the fact.[45] Reality was not just more complicated. It was, first of all, much tenser, not the least because the SA was prohibited by order of the Führer from participating in military training programmes.[46]

The basic problem consisted in the *Reichswehr*'s need of a great number of men in the *Grenzschutz* (border militia); in fact they needed everybody, men and women, along the border, but many decided to leave during the crisis of agriculture. Worse, with the agricultural crisis the old social structure began to crumble. With it the social infrastructure that reinforced the voluntary structure of the *Grenzschutz* fell apart as well. If one adds that the *Reichswehr* put in increasingly their own retired officers after 1929 and gave the *Grenzschutz* a formal structure outside of the existing social hierarchy – without having an instrument of compulsion – one might start to understand the difficulties of the local *Reichswehr* units and their officers. In fact, the only one group which fits the *Reichswehr* ideally and steadily gained in strength (though in Catholic areas matters looked differently) was the SA with its free-wheeling mobilisation of the countryside. However, the SA was not caught easily. The SA leadership proved to be exceedingly stubborn down to the smallest units, because they justly feared for their positions. Moreover, a *rapprochement* with the SA also involved a choice against the established ultra-conservative social order in the East, which had been the mainstay of the *Grenzschutz* from its earliest days in 1919.[47] It also involved a choice against the Prussian state, though that cost less heartbreak.

Nothing forced the *Reichswehr* to move into the direction of the SA. There were other choices and the local officers who actually faced the 'mob' knew all too well (just as the SA leadership) that it was either them or the SA leaders. They were engaged in a low-level struggle over command and authority which lasted well into 1934. In many ways, though, engaging the SA was the *easiest* solution – the SA being right mobilisation at the right places – and it was the 'less' class-bound solution – the SA being based not on the dominant social group in the East, but on a fairly wide spread of social groups. Moreover, the average SA man seemed to have been more readily available for what no other social group wanted to do. He wanted to join the army. It is not for naught that over 50 per cent of all new recruits of the army in 1934 came through the SA. Incidentally this may also make understandable the social roots of the *Reichswehr* leadership's anxiety about the SA which led to the bloody purge in 1934.

As it was, the *Reichswehr* had very ambitious plans for recruitment. But even without such plans, the crisis of the countryside would have forced the *Reichswehr* to act. Without being able to resort to compulsion the *Reichswehr* had to rely on social mobilisation which it could not create on its own. Doing so, it had to enter the social struggles in the countryside. This was the basic tension, which led to the more famous and sometimes bizzare negotiations on a top level between the SA and the *Reichswehr* with Hitler and Gregor Strasser waiting on the sidelines. The *Reichswehr*, ultimately, decided to go with the SA in 1933 not because the officers liked the SA men. In fact, these poor men were put through gruelling paces and had their noses rubbed during their basic training under the leadership of military officers and NCOs.

Material rearmament was another case. Once again, it was the *Reichswehr* which was forced to move, if it wanted to stick even to its limited plans. The world economic crisis had all but destroyed the military's supply and procurement base among the small and medium-sized producers of central Germany. If it did not want to wreck this base entirely, armaments had to be stepped up considerably in order to hold these firms over water. It was the military more than anybody else which ventured ahead with plans for deficit spending in 1931/2.[48]

Big business, on the other hand, was less involved, and the *bête noire* of German economic history, heavy industry, least of all. The reasons for this were simple enough. A massive, unilateral rearmament drive only would have threatened the complex infrastructure of the cartelised organisation of heavy industry. Furthermore, it threatened the soft structure of the international iron cartel at a point at which the continental European heavy industrialists were busily engaged in closing one of the major loopholes of the international cartel by including Britain. Heavy industry quite naturally was not the champion of rearmament, though it had other strong reasons (for example, the social costs of production) to consider the National Socialists as a most useful tool.[49] On the other hand, the machine-tool industry, the motor and aircraft industries, and the electrical industry (particularly Siemens which was successfully ousted from the *Reichsbahn*'s plans for electrification by its competitor AEG) were pressing hard.[50]

The final political deal is well known. Long-term and massive rearmament under the joint control of heavy industry, *Reichswehr*, and Schacht, possibly on the basis of bilateral arms control agreements with France and Britain, could offset the continuing slump of the international economy. Adolf Hitler, the new Chancellor, proved to be most promising in this respect. After the spring round of negotiations in Geneva in 1933 and after the violent repression of labour it seemed to be most likely that he could do what most had thought to be impossible only months before: massive and long-term rearmament (because only that would suffice in order to reorient entrepreneurial strategies) without disrupting entirely the links to France and Britain which, after all, remained the primary export markets. The National Socialist Party had demanded rearmament all along; but the decisive point does not consist in those demands and promises of which there were many, but in Hitler's ability to position himself at the crucial interface of domestic and foreign policy and to provide the decisive links between *Reichswehr* and industry by guaranteeing (through the repression of any opposition) long-term rearmament. The Nazi leadership facilitated and guaranteed the fusion of *Reichswehr* and industrial interests.

Hitler himself did not enter the professional and technical negotiations about future armaments at this point. He remained remarkably aloof – after all he was the Chancellor. But he worked hard on placing international relations back on the basis of military force and force alone. By occupying the realm of foreign policy, he not only gained support in the army, but also step by step began to shape and to reshape the domestic arrangements between the armed forces, Schacht, and industry. He moved into domestic affairs with the pressures of the incipient international rearmament – itself a reaction to the German militarisation of foreign policy – in his back.

It may be disappointing to some that rearmament was not the first choice of heavy industry.[51] But industries are industries. They know a good deal when it comes and they seize it, especially if the price is paid by someone else. More importantly, only if we give up the notion that rearmament was a foregone conclusion do we begin to understand the long and quite disjuncted negotiations[52] about the ways to overcome the world economic crisis which ended in the armaments boom of the Third Reich. Had everyone been committed to rearmament from the beginning and had rearmament been without tremendous social costs and political–economic choices, it would not have needed an Adolf Hitler and the National Socialist movement. However, rearmament carried very heavy social costs and large-scale rearrangements in the productive apparatus. It became increasingly evident and openly visible in 1933, that only the new Chancellor and his movement would be able and willing to carry the burden and to distribute it in a 'favourable' way. Even though the Nazi leadership did not openly engage at this point in defining the course and the extent of rearmament, without them there would have been no rearmament.

It should now be more evident what we are aiming at. The relationship between National Socialism (and National Socialists) and the *Reichswehr* indeed cannot be explained by the mere stringing together of political events. This relationship begins to make sense only in the light of the material conditions of the *Reichswehr* which were uniquely shaped by the dynamics and contradictions of rearmament. This not only allows a 'truer' picture of the relations, but also dispenses with the frantic search for sinister conspiracies. The development of the *Reichswehr* opened up a number of areas in which the military's work and attitudes intersected with the activities and attitudes of the Nazis. However, the *development* of the relations cannot be understood in terms of a partial identity of interests alone. Both sides came together reluctantly – after all, 1923 was

not forgotten easily and they remained fundamentally different organisations – because a number of vital choices had to be made. In the process
of choosing, the National Socialists proved to be increasingly essential
for the *Reichswehr*. The link to the Nazis helped to solve some vital
problems of rearmament, which had become evident, even paralysing in
the course of the world economic Depression in Germany. Whereas these
problems reflected the political and social – not to mention the
international – tensions of the time, they were compressed in the work of
the military, that is, rearmament and the preparation of war. The nature
of this work, however, had changed and demanded new solutions. The
Third Reich seemed to provide them.

It is in those shaded areas of common concerns where we could now
place the events, because this is where the relations between the two
protagonists took shape. The drama of words and symbols which were
manifested in these events – mostly top-level meetings – would be
replaced by an altogether grander and more original one: we see the
tensions at work, with some additional strokes we could add the essential
differences of military work and authority on the one hand and
Right–radical mobilisation and political cohesion on the other. Then, we
can bring in the personae who actually made the events. Half knowingly,
half not, they were driven by the material tensions behind their activities,
and yet it was up to them to make choices and to give the tensions a
concrete outcome.

It is this struggle – and it is a struggle over power – which brings
political history into its own and lets it surpass all those plastic substitutes
which are offered in its name. The latter only live by meekly associating
with once-great and vivid ideas and thoughts – as it is the case with
militarism which was a way of political and practical thinking about the
military and civil society, but which has been successfully destroyed by
historical and social-scientific entrepreneurs who use the past as raw
material in order to produce palatable products of history. They use up
historical reality rather than enlivening it.

However, we have not finished our task yet. It has been assumed
previously (and wrongly) that one could come to an understanding of the
growing predominance of the military by looking at the dynamics of their
activities.[53] While the push of the military is out of the question, this is an
all-too linear a view none the less. It is the national and international
struggle over power that shaped the military's status and role in state,
society, and economy and shaped its ability to pursue its main concern,
rearmament.

In 1928/9 the *Reichswehr* had finally concluded peace with Weimar
governments. It had formalised a practice that had been growing for
some years, namely, that the military activities were not to be conducted
extra-constitutionally, but as an activity of the German government,
which was decided over and legitimised by the Cabinet and was binding

for the whole executive.[54] The material content of these arrangements were the armaments programmes, the *Landesschutz-Organisation*, and the *Grenzschutz*, the latter being the preparation for mobilisation on a national scale and the formal though secret and actually illegal institutionalisation of a border militia. All sides drove a hard bargain in the process of negotiations. The *Reichswehr* did not get everything it wanted, nor even what it thought to be necessary or vital. However, a compromise was reached and, even though there is some uncertainty about details, ultimately even the Prussian government and the more stubborn territorial (that is, *Reichswehr* divisional) commanders seem to have given in.[55] The *Reichswehr*'s activities were fully integrated into domestic foreign affairs of the Reich, which was at that point a singular achievement in German military history.

The arm-wrestling over advantages, of course, continued unabated. Prussian police commanders continued to be exasperated about the aloofness and the social connections of the *Reichswehr* and exposed them where they could. The *Reichswehr* did not stick to the agreements in every detail and tried to squeeze out every possible advantage.[56] But this is normal politics in a fractured society. It is not normal politics that within two years the *Reichswehr* was a predominant force in German politics, that its political representatives could make and unmake governments, and that it could begin to redress the arrangements of 1928/9 unilaterally. What had happened?

It is difficult to resist making the leading *Reichswehr* politicians into the main 'movers' and 'shakers', because they were so intimately involved at every stage of the formation of all presidential regimes. However, we need restraint: whereas the *Reichswehr* had a great interest in the formation of a presidential regime, it was by no means the only one and not even the prime mover in bringing it about. Moreover, it was not the *Reichswehr* that moved the presidential regimes, but the decaying presidential regimes that increasingly moved the *Reichswehr*.

Schleicher was one of the handymen in 1929/30 who helped to bring about the Brüning government. He had special interests and special grudges. However, Schleicher, who had pursued a similar course already in 1926/7 without success, would not have been successful in 1929/30, had there not been a growing consensus that the political arena needed restructuring and reorientation.[57] Nobody quite knew what the new political arena should look like, but it had clearly become part of the antagonism in society, rather than being a site for mediation of widely differing interests. The state apparatus was thrown into the mounting antagonism in society and economy. From a mediating state Weimar moved to a partisan one. The political tug-of-war over how openly the state with its resources was to take sides continued until well into 1932 (and was really resolved only in 1933), but the essential borderline was crossed in 1930.

The *Reichswehr* gained here and there in this situation, but overall it gained remarkably little and only late in 1932.[58] Its gains were especially meagre in view of the political prominence and notoriety of its leadership. The *Reichswehr* was pulled into the political limelight, because the military organisation of violence – and other *Herrschafts-betriebe* such as the police, but also large corporations – were the only ones that could back up a government that entered conflict, lost its non-partisan character overtly, and with it lost its legitimacy. The partisan state shrank, in turn, to a state of coercion.

There is more than one example in recent history that authoritarian and military regimes went through this cycle, being subsequently restructured and redemocratised. It is unwarranted to think of the development in 1931–3 as a necessary one that could not have been stopped. Indeed, it might be quite useful to think of the developments between 1932 and 1933 as highly unlikely to have happened. We should wonder why the presidential regime did not turn towards a stabilised authoritarian regime with some organised social backing, but into a state of permanent counter-revolution that drove Germany into war and defeat.[59]

Obviously the major part of the story has to do with the army's and other élite groups' initially high-handed and irresponsible, and subsequently increasingly desperate attempts to form a new dominant political alliance.[60] We know the issues at stake in considerable detail. But we should also emphasise that it is not just the issues which made the formation of a new political alliance so difficult. The political process was just not conducive to such alliances, because it lacked a firm common ground either in national or international politics. In the German case the collapse of international relations may have been even more important than the collapse of the domestic ones. Mediation of interests and political debate which are primarily backed by producers of domination of all kinds reach just as far as coercion reaches – and that is not very far. Coercion only reinforces partial interests, which counteract rather than strengthen the formation of political alliances. Both the costs and benefits of stabilisation seemed uncertain. Social groups were held together more by the dynamics of the continuing struggle than by stabilising arrangements. Papen and Schleicher tried desperately to break this vicious cycle, but neither was a cunning politician or even had the means to act 'politically'. They were unable to lead the partisan state beyond coercion.

It is a well-known figure of interpretation that the Nazis entered the picture as potential allies who were – among others – to provide the 'social underpinning' for the conflict-oriented regime. This is what Schleicher thought, and this is where he failed. In their very own and ruthless way the Nazis were not 'social underpinning', but they were the only ones – given the continuing predominance of a partisan state –

which could re-establish a political arena. They succeeded, using their social mobilisation in order to reconstitute (and to restructure) the political arena. On the other hand, the rule of the *Reichswehr* in late 1932 produced dissent faster than it could produce consent inside and outside the armed forces. It is only characteristic for the state of affairs that a highly dubious deal between Strasser, Schleicher, and possibly Leipart (trade unions) was to save a nation and a state. This shows the advanced degree of decomposition of the political arena and very little else. This, however, can be observed elsewhere as well and it does not necessarily foreclose a return to 'normalcy'. The difference – among others – consisted in the *Reichswehr*'s needs.

The state of affairs affected the *Reichswehr* itself beyond the unease of officers about being drawn into politics too overtly. The organisation of violence, the military, does not just exist in order to be used. Rather organising violence is a continuing social, economic, and political activity. While the *Reichswehr* leadership favoured a conflict-oriented state and while it was pushed into a predominant position in it, the reality of conflict, the endemic social, economic and political struggle over power in its increasingly raw and unchannelled force undercut the ability of the *Reichswehr* to do exactly that for what it was called for. Once more as in 1923, the *Reichswehr* was nearing a stage where it had all the power in the state to organise violence according to its own designs. However, the very fact of having power in a warring polity undid the use of it. At the height of the Papen government the *Reichswehr* could push through its own strategies for rearmament domestically and in foreign affairs, but all it had in the end were orders of a government which could not be implemented because they were swallowed in the raging political and social conflict.

The military felt that social and political conflict had reached such a level that they sooner or later were forced to intervene openly. The decision to intervene was imminent in late 1932. The *Reichswehr* was systematically preparing for this case realising in the process that it may very well lose. An actual defeat of the military was highly unlikely, particularly after the army had begun to draw in the Prussian police.[61] But the militarisation of the endemic civil strife would have threatened (or at least interrupted) the process of rearmament by deepening the unresolved conflicts in society. Preparation for war and rearmament on the one hand and open military engagement in civil strife on the other were incompatible. The *Reichswehr* might have saved a decaying authoritarian state, but it would have lost the advantages of rearmament which have accrued since 1924. The partisan state destroyed one of the very fundaments of modern rearmament, namely, the 'unity of the people'. An open militarisation might have been a military success, but it would have perpetuated the conditions of the partisan state.

In the situation of December/January 1932/3 the *Reichswehr* was faced with its most difficult choice since 1923: in order to achieve what it wanted (rearmament), it had to give up what it had (its prominent but self-destructive position in politics). Adolf Hitler made the difference at this special moment, whatever the prehistory of the two protagonists was. The National Socialists desperately needed to enter the state, the *Reichswehr* desperately wanted to gain social unity and uniformity – the *Volksgemeinschaft* – without losing the advantages of a partisan state. This was the condition for change in 1933. The *Reichswehr* could withdraw from the conflicting state *and* rearm. The creation of a *Volksgemeinschaft* was taken over by the National Socialists. The partisan state became institutionalised and re-instrumentalised (it seemed) in the SS and Gestapo. It was not until 1938 that some officers began to realise that protection had a price.

Notes

* This essay was written during a sabbatical at the Woodrow Wilson International Center for Scholars in Washington, DC. I would particularly like to thank Walter McDougall for our stimulating discussions on political history, and him and James Vann for their very thorough and helpful editing of this essay.

1 John Wheeler-Bennett, *The Nemesis of Power. The German Army in Politics* (London: 1953); see also his *Knaves, Fools and Heroes in Europe between the Wars* (London: 1974); Karl-Dietrich Bracher, *Die Auflösung der Weimarer Republik. Eine Studie zum Problem des Machtverfalls in der Demokratie* (Villingen: 1964); Hans Herzfeld, 'Zur neueren Literatur über das Heeresproblem in der deutschen Geschichte', *Vierteljahrshefte für Zeitgeschichte*, 4, 1956, pp. 361–86.

2 This tendency is most clearly expressed in Herbert Rosinski, *The German Army* (New York: 1966); Hans Gatzke, 'Russo-German Military Cooperation during the Weimar Republic', *American Historical Review*, 63, 1958, pp. 1–29; its high point is Francis L. Carsten, *Reichswehr and Politics 1918–1933* (Oxford: 1966); an opposing view is presented by Hans Meier-Welcker, *Seeckt* (Frankfurt: 1967).

3 Otto-Ernst Schüddekopf, *Das Heer und die Republik. Quellen zur Politik der Reichswehrführung 1918–1933* (Hanover: 1955), pp. 265–378. See, as one example among many, the brief report on 'Reichswehr and Nazism' by the British Military Attaché in Berlin, Col. J. H. Marshall-Cornwall, of 4 March 1932; Public Record Office London, (PRO), FO 371/15943.

4 Manfred Messerschmidt, *Die Wehrmacht im NS-Staat. Zeit der Indoktrination* (Hamburg: 1969); W. Deist, Manfred Messerschmidt, Hans-Erich Volkmann and Wolfram Wette (eds), *Das Deutsche Reich und der Zweite Weltkrieg*, Vol. 1, *Ursachen und Voraussetzungen der deutschen Kriegspolitik* (Stuttgart: 1979); Klaus-Jürgen Müller, *General Ludwig Beck. Studien und Dokumente zur politisch-militärischen Vorstellungswelt und Tätigkeit des Generalstabschefs des deutschen Heeres 1933–1938* (Boppard: 1980).

5 Harold C. Deutsch, *Hitler and his Generals. The Hidden Crisis, January–June 1938* (Minneapolis, Minn: 1974); Harold J. Gordon, *The Reichswehr and the Republic 1919–1926* (Princeton, NJ: 1957); but also Basil Liddell-Hart, *The German Generals Talk* (New York: 1948); however, contrast these with the magisterial conservative view of Gordon Craig, *The Politics of the Prussian Army* (Oxford: 1955).

6 Christian Streit, *Keine Kameraden. Die Wehrmacht und die sowjetischen Kriegsgefangenen 1941–1945* (Stuttgart: 1978).

7   Horst Drechsler, *Südwestafrika unter deutscher Kolonial-herrschaft* (Berlin/GDR: 1966); Helmut Bley, *Kolonial-herrschaft und Sozialstruktur in Deutsch-Südwestafrika* (Hamburg: 1968); Jon M. Bridgman, *The Revolt of the Hereros* (Berkeley, Calif: 1974); Georg Eliasberg, *Der Ruhrkrieg von 1920* (Bonn-Bad Godesberg: 1974); Jürgen Tampke, *The Ruhr and Revolution. The Revolutionary Movement in the Rhenish Westphalian Region, 1912–1919* (Canberra: 1978); Erhard Lucas, *Märzrevolution im Ruhrgebiet* (Frankfurt: 1970); Michael Geyer, *Aufrüstung oder Sicherheit. Die Reichswehr in der Krise der Machtpolitik* (Wiesbaden: 1980), pp. 85–91.

8   New evaluations in Gordon Craig, *Germany 1866–1945* (New York: 1978), pp. 560–7; Peter Hayes, 'A Question Mark with Epaulettes? Kurt von Schleicher and Weimar Politics', *Journal of Modern History*, 52, March 1980, pp. 35–65; Axel Schildt, *Militär-diktatur mit Massenbasis? Die Querfrontkonzeption der Reichswehrführung um General von Schleicher am Ende der Weimarer Republik* (Hamburg: 1981).

9   Thilo Vogelsang, *Reichswehr, Staat und NSDAP. Beiträge zur deutschen Geschichte 1930–1932* (Stuttgart: 1962); and his *Kurt von Schleicher. Ein General als Politiker* (Göttingen: 1965); see also the much earlier Gordon Craig, 'Reichswehr and National Socialism. The Policy of Wilhelm Groener 1928–1932', *Political Science Quarterly*, 43, June 1948, pp. 194–229 on the sources of the issue. Finally, the magisterial summary on this issue Karl-Dietrich Bracher, Wolfgang Sauer and Gerhard Schulz, *Die nationalsozialistische Machtergreifung. Studien zur Entwicklung des totalitären Herrschaftssystems in Deutschland 1933–1934* (Cologne: 1960).

10   Particularly evident in Bracher, *Auflösung der Weimarer Republik.*

11   At one point this notion had a cathartic meaning; see Friedrich Meinecke, *The German Catastrophe. Reflections and Recollections* (Cambridge, Mass: [1946] 1950).

12   Dick Geary, 'Identifying Militancy. The Assessment of Working Class Attitudes towards State and Society', in Richard J. Evans (ed.), *The German Working Class 1888–1933* (London: 1982), pp. 220–46 has most recently pointed to this problem. He may underestimate the difficulties of such a venture. The writer who will be able to analyse only one incident in the struggle from both sides will make a quantum leap in historiography. He or she will face the extraordinary difficulty of bringing together two entirely different worlds, in which even the physical landmarks – streets, buildings, people – appear in a different light. The writer would, moreover, have to deal with the danger of synthesising antagonisms in the 'higher-order' coherence of an essay or book. But most of all, he or she would have to overcome the logistics of the historical profession. The two sides share neither notes nor enthusiasm.

13   Kurt Gossweiler, 'Der Übergang von der Weltwirtschaftskrise zur Rüstungskonjunktur in Deutschland 1933 bis 1934. Ein historischer Beitrag zur Problematik staatsmonopolistischer Krisenüberwindung', *Jahrbuch für Wirtschaftsgeschichte* (1966/ II), pp. 55–116 and his *Grossbanken, Industrie-monopole und Staat. Ökonomie und Politik des staatsmonopolistischen Kapitalismus in Deutschland* (Berlin/GDR: 1971).

14   Karl Nuss, *Militär und Wiederaufrüstung in der Weimarer Republik* (Berlin/GDR: 1977); more clearly Heinz Sperling, 'Aspekte der Rolle des Reichswehr-Führung beim Übergang von der revolutionären Nachkriegskrise zur relativen Stabilisierung des Kapitalismus in Deutschland 1923/24', *Militärgeschichte*, 12, 1973, pp. 694–705.

15   Most clearly shown for the National Socialists by Timothy Mason, *Arbeiterklasse oder Volksgemeinschaft. Dokumente und Materialien zur deutschen Arbeiterpolitik 1936–1939* (Opladen: 1975); for the military the same argument is most succinctly stated by Carsten, *Reichswehr and Politics.*

16   See my forthcoming essay on the 'Verwendung im Reich, 1924–1933', *Militärgeschichtliche Mitteilungen*, 24, 1983.

17   As alleged by Frank Müller, 'Zum Anteil der Reichswehr an der Vorbereitung des Faschismus', in Reinhard Kühnl and Gerd Hardach (eds), *Die Zerstörung der Weimarer Republik* (Cologne: 1977), pp. 142–80.

18   Edward W. Bennett, *German Rearmament and the West, 1932–1933* (Princeton, NJ: 1979); Michael Geyer, 'Professionals and Junkers. German Rearmament and Politics

in the Weimar Republic', in Richard Bessel and E. J. Feuchtwanger (eds), *Social Change and Political Development in Weimar Germany* (London: 1981), pp. 77–133.

19   As in Alfred Vagts, *History of Militarism* (New York: 1959); a most telling example of the futility of this kind of approach is Dimitri K. Simes, 'The Military and Militarism in Soviet Society', *International Security*, 6, Winter 1981/2, pp. 123–43. On the debate in political science Amos Perlmutter, *The Military and Politics in Modern Times. On Professionals, Praetorians, and Revolutionary Soldiers* (New Haven, Conn: 1977).

20   Bennett, *German Rearmament*, pp. 169–75. His argument is all the more striking, since he uses a fairly conventional approach.

21   This has been the case in Michael Geyer, 'Der zur Organisation erhobene Burgfrieden', in Klaus-Jürgen Müller and Eckart Opitz (eds), *Militär und Militarismus in der Weimarer Republik* (Düsseldorf: 1978), pp. 15–100.

22   See the differing conclusions in Werner Conze, Michael Geyer, Reinhard Stumpf, Art. 'Militarism', in Werner Conze, Otto Bruner and Reinhart Koselleck (eds), *Geschichtliche Grundbegriffe* (Stuttgart: 1979) IV, pp. 1–47.

23   Judith M. Hughes, *To the Maginot Line. The Politics of French Military Preparations in the 1920s* (Cambridge, Mass: 1971); Mary Kaldor, *The Baroque Arsenal* (New York: 1981).

24   Geyer, 'Burgfrieden', pp. 28–50.

25   This caused tremendous frictions in the officer corps which found an expression in Seeckt's dismissal in 1926. Seeckt had held on to older officers, who were subsequently retired. See Joachim von Stülpnagel, *75 Jahre meines Lebens*, pp. 230, 241, 245–54.

26   Donald C. Watt, *Too Serious a Business. Armed Forces and the Approach to the Second World War* (London: 1975); John Gooch, *Armies in Europe* (London: 1980).

27   Andreas Hillgruber, 'Militarismus am Ende der Weimarer Republik und im Dritten Reich', in Andreas Hillgruber (ed.), *Grossmachtpolitik und Militarismus im 20. Jahrhundert* (Düsseldorf: 1974), pp. 37–52.

28   This is the root for the military's search for a 'Volksgemeinschaft'. Hajo Herbell, *Staatsbürger in Uniform 1789–1961. Ein Beitrag zur Geschichte des Kampfes zwischen Demokratie und Militarismus* (Berlin/GDR: 1969); Walter Görlitz (ed.), *Generalfeldmarschall Keitel. Verbrecher oder Offizier* (Göttingen: 1961), pp. 154–69; Konrad Prümm, *Die Literatur des Soldatischen Nationalismus der 20er Jahre (1918–1933). Gruppenideologie und Epochenproblematik*, 2 vols (Kronberg/Ts.: 1974).

29   Andreas Hillgruber, 'Die Reichswehr und das Scheitern der Weimarer Republik', in Erdmann and Schulze (eds), *Weimarer Republik*.

30   Wilhelm Deist, *The Wehrmacht and German Rearmament* (London: 1981).

31   Geyer, *Aufrüstung oder Sicherheit*, pp. 177–87.

32   Ernst Deuerlein, 'Hitlers Eintritt in die Politik und die Reichswehr', *Vierteljahrshefte für Zeitgeschichte*, 7, 1959, pp. 177–227; Harold J. Gordon, *Hitler and the Beerhall Putsch* (Princeton, NJ: 1972); Heinz Hürten, *Reichswehr und Ausnahmezustand. Ein Beitrag zur Verfassungsproblematik der Weimarer Republik in ihrem ersten Jahrfünft* (Opladen: 1977); Thilo Vogelsang, 'Die Reichswehr in Bayern und der Münchener Putsch 1923', *Vierteljahrshefte für Zeitgeschichte*, 5, 1975, pp. 91–101.

33   Ernst W. Hansen, *Reichswehr und Industrie. Rüstungswirtschaftliche Zusammenarbeit und wirtschaftliche Mobilmachungsvorarbeiten 1923–32* (Boppard: 1978).

34   Geyer, 'Burgfrieden', *passim*.

35   Jost Dülffer, *Weimar, Hitler und die Marine. Reichspolitik und Flottenbau 1920–1939* (Düsseldorf: 1973).

36   Holger H. Herwig, 'From Kaiser to Führer. The Political Road of a German Admiral', *Journal of Contemporary History*, 9, April 1974, pp. 107–20.

37   Bracher, *Auflösung der Weimarer Republik*, pp. 227–34; Karl Demeter, *Das deutsche Offizierkorps in Gesellschaft und Staat* (Frankfurt: 1968, 4th edn); Hans Meier-Welcker, 'Der Weg zum Offizier im Reichsheer der Weimarer Republik', *Militärgeschichtliche Mitteilungen*, 19, 1976, pp. 147–80; Gotthart Breit, *Das Staats- und*

Gesellschaftsbild deutscher Generale beider Weltkriege im Spiegel ihrer Memoiren (Boppard: 1973).

38   See the fascinating study by Eric J. Leed, *No Man's Land. Combat and Identity in World War I* (London: 1981), who explores the changes in military identity during the First World War.

39   This view is confirmed by Hans Meier-Welcker, 'Aus dem Briefwechsel zweier junger Offiziere des Reichsheeres 1930–1938', *Militärgeschichtliche Mitteilungen*, 14, 1973, pp. 7–100. Detlef Bald, 'Sozialgeschichte des deutschen Offizierskorps von der Reichsgründung bis zur Gegenwart', Sozialwissenschaftliches Institut der Bundeswehr (ed.), *Berichte*, Vol. 3 (Munich: 1977), pp. 15–47.

40   'The German Reichsheer [army] according to the census of November 1922'; Bundesarchiv-Militärarchiv: RW6/v. 48.

41   Hans Ebeling, *The Caste. The Political Role of the German General Staff between 1918 and 1938* (London: 1945).

42   See, for example, Adolf Hitler, 'Reichswehr und deutsche Politik', *Nationalsozialistische Monatshefte*, 1, June 1930, pp. 97–103.

43   Peter Bucher, *Der Reichswehrprozess. Der Hochverrat der Ulmer Reichswehroffiziere 1929–1930* (Boppard: 1967).

44   Keith W. Bird, *Weimar, the German Naval Officer Corps, and the Rise of National Socialism* (Amsterdam: 1977).

45   Vogelsang, *Reichswehr, Staat und NSDAP*, pp. 216–20.

46   Thilo Vogelsang, 'Zur Politik Schleichers gegenüber des NSDAP 1932', *Vierteljahrshefte für Zeitgeschichte*, 6, 1958, pp. 86–118; Andreas Werner, 'SA und NSDAP. SA: "Wehrverband", "Parteitruppe" oder "Revolutionsarmee"? Studien zur Geschichte der SA und NSDAP 1920–1933' (Phil. Diss., University of Erlangen, 1965); Richard Bessel, 'The SA in the Eastern Regions of Germany, 1925–1934' (Dissertation, University of Oxford, 1980).

47   Carsten, *Reichswehr and Politics*, pp. 350–63; see also the revealing rationale of Col. Reichenau: 'The Reichswehr . . . could never employ organizations like the Stahlhelm, the Nazi SA, and the Reichsbanner in separate units, simply because it would be highly dangerous to do so owing to the jealousy existing between some and the hatred between others. Germany was already divided enough, but units with separate private aims within a national army would be fatal to its morale'. Report by A. F. Yencken on a conversation with Col. v. Reichenau at Finckenstein/East Prussia, 18 May 1932; PRO, FO 371/15944.

48   Michael Geyer, 'Das Zweite Rüstungsprogramm', *Militärgeschichtliche Mitteilungen*, 17, 1975, pp. 125–72.

49   Bernd Weisbrod, *Schwerindustrie in der Weimarer Republik. Interessenpolitik zwischen Stabilisierung und Krise* (Wuppertal: 1978). It should be mentioned that heavy industry and armaments industry, as a matter of course, pressed for lifting the ban on armaments production (Hansen, *Reichswehr und Industrie*, pp. 166–88; Nuss, *Armee und Wiederaufrüstung*, pp. 276–80).

50   Some of the documentary evidence is in Dieter Eichholtz and Wolfgang Schumann (eds), *Anatomie des Krieges. Neue Dokumente über die Rolle des deutschen Monopolkapitals bei der Vorbereitung und Durchführung des Zweiten Weltkrieges* (Berlin/GDR: 1969).

51   George W. F. Hallgarten, *Hitler, Reichswehr und Industrie. Zur Geschichte des Jahres 1918–1933* (Frankfurt: 1955, 2nd edn).

52   Work creation was only a marginal issue in this context, the major one being the social costs of production and price and market control. Michael Wolffsohn, *Industrie und Handwerk im Konflikt mit staatlicher Wirtschaftspolitik? Studien zur Politik der Arbeitsbeschaffung in Deutschland 1930–1934* (Berlin: 1977).

53   Geyer, 'Burgfrieden', *passim*.

54   Hansen, *Reichswehr und Industrie*, pp. 191–202; Nuss, *Armee und Wiederaufrüstung*, pp. 205–31; Carsten, *Reichswehr and Politics*, pp. 265–74.

55 Hagen Schulze, Otto Braun oder Preussens demokratische Sendung (Frankfurt: 1973), pp. 610–17, 738–40.

56 Bennett, *German Rearmament and the West*, pp. 176–201 with the essential emphasis on foreign policy.

57 Josef Becker, 'Zur Politik der Wehrmachtsabteilung in der Regierungskrise 1926/27', *Vierteljahrshefte für Zeitgeschichte*, 14, 1966, pp. 68–78; Gerhard Schulz, Ilse Maurer and Udo Wengst (eds), *Politik und Wirtschaft in der Krise. Quellen zur Ära Brüning*, 2 vols (Düsseldorf: 1980), I, pp. 1–102.

58 This view may surprise considering the second armaments programme, the circumvention of fiscal cuts, the Reich's defence order of October 1932 and similar orders, and last but not least the German foreign policy. However, compared to the power and importance of its role in the state the Reichswehr made very little material progress.

59 See the forthcoming essay by Michael Geyer, 'The State in National Socialist Germany', in Charles Bright and Susan Harding (eds), *The Making of the State* (1983).

60 Vogelsang, *Reichswehr, Staat and NSDAP*, pp. 280–2 and his 'Neue Dokumente zur Geschichte der Reichswehr 1930–1933', *Vierteljahrshefte für Zeitgeschichte*, 2, 1954, pp. 397–436.

61 Fritz Arndt, 'Vorbereitung der Reichswehr auf den militärischen Ausnahmezustand', *Zeitschrift für Militärgeschichte*, 4, 1965, pp. 195–203.

8 National Socialism and the Christian Churches during the Weimar Republic

JOHN S. CONWAY

The story of the German churches during the short life of the Weimar Republic (1918–33) is one of confusion, disorientation, and lack of clear purpose. Paradoxically it was also the period during which the churches achieved an unprecedented freedom to control their own institutional affairs. In the realm of ideas, however, the churches perhaps more than other social institutions suffered a crisis of credibility, which threatened their historic stance as the guardians of the nation's spiritual and moral health. This 'shaking of the foundations' must in part be held responsible for the eagerness with which the majority of German churchmen welcomed the advent to power in 1933 of Adolf Hitler. For most of Germany's churchmen, as of the majority of all other Germans, Hitler was conceived as the leader of an authoritarian nationalist government, which would bring clarity out of confusion, restore morality in place of decadence, and national self-respect instead of guilt and humiliation. Broadly speaking, it can be argued that it was this longing to be once again fully integrated into the whole national life of the German community and to participate in the rebuilding of a national society which created the wave of enthusiasm in the churches for the *Machtergreifung* of 1933.

The traumatic events of November 1918 in Germany can now be seen to have led to not only a dramatic rupture but also an unexpected continuity in German history. On the one hand, the overthrow of the Hohenzollern monarchy and its associated dynasties marked the end of the authoritarian, Prussian-dominated and hierarchical order of society which had characterised the German empire as created by Bismarck and opened the way for mass populist political movements. On the other hand, the continuity of Germany's geographical entity (with minor excisions), the maintenance of its technical, industrial and economic resources, and the preservation of its social institutions, left intact the framework which, when mobilised by the ideological forces of revenge, and revived aspirations for great power status, were to lead once again within twenty years to a renewed attempt at world domination.

In this situation the German churches were to play a significant role in the reformulation of ideas about Germany's national identity and mission. On the one hand, the shock of defeat necessitated a rethinking of the place of the churches in the political and social spectrum. On the other hand, the freedom to organise their own institutional structures led to a continuing tension in the relationship between the churches and the state, which was still unresolved in 1933. To a considerable extent the desire to achieve a more secure institutional framework was responsible for the failure of the church leaders to alert their congregations to the more dangerous aspects of the political extremism of the right-wing variety which made such rapid advances after 1930. However, the theological and intellectual currents in the 1920s must also be held responsible for the climate of opinion in the churches which made churchmen so susceptible to the professed aims of National Socialism, especially among German Protestants. In particular, the rise of the school of nationalist or *völkisch* theologians was to cause fateful repercussions and to prevent the growth of alternative theologies. Their influence significantly affected the mass of Protestant, and to a lesser extent of Catholic, voters in favour of the anti-democratic and anti-republican developments on the political scene.

Both these developments, in the institutional and intellectual aspects of church life, have been authoritatively analysed in the excellent study by Klaus Scholder, which is the first attempt to portray the history of both of Germany's major Churches, Catholic and Protestant, together, rather than in the segregated manner hitherto.[1] Although Scholder has his own critical and sometimes polemical points of view, and entirely ignores the lesser role of the small handful of free churches, his insights are valuable in stressing the relationship between the particular institutional developments and the wider framework of political and social trends of the 1920s before he launches into a detailed study of the conflicts within the churches after the Nazi take-over of power. Two other recently published studies in English, although more limited in scope, also deserve attention, namely Jonathan Wright's[2] and Reg Ward's[3] stimulating discussion of the social reform movements. The American author, Ernst Helmreich, has further written a broader survey which gives a factual picture of developments during the Weimar Republic.[4] The latest contribution to this literature has been written by a younger historian of the East German Church, Kurt Nowak, which presents an admirably comprehensive description of the various church parties and pressure groups, and their reactions to the turbulent political events of these years.[5] Developments in German Catholicism have not so far been the subject of any major monograph in English.

Perhaps inevitably these studies have concentrated on the institutional life of the churches, and drawn attention to the actions and policies of the major leaders and thinkers. Far more difficult is an assessment of the inner life of the average man or woman in the pew. Yet the astounding extent to which the NSDAP successfully captured the allegiance of

ordinary laymen – both Catholics and Protestants – and the envious
attention given by certain sections of the Nazi Party to the churches as
agencies of instruction and propaganda, both deserve further examination. If the Nazi interest in church members was skilfully orchestrated,
the churchmen's desire to reinforce their cultural and social relevance
played an important role. It is undeniable that there was a considerable
amount of wishful thinking in such a position. The readiness with which
the churches approved the new Nazi regime in 1933 made it all the more
difficult afterwards to admit that they had been mistaken. This in turn
has conditioned the response of church historians, most of whom
have loyally sought to exonerate their church's participation in the
Third Reich, and to minimise the elements of popular collaboration.
Tentatively it may be suggested that the Nazi authoritarianism and
moral rigidity were widely welcomed amongst the laity whose refusal to
admit the claims of a pluralistic democratic society was reflected in their
stubborn resentment against reform, both inside and outside the
churches.

The revolutionary events of 1918 affected the German Evangelical
Churches in four significant ways: they influenced their organisational
structures, altered the basis of their congregational and public support,
modified their functions in society, and ultimately led to striking and
frequently contradictory theological reassessments.

The sudden disappearance of the German monarchies presented all
the Evangelical Churches with a major crisis of authority, not only in its
legal form but equally in their future stance in public life. For centuries
these churches had seen themselves as the most loyal subjects of the
monarchical order, and the majority of pastors and laity alike had
traditionally supported the policies of their political superiors, for which
the particularly Lutheran interpretation of Romans 13:1 was widely
adopted. The organisational crisis took an acute form in the first days of
the Republic, especially in Prussia, when the new Socialist government
immediately claimed for itself the legal inheritance of the royal
prerogatives of control over the churches. The appointment of Adolf
Hoffmann to the *Kultusministerium*, as one of the fiercest opponents of
the churches who for nearly thirty years had been an ardent advocate of
the church's overthrow, raised every possible fear of the likely consequences. Nor were these slow in forthcoming. Within the next few weeks
Hoffmann issued a rapid series of decrees, declaring the enforced
separation of church and state, the abolition of state subventions, the
ending of compulsory religious education in schools and the alleviation of
measures by which citizens could officially leave the church. The
enormous wave of protest these measures produced soon forced the
Social Democratic government to dispense with Hoffmann and to retract
the decrees. But the damage was done. Hoffmann became a symbol of
the revolution and its anti-clericalism, and confirmed the already

virulent suspicions amongst churchmen against Social Democracy and its 'godless atheist' policies. In fact the provisions of the Weimar Constitution, as established in 1919, were far more moderate and indeed favourable to the churches. The major churches retained their legal and historical pre-eminence and financial advantages. They were no longer to have exclusive jurisdiction in such matters as education, but were granted wide powers of self-government without state interference. The apprehensions of a radical separation were dispelled and the existing legal protection for church life was assured. Subsequently it was left up to each regional church to appoint its own officials and structures, which took place over the next two years. As Scholder has pointed out, this had the effect of greatly strengthening the local *Landeskirchen*, and the efforts from 1922 onwards to create a national or at least a federal structure to centralise the affairs of the German Evangelical Church ran into strong and consistent opposition. As is well known, this problem was to form one of the major controversies of 1933 when the Nazi take-over created a new political climate for the establishment of a Reich Church, this time to be dominated by Nazi sympathisers.

The 1919 settlement also paved the way for the consolidation of control on the various church synods, executive bodies and administrative boards, by the representatives of the former 'establishment', especially after the church leaders resolutely opposed a democratic basis. Instead a careful system of indirect elections secured the position of those traditional classes who had long regarded themselves as the 'pillars of the church'. This has led such critics as Friedrich-Martin Balzer[6] to regard the outcome as nothing more than a deliberate attempt to preserve the feudal–hierarchical character of the church as an instrument in the wider class warfare of the period, in which the churches' class interests were only thinly disguised by their religious terminology.

Other critics, especially from East Germany, such as Walter Bredendiek[7] have drawn the conclusion that such attitudes led directly to the widespread support given to the Nazi movement. But this is to short-circuit the course of events. The prime concern of the early years of the Weimar Republic was to erect defences against the negative impact of the revolution, of which Hoffmann's onslaughts were seen only as a forerunner. This is the theme adopted by Claus Motschmann in his study of the Evangelical Church and the Prussian state at the beginning of the Weimar Republic.[8] Although he sought to prove that the churchmen were prepared to take up a positive role towards the new state, the evidence he cites of the organised mass protests against Hoffmann's measures and of the victorious manoeuvres by which liberal churchmen were excluded from the governing bodies of the church, suggests that his argument is more apologetic than historical. On the other hand, Motschmann rightly pointed out the critical nature of the loss of the monarchy in evangelical polity. The attempt of the new regime to place the office of *summus episcopus* in the hands of state ministers met with stiff opposition. It is interesting to note that some liberal churchmen welcomed this proposal, since they were well aware of the weakness of any campaign to insist on a fully democratic reform of the church structures. All attempts to introduce more popular forms of synodical government, or to recognise the rights of women, were thwarted by the conservatives. When in 1920 the Prussian state government granted a special general synod of the church the right to enact its own constitution, the conservative majority effectively blocked the reformist trend, either from above or below. More positively, the consolidation of the church's structures in the hands of watchful, if conservative, vigilants stemmed from a belief in the continuing responsibility for the defence of the values of a Christian society at a time of unprecedented crisis in the life of the nation.

This point is well illustrated in the account by Jochen Jacke of the Protestant Church's positions in the early years of the Weimar Republic.[9] He points out how strongly the idea of a *Volkskirche* was stressed. In part, encouraged by the evidence of national unity during the war years, many clergy saw the need for a vibrant social engagement as a substitute for the hierarchical and authoritarian patterns of the past. By trying to claim the title of being the moral guardians of the state, and by identifying the church with all classes of the people, this *Volkskirche* could be the vehicle for reversing the disastrous loss of so many of the workers as well as of the educated classes, which had so obviously weakened the church's witness in earlier years. This ambition could thus vindicate the claims for church privileges in the new and pluralistically democratic Republic, as well as justifying the large and expensive church bureaucracy which allegedly existed to serve the needs of all the people through the *Volkskirche*.

The revolution of 1918 had apparently broken the organisational link between the church and the nation's rulers. The church was therefore called to create and keep alive a better concept of the state than that offered by the Republic with its multiplicity of quarrelling parties. To be 'above parties' was to act as the collecting point for all who saw in the church the one structure which would remain true to Germany's historic traditions, and, like the army, to become in effect a 'state within a state'. This attitude was only accentuated by the fact that, following 1918, a large number of military officers, like Martin Niemöller, became clergymen, and reinforced the dislike of the Republic in the ranks of their followers. Such men remained committed monarchists, not so much out of sympathy for Wilhelm II, but because the authoritarian pattern before 1914 seemed to represent the ideal closer to their hearts. It followed that the revolution of 1918 was regarded as the moment when this pattern was broken, loosing into Germany all those forces of darkness and evil against which the church was called to campaign. The

Republic was deprecated and abhorred implicitly or explicitly from pulpits throughout the land. It was to be treated, not as the state to which the church was called to be loyal, but merely the 'system' whose disappearance or replacement was much to be desired. After the election of Hindenburg as President in 1925, the shrewder leaders saw little hope for the restoration of the monarchy. They were therefore all the more susceptible to the claims of a substitute leader, whose personal charisma appeared to restore the old order while guaranteeing the defeat of the revolutionary hordes.

Organisationally then, the churches remained what they had always been: monarchist, anti-revolutionary, anti-socialist, anti-democratic. But it is necessary to note that these tendencies were in fact stronger in the laity than in the leadership, as was evidenced by the heavily conservative majorities in the various synods established in 1919.[10] The illusion that direct democracy in the churches would have produced a more liberal policy was soon abandoned, except by the partisan supporters of the Religious Socialist movement, who continued to believe that the electoral majority of socialist voters in the state could be mobilised to achieve a parallel victory in the church structures. In reality, the disinterest of the majority of nominal supporters and the weakness of the few liberal voices in the churches, ensured a continuing domination by the conservative elements. Even more than in England, the German Evangelical Churches could be regarded as 'the conservative classes at prayer'.

Both Wright and Scholder, however, point out that in subsequent years the political attitudes of the church hierarchies were more moderate than those of the lay synods. The Prussian Evangelical *Oberkirchenrat*, the most influential of the churches' leading organs, soon realised that the 1919 settlement had treated the churches generously, and sought to work out a *rapprochement* with the new Republic. The aim of its President, Kapler, was to prevent the church from being imprisoned by backward-looking longings for a restoration of the monarchy. He sought a gradual improvement of the churches' position in such matters as educational privileges, and threw his weight unreservedly behind President Hindenburg. Under his guidance the Protestant leadership argued that the concessions given to the Roman Catholics, which were seemingly prompted by reasons of political advantage, should be matched by equal benefits to the Protestants. He sought to bring the church membership to recognise the advantages given by the Republic and to prove to the republican governments that the Protestants could be a source of support. He tried to keep in check the more intemperate of the clergy, and argued that these were no more representative than the extremists on the Left who called for a root-and-branch abolition of church privileges by the socialist governments.

But such attempts were effective only on a limited scale at the highest level of church government. Much more influential in determining the political attitudes of the congregations were the often vehemently expressed opinions of the delegates to the local synods. It was here that all attempts to reorient the church away from its authoritarian heritage were blocked. Reform had become synonymous with revolution, and the experiences of 1918 were allowed to become mythologised in the minds of the congregations as the ultimate threat to the church's existence. The whole history of the 1920s, and indeed of the 1940s, cannot be explained unless the refusal of the church leadership to challenge these assumptions is made clear. The readiness of the church to see itself as a bulwark against new ideas was indeed uppermost even after 1945, as the character of the church in West Germany since then has amply demonstrated. Wright for example does not give enough attention to the hold of the anti-revolutionary, anti-socialist, and anti-democratic elements at this level. So far from being 'above parties', the fact was that the majority of the posts in the church's governing bodies were held by advocates of a conservative authoritarianism, whose members unequivocally supported right-wing political parties such as the DNVP. For instance, the executive of the church senate in 1930 consisted of six persons, four of whom were elected. All four, Winckler, Wolff, von Armin-Kröckendorff, and von Berg, were leading members of the DNVP, and either present or past members of the *Reichstag* or Prussian *Landtag*. The president of the German Evangelical *Kirchentag*, which was the umbrella organisation for all the provincial churches, was Freiherr von Pechmann, an aristocrat and ardent monarchist, who was succeeded in 1930 by a retired general, Graf von Eckstadt. These men successfully headed off the ineffectual attempts to turn the church towards a more liberal, let alone democratic, stance, and reinforced the tendency to think in terms of localism, tradition, self-preservation, and reaction.

The continued hostility to the Republic and to all aspects of socialism on the part of the majority of Evangelical Churchmen can thus in part be attributed to the reactionary influences of the lay leadership, and to the desire to defend the bulwarks of a well-beloved institution. It is noteworthy that very similar attitudes were to be found in the majority of the other professions, the army, the civil service, the judiciary, the doctors and the teachers, whose members feared above all the loss of status, as well as wealth and income, which the threat of the abortive revolutions of 1918 had posed.

The position of the Roman Catholic Church was no less ambiguous. To the elder generation, the memories of the period of disparagement and oppression of the *Kulturkampf* were not entirely dispelled by the overthrow of the Bismarckian Protestant-dominated empire and of the Prussian Hohenzollern monarchy. The defensive mentality which most of the church leaders had inherited left the impression that German

Catholics were second-class citizens, whose rights had to be safeguarded and secured. The evident enthusiasm which Catholics had displayed during the war, and the successes which their political wing, the Centre Party, had achieved in remedying the most grievous disabilities, had certainly ameliorated their position. On the other hand, Catholics were equally fearful of the onslaughts of a rampant socialism, which drew them together into a rather uneasy 'Holy Alliance' with the Protestants against the radical measures of the short-lived Hoffmann era. Denunciations of revolution in general and Bolshevism in particular were as common in Catholic as in Protestant pulpits. In addition, the feeling that Catholics were still disadvantaged in the political and social arenas led to the maintenance of a minority complex, which was allied to the dislike of those trends and personalities who were presumed to be undermining the essentially rural-based and static concepts of society widely prevalent in Catholic circles. At the level of ordinary Catholics, these feelings were expressed in widespread resentment against the alleged agents of change, often equated with decadence, capitalist exploitation or urban-based manipulation of the media. Hence the frequency of anti-Semitism in such milieux, and the support given to the nationalist movements which promised to rid Germany of these vitiating excesses.

Both Scholder and Helmreich point out that the real initiative in Catholic affairs was taken by the Vatican, whose young and skilful Nuncio, Eugenio Pacelli, later Pope Pius XII, held successively the posts in Munich from 1917 and in Berlin from 1920, until his promotion in 1929 to be Cardinal Secretary of State. Scholder indeed considers Pacelli's appointment to be one of the most important dates of German Catholicism in this century, since no one else influenced the German Catholic Church's policy so decisively as this energetic and ambitious Roman. Pacelli quickly realised that the provisions of the new Weimar Constitution gave the Catholics much greater freedoms and equality than the German empire had done. But at the same time, he pursued a single-minded course to secure these advantages, not by the will of a possibly transient political system, but by legally binding treaties between the Vatican and both the state and Reich governments. These persistent efforts led first to the creation of a Nunciature for the whole Reich in 1920, and subsequently to the signing of a Concordat with Bavaria in 1924, which Pacelli believed could act as a model for the other states and finally for the Reich itself. The very favourable terms obtained from the Bavarian government were then used by Pacelli as a lever to demand similar concessions elsewhere. In Prussia, however, the opposition to his plans, both from the Protestants and from the secularists, led to a less satisfactory settlement, which excluded school questions from the Prussian Concordat signed in 1929. A similar Concordat was arranged with Baden in 1932.

Pacelli's main goal was, however, the achievement of a Reich

Concordat. The Vatican hoped thereby not only to consolidate the legal position of German Catholics but also to secure a tighter grip over this largest and most significant group of its supporters in central Europe. The Vatican also hoped to exploit the Reich's desire for diplomatic assistance in its quarrels with France over the Saar and with Poland over Silesia. A Reich Concordat would remove once and for all the danger of a renewed *Kulturkampf*. These plans were, however, constantly thwarted by the opposition in the republican governments and ministries. Not only were the Vatican terms considered too exacting, but also the legally binding privileges which Catholics would enjoy, especially in such matters as education or state subsidies, threatened to divide the nation even more irrevocably. Furthermore these extended negotiations inevitably came to the notice of the Protestant authorities, who not surprisingly demanded that their rights should also be guaranteed by similar legislation. Such proposals only made it more difficult to mobilise political support in the ranks of the ruling coalition of Social Democrats and members of the Centre Party during the final years of the Weimar Republic. The negotiations for a Reich Concordat languished.

Scholder is particularly critical of Pacelli's handling of these affairs. In his view, the nuncio's policy was marked by the following considerations: an excessive concentration on the legal forms of a Concordat; an inclination to exploit ruthlessly a relatively favourable political climate; an almost complete lack of interest in the specifically German problems and difficulties, and not least a tendency to ignore the German ecclesiastical hierarchy. All these factors, Scholder claims, were to be accentuated in 1933 when the unexpected Nazi offer to conclude a Reich Concordat prompted Pacelli's fateful acceptance in the remarkably short time of three months.[11]

Not surprisingly these criticisms have evoked a considerable response. In particular the alleged readiness of the Catholic Church to capitulate in face of the Nazi promises for a Reich Concordat have aroused strong counter-attacks. Scholder is accused of over-simplifying the issues and of ignoring crucial factors, such as the attitude of the Centre Party. Konrad Repgen, for example, in a lengthy rebuttal of Scholder's arguments, refutes the idea that the opposition of the Centre Party to the passing of the notorious Enabling Act of 23 March 1933 was bought off by the promise of a Concordat.[12] He holds that the two developments were quite separate. One point of dispute, still unresolved, lies in the policies of the chairman of the Centre Party, Mgr Ludwig Kaas, whose departure from Germany to Rome and subsequent participation in the Concordat negotiations, was clearly of great significance. Scholder believes that Kaas was much influenced by the successful conclusion of the Lateran Treaty of 1929 between the Vatican and the Fascist dictator, Mussolini. Equally he was disillusioned by the weakness of the German Centre Party, which he abandoned to its fate in April 1933, never to return. It is certainly true that Pacelli had no great respect for the Centre Party or for its parliamentary leader, Heinrich Brüning. Brüning's cautious behaviour as Reich Chancellor and his refusal to arouse the danger of a *furor protestanticus* by initiating proposals for a Concordat for the Catholics were not acknowledged by Pacelli. Furthermore the collaboration of the Centre Party with the Social Democrats was regarded in the Vatican as leading dangerously down the slope to proto-Marxist measures. The subsequent replacement of Brüning in 1932 by the more flamboyantly right-wing Catholic aristocrat, von Papen, was undoubtedly to the Vatican's liking. On the other hand, it is also true that the official organs of the Catholic Church were much less eager to give evidence of support to the rising cause of Nazism than were the Protestants. No substantial number of priests joined the Nazi Party or gave it uncritical support as did a wide variety of Protestant pastors.

How far this reluctance can be adduced to the timely conclusion of a Reich Concordat is much debated. It certainly did not prevent both the Catholic hierarchy and the majority of laity from supporting the nationalist goals of German renewal. When the Nazis' true goals of subordinating the churches became clearer, the Concordat not only gave some protection, but also afforded a rallying point around which to defend the church's interests. However, as Gordon Zahn has made clear, the willingness of the Vatican and the German bishops to extend recognition to the new regime early in 1933 effectively removed the basis upon which any later more far-reaching moral protest might have been based.

At no time was the German Catholic population released from its moral obligation to obey the legitimate authority of the National Socialist rulers under whom those Catholics were placed by the 1933 directives of their spiritual leaders; at no time was the individual German Catholic led to believe that the regime was an evil unworthy of his support.[13]

All subsequent evaluations of the Reich Concordat have inevitably been written in the light of later events. While its defenders claim that it provided German Catholics with an unprecedented and favourable recognition of their rights, and point out that the Nazi intentions at the time were carefully concealed from all observers, the critics can point to the outmoded thinking of the Roman Curia which still believed that the position of the church could be strengthened by such measures, when in fact the rise of totalitarianism called for an entirely different and much more militant defence of Christian values against the nihilism which so soon engulfed the world. Some critics of the Papacy, notably Rolf Hochhuth,[14] were later to believe that Pacelli's conduct was motivated by his sympathy for National Socialism, which continued over into the still more controversial period of his reign as Pope Pius XII. There is no evidence at all for this calumny. Alternatively it is argued that a more prophetically minded statesman should have foreseen the coming disaster, and have aroused the German Catholics to a more vigorous defence not only of the church's legal position, but more significantly of human rights, especially of the Nazis' victims, most of all of the Jews. Such criticisms are however not free from a romantic wishful thinking about the potential influence of the church. The evidence from the 1920s suggests that the power of the church leaders to limit or prevent the rise of extremist nationalist politics was restricted by social and political factors over which they had little control. Whatever mistakes and miscalculations the church leaders made, their position rested on a basis of support which was increasingly undermined as Catholics and Protestants alike were caught in a crisis of credibility, in which the familiar landmarks and norms were ruthlessly swept away. To rely on legal guarantees, as the Catholics did, or on the moral sense of German decency as most Protestants affirmed, proved quite insufficient in the turbulent currents let loose by Nazi fanaticism.

What were Hitler's own policies towards the churches during the years of his rapid rise to fame and power? Was he from the first determined on the ruthless persecution of Christianity which later marked the Nazi treatment of the churches, or were his attitudes tactically guided by the exigencies of political pressures? As with the parallel arguments about Hitler's hatred of the Jews, no satisfactory conclusion has yet been reached. Psychologically Hitler had undoubtedly shed any lingering loyalties to the Catholicism of his youth. But his frequent references to 'Providence' and his well-known claim in *Mein Kampf* to be carrying out 'the work of the Lord' in fighting the Jews[15] were more than accidental. As late as 1944, in one of his recorded table talks, Hitler could still speak approvingly of Jesus for having fought against the destructive materialism of his time and thus against the Jews.[16] The evidence is that Hitler, as Scholder convincingly shows, gained most of his ideas on religion from the writings of the propagandists of the *völkisch* movement. The salvation of Christianity from the perverting taints of Judaism and its reformulation as the purified basis of German nationalism were constant themes in the books and pamphlets Hitler is known to have read, and in the ideas of his early close associates, such as Dietrich Eckart. With rhetoric drawn from Fichte, Lagarde, Houston Stewart Chamberlain or Lanz von Liebenfels, these *völkisch* campaigners combined a sectarian fanaticism with a Messianic zeal for their conflation of German nationalism and anti-Semitic racism. Hitler himself contributed nothing original to this frothy brew of half-baked ideas which formed the basis of the Nazi Party's official programme, especially in Point no. 24, where the Party's acknowledgement of a 'positive Christianity' was elaborated as early as 1920.

We demand freedom for all religious denominations in the State so far as they are not a danger to it and do not militate against the customs and morality of the German race. The Party as such stands for positive Christianity, but does not bind itself in the matter of creed to any particular denomination. It fights the spirit of Jewish materialism *inside* and *outside* our ranks and is convinced that our nation can achieve permanent health from within only on the principle: 'Common welfare comes before individual welfare'.[17]

Hitler's most significant development in these early years was his realisation that the goals of a nationalist *völkisch* renewal would not be achieved by the sectarian and pseudo-philosophical pamphleteering which marked the activities of so many of the *völkisch* agitators. Instead victory for these ideas was to be achieved by the organisation of a political movement. His statement in *Mein Kampf* that the task of the Nazi movement was not to undertake a religious reformation, but rather a political reorganisation of the German people[18] meant a decisive change in strategy. Subsequently Hitler drew the conclusion that he should dissociate himself from all those whose enthusiastic endorsment of *völkisch* ideas led them into interminable disputes with the upholders of Christian orthodoxy. This decision can be directly related to the conclusions Hitler drew from the ignominious failure of the attempted *Putsch* of November 1923. Whereas his hero and in part mentor, General Ludendorff, believed that the failure was due to the mistaken loyalty of Bavarian Catholics to the regime, and sought to attack their faith under the banner of the new creed of the Tannenberg League, Hitler distanced himself rapidly from such a stance. When Ludendorff in turn challenged Hitler on his lack of explicit anti-Christian condemnation, Hitler replied:

> I entirely agree with his Excellency, but his Excellency [Hitler spoke to the General always in a servile and devoted way and addressed him always in the third person as he had learnt to do as a corporal] can afford to announce to his opponents that he will strike them dead. But I need, for the building up of a great political movement, the Catholics of Bavaria just as the Protestants of Prussia. The rest can come later.[19]

A few years later, in 1928, Hitler took the further remarkable step of ordering the expulsion from the Nazi Party of one of its foremost propagandists, Artur Dinter. As the Party's *Gauleiter* in the important state of Thuringia, Dinter had risen rapidly in the ranks of the Party on the strength of his early devotion to the *völkisch* cause and his undoubted gift for vituperative agitation. But when he concentrated his advocacy on the need for a religious reformation and an all-out campaign against both Catholicism and Judaism, Hitler asserted his own leadership and ordered his removal.[20] This was a clear demonstration of Hitler's determination to avoid all religious disputes between the Nazi movement and the potential adherents he sought amongst both Catholics and Protestants.

Hitler's instructions to avoid all religious polemics during the remainder of the pre-1933 period were strict and unequivocal. Equally he refused to define exactly what was intended by the Party's platform on religion, thereby deliberately avoiding a contentious and potentially divisive issue. Success proved Hitler right. The creation of a mass party would never have been achieved if the potential opposition of church members had been successfully mobilised against Nazism. Power could be won *without* the support of German Christianity, but not *against* it.[21]

The success of this tactically dictated reticence was already apparent before 1933. Increasing numbers of churchmen supported the Nazi Party as the only perceived defence against communism and Judaism, and out of disillusion with the lack-lustre democratic regime. Even in the ranks of the Catholic supporters of the Centre Party, defections took place, particularly among the young, and in the urban areas. As Peter Stachura has shown, the Centre Party retained its following in its traditional strongholds of the rural Catholic districts, and amongst women.[22] But the readiness by 1932 of the Centre Party's leaders to consider entering a possible coalition with the NSDAP undoubtedly weakened the barriers to more sympathetic evaluations of the Nazi propaganda, especially when the disasters of the Depression further destabilised the German political scene.

The reaction in the churches to the Nazi Party's advance became notable after its striking victory in the 1930 elections. Significant differences emerged which prevented any clear united opposition. Some far-sighted Catholic theologians and bishops warned their followers against the insidious dilution of Christian doctrine in the Nazi creed of 'positive Christianity', and issued messages declaring that extreme nationalism, by glorifying the Race, would lead to ignoring the revelation and commandments of God. But an increasing number of Catholics were attracted by the hope of a nationalist renewal along authoritarian lines, and were impatient with the negative attitudes adopted by their ageing leaders. The disillusionment with an imposed democracy and with Germany's alleged humiliations in the international arena were combined with dreams of the re-creation of an organic society which would reverse the deplorable heresies of individualism, liberalism and democracy which had been unleashed since the French Revolution. Marxism and Judaism seemed to many Catholics to have been the chief beneficiaries of the overthrow of the Hohenzollern empire. What was now required was a leader who would effectively tap the German Catholics' desire to be fully integrated into the mainstream of German life. Such views were only strengthened by the evident distrust which had grown up between the Centre Party, with its readiness to compromise with Social Democracy, and the ecclesiastical hierarchy, under the influence of the Nuncio, Pacelli, who, as we have seen, opposed any such trend. The Nazis cleverly exploited this difference by claiming that their campaign was directed only against 'political Catholicism' and the divisive impact of denominationally based parties, while at the same time denouncing, especially in Protestant areas, the 'clericalism' of the priests who were held to be less than truly German by being tied to their allegiance to Rome.

Similarly the Nazi polemic sought to show that the true interests of the church could not be defended by the Centre Party, which allied itself with 'godless Marxism', but only by a resolute anti-communist front of which the Nazis were the most prominent activists. To this end in 1930 the reputed physics professor and Nobel Prize winner, Professor Johannes Stark, wrote a pamphlet, *National Socialism and the Catholic Church*, which sought to remove the doubts in the minds of Catholic voters by showing that in reality the Nazi party was more Christian in its anti-communist stance than the Centre Party.

The Catholic leaders' response to these attacks was at best muted. Aware of the strong tide of nationalist sentiment, they were fearful of the danger of a renewed *Kulturkampf* and of the possible defection of many of their followers to the much more militant camp of the Protestants. They limited their opposition to ideological questions by defending traditional Catholic doctrines against the uncritical enthusiasm for the new charged racism of the Nazis, and clamped down on any endorsement of Nazi party politics by members of the clergy. Up to 1933 the official attitude was one of reserve. With a few minor exceptions the Catholic clergy gave no open support to the Nazi movement, and the Catholic doctrinal position remained unaltered.

In the ranks of Protestant Churches, however, there were striking differences. In contrast to the Catholics, there was no authoritative hierarchy, no one Protestant political party, and no firm doctrine of ideological opposition. Instead an enormous variety of standpoints emerged. Each church group, each local church synod, each theological party was seeking for a new orientation in order to make up their minds. After the 1930 elections, the theme of the church and National Socialism became one of the most frequent and controversial topics in Protestant circles. The advantage lay with those who proclaimed the necessity of working with, rather than against, the tide of events. As a result, by the early 1930s, many Protestants had come not only to accept the rightness of Hitler's political ambitions but also to justify them in the theoretical field as well. Not only had the evident disarray of the republican governments increased the longing for an authoritarian solution to Germany's problems' but also the defensive backward-looking attitudes of many of the Protestant Church leaders led some of the younger more activist clergy openly to support the NSDAP, and even to believe that the leadership of the Protestant Church could be reasserted in its ranks by demonstrating the commitment of the church to the Nazis' anti-Bolshevik and anti-Semitic policies. In 1932 the founding of the *Glaubensbewegung Deutsche Christen*, under the leadership of a radical young pastor, Joachim Hossenfelder, signalled this attempt to align the 'progressive' forces in the church with the new dynamic political party, in a common search for a renewal of German national life.

If numerically these hotheads were prominent only in such areas as Thuringia, their uncritical adoption of a policy of Christian activism and engagement drew a great deal of attention to their campaign for a more socially relevant Protestantism. In place of pietistic preaching, they demanded the church's complete commitment in political affairs. The Nazi Party was hailed as the vehicle for true Christian fellowship. As against the provincialism and dogmatic orthodoxy of traditional Lutheranism, they called for the whole-hearted devotion to the Messianic figure of Adolf Hitler. The Führer, they claimed, was 'the redeemer in the history of the Germans. Hitler stood there like a rock in a wide desert, like an island in an endless sea. In the darkest night of our Christian Church history, Hitler became for our time that marvellous transparency, the window through whom light fell on the history of Christianity'.[23]

It was notable that these enthusiastic endorsments did not meet with the entire approval of the Nazi leaders. Hitler's desire for confessional neutrality led him to forbid the creation of a special Nazi League of Pastors. On the other hand, he was equally quick to disavow the more radical anti-Christian views of his close associate, and editor of the *Völkischer Beobachter*, Alfred Rosenberg, whose book *The Myth of the Twentieth Century*, published in 1930, was a clear attempt to push the Party into a hostile stance against all the 'surviving relics of discredited creeds' in the cause of a re-established German paganism. But those Nazis who believed that the Protestant voters could be mobilised in the service of the Party, such as the outspoken Prussian *Gauleiter*, Wilhelm Kube, dismissed Rosenberg as an unimportant scribbler. Kube's campaign soon produced results. Throughout 1931 and 1932 he organised frequent meetings of Protestant laymen to infiltrate Nazi sympathisers on to parish church committees, and gave strong if concealed support to Hossenfelder's *Glaubensbewegung Deutsche Christen*. In a fiery article published in the *Völkischer Beobachter* in January 1932, Kube called on Nazi supporters to conquer the church from below.

The church must not be left as a sinecure for these christian socialists and conservative General Superintendents. We need an evangelical national church for the whole of Germany, which will finally put an end to the divisive splintering between a dozen and a half local provincial churches. . . . National Socialists! Don't let anyone slam the doors of your churches in your faces. . . . Conquer the church for yourselves and fill it with the living Christian spirit of an awakened Germany.[24]

The results were evident in the local parish elections carried out in September and October 1932. Although in fact only about one-third of the church committee places were filled with *Deutsche Christen*, despite every effort to mobilise potential voters to turn out, the impact was impressive enough. As one internal report to the church leaders stated: 'No church group has been able to reach so large a number of votes in so short a time after the creation of its organisation and programme'.[25] As Scholder rightly remarks, these elections were clearly a result of the deliberate introduction of political values and tactics into the church structures.[26] Even if their 'conquest' of the church had to wait another nine months until July 1933, the success of these measures showed how far the Nazis had achieved the goal of attracting support. There can be no doubt that the skilful propaganda of the *Deutsche Christen* with its optimistic claim to be riding the tide of German affairs, its radical anti-Semitic tirades, its fervent support of the rising Nazi Party, and its call to all Protestants to join in the cause of national renewal and loyal service to the *Volk* under the inspiring leadership of Adolf Hitler, gathered in many followers at this juncture.

These seeds of radical extremism, to no little extent, showed a remarkably rapid outburst of growth because they fell into fertile ground already well tilled by much more respectable Protestant theologians. Scholder gives a masterly and trenchant analysis of the increasingly significant theologians of the *völkisch*–nationalist school, such as Reinhold Seeberg, Emanuel Hirsch, Paul Althaus and Wilhelm Stapel.[27] During the 1920s these men undertook the reformulation of Lutheran theology by rejecting the traditional loyalties to throne and altar, and instead substituting nationality and *Volk*. Not only was nationality to be seen as a direct product of God's creation, but God's revelation was to be found not solely in the pages of the Bible, but also in a nation's history. As Paul Althaus stated in a famous address in 1927: 'Nationalities as totalities have their vocation in divine history'. Wilhelm Stapel and Emanuel Hirsch developed their ideas of the special spiritual–political mission of the German nation, and called for dedication to this new ideal in contrast to the selfish individualism of the pietists or the vague cosmopolitanism of liberal theology. This 'political theology', Scholder claims, shows what happens when 'political' ethics becomes the key to theological understanding rather than the other way round.[28] By contrast, Scholder upholds the theological approach of Karl Barth, the Swiss theologian then teaching in German universities, who stressed the necessity of subjecting all human political creeds to a prior proclamation of the 'word of God', as he tried to do in his 'dialectical' theology in the 1920s, which however at that time remained effective only within the ranks of a limited following of pastors.

These *völkisch*–nationalist theologians were not, for the most part, as Scholder rightly points out,[29] early adherents of the Nazi Party. As respectable professors they deplored the revolutionary excesses of the extremists, but seemed unaware how much their virulent incitements to hatred and denunciations of their opponents debased the level of theological argument. This strident invective, in the name of a popular 'political theology', must be held responsible for making Protestant churchmen receptive to Nazi ideas, not least by the prevention or exclusion of more rational or liberal alternatives.

With the advantage of hindsight, it can now be seen that one of the most pernicious effects of this 'political theology' was its legitimisation in Protestant circles of the *völkisch* movement's and the Nazi Party's rampant anti-Semitism. Many scholars are now agreed that the radical prejudice against Jews and Judaism in Germany, whether from religious roots as expressed by Adolf Stoecker in the 1880s, or from nationalist sources, was on the wane by 1914. The war and the defeat, however, gave an opportunity for its revivification, most notably in the educated classes which provided the leadership in the professions. Particularly in the Protestant Churches, the search for an explanation for Germany's catastrophic losses led to the widespread acceptance of a dualistic world picture, in which the forces of light were equated with the *völkisch*–nationalist principles, and the forces of darkness with Judaism, materialism and liberal internationalism. Such rhetoric marked the transition from the earlier anti-Judaism drawn from Christian tradition, not least from Luther, and the newer pseudo-biological racist anti-Semitism. After 1945 some attempts were made to try and draw a sharp dividing line between the ancient prejudice of the church and the new fanaticism of the Nazi Party, in order to exculpate the former, and lay the blame for the later Holocaust solely on the latter. But, as Uriel Tal has shown,[30] there was already a subtle blending of the arguments, when Protestant theologising came increasingly to draw its metaphors from the racist sources, especially in the use of the ideas of racial segregation and discrimination. As Richard Gutteridge commented, anti-Jewish attacks which combined invective with religious phraseology were commonplace in Protestant pulpits.[31] The Evangelical press constantly spread the caricature of the Jews as corrupt and degenerate, eager to demolish the traditional morality of the Christian national state. The Nazis also frequently used the Christian religious vocabulary to enhance their racist polemics, and made repeated references to the need for national salvation, redemption or renewal by the ousting of the Jews from Germany's national life. This permeation of Protestantism by radical racist ideas was helped by the support given by prominent church leaders and theologians, who, while deploring the excesses of violence against the Jews, nevertheless condemned the alleged materialism and intellectualism of Judaism on racial grounds. In 1928, for example, one of the more prominent younger church leaders, the General Superintendent of the Kurmark, Otto Dibelius, sent his clergy the following Easter message:

> We will all have not only understanding but also full sympathy for the final motives which have given rise to the nationalist movement. Despite the ugly sound which has often attached itself to the work, I have always regarded myself as an anti-semite. The fact cannot be concealed that the Jews have played a leading role in all the symptoms of disintegration in modern civilisation.[32]

Or again, the attitude of the more conservative pietist tradition was expressed in the following year by one of Germany's most venerable New Testament professors, Adolf Schlatter:

> Reverence for Race which enhances the fullest respect for the barriers it imposes, and attention to the necessities laid down by Nature that condition our life as a People, ought for every Christian to be a matter of course.[33]

If such remarks can be taken to have been part of a long tradition of church prejudice, there can be little doubt such declarations from respected church leaders continued to provide the ordinary layman with 'not only the excuse but also the sanction for animosity and persecution'.[34] During the whole of the Weimar Republic, the Protestant Church leaders failed to take steps to check the growth of radicalism in both clergy and laity on this issue, or to warn their followers against the increasing agitation to regard the problem as one of race. Only a few isolated voices took their stand to proclaim the irreconcilability of anti-Semitism with Christian doctrines, and to stress instead the debt of gratitude Christians ought to show to the cradle of Christianity.[35]

In the Catholic Church, the same anti-Semitic prejudice and racist overtones could be observed. This was mixed also, especially in conservative rural areas such as Bavaria, with a strong feeling of xenophobia, so that the popular discontent against the influx of Eastern Jews from Poland and Russia after 1918 could be exploited. While there were some notable opponents of this trend, such as the Catholic Bishop of Mainz, who banned Nazi Party members from the sacraments in 1930, there was virtually no reassessment of traditional Catholic theology on this thorny issue. Far more crucial, as Donald Niewyk has pointed out,

> were the great masses of ordinary Christians of both persuasions who were either indifferent to the Jews or influenced to varying degrees by

the criticisms of Jews as bearers of secularism. Those criticisms, more than any other single contribution, neutralised much Christian opposition to anti-Semitism and helped open the way to Christian support for National Socialism.[36]

With the advantage of hindsight, it can now be seen that these various trends, both institutional and intellectual, were of great significance in preparing the ground for the churches' ready acceptance of Nazism. But it may be argued that possibly the most influential factor in the minds, not just of churchmen, but of a very wide spectrum of bourgeois opinion throughout the country in these crucial years of the early 1930s was the longing for a strong leader or father figure. This is the argument lately and convincingly advanced by Ian Kershaw.[37] His evidence shows that churchmen of all varieties, like the majority of the educated élites, were particularly susceptible to the wishful thinking which swept the country in the wake of the onset of the Depression. The Catholic desire to return to an authoritarianism of the pre-Enlightenment period was matched by the Protestant longings for a restoration of the monarchy, or, if not, then of a substitute figure. These projections of expectations of a Messianic character on to a political leader were the product of a crisis of identity, when the certainties of religious faith seemed to have been shattered, and the surviving institutions lacked the appeal of former years.[38] The belief in the possibility of national and social renewal fostered a Utopian yearning for a leader who could by his charismatic personality, his decisiveness and popular appeal unite rather than divide all sections of the community. Particularly in the professional classes, whose resentment against the post-1918 situation was so constantly maintained, the hope for an outstanding Führer seemed increasingly to be the answer to Germany's political, economic and social turmoil. This delusion, Kershaw believes, is the only way in which to explain the unprecedented metamorphosis of Adolf Hitler from a provincial sectarian agitator to the leader of the whole nation within so short a time. It was not so much the cleverly orchestrated propaganda of the Nazi movement which 'created' Hitler as Führer, but the projection of wishful thinking on the part of so many of the populace.

Kershaw also points out how many of these projections were couched in pseudo-religious terms, a factor which evoked great response in the ranks of the churches. Furthermore this trend was enhanced by the remarkable and rapid growth of a subtle differentiation between the Führer and the Party he led. There was an eager readiness to believe in the good intentions of Hitler, who, it was widely held, would discard the radical rhetoric of his speeches once the experience of power brought with it an acceptance of responsibility. At the same time, the revolutionary excesses of the Party could be frequently criticised, or excused as the incidental accompaniments of an inexperienced political movement.

Thus the idolisation of the Führer's personality could be upheld by churchmen as a patriotic duty right up to the end of the Nazi era, while the disillusionment which was to follow could be focused on to lesser figures in the Nazi entourage. But already before 1933, this 'cult of personality' had reached such proportions that a superexalted nimbus surrounded and idolised the man Hitler so that the reality of his actions and thoughts cannot be separated from the myth, which he himself so eagerly cultivated. It can be argued that this excessive national–political divinisation of a single leader was a result of the distorted or deformed political consciousness of the German people, and a kind of compensation for the disintegrative developments in Germany since 1870 or 1918.[39] But it is undoubtedly true that the massive political irrationality of this belief in the Führer was far more responsible than the Nazi Party's organisation or its ideology for the remarkable cohesion of the Third Reich, and for the loyal, if deluded, service given by so many churchmen in the subsequent years.

As I have pointed out elsewhere, the failure of the churches to take a stand against Nazism and its nihilistic policies was both historically and theologically conditioned.[40] The period of the 1920s was one of enormous stress and strain for all aspects of German society. The leaders of the churches shared with almost all the other élites the same crisis of identity, unwilling or unprepared to face the demands of the post-1918 situation. The ingrained traditions of pietism, the lack of any critical theology sufficient to sustain a prophetic protest against nationalism and racism, the submissive attitude towards the state, the basically conservative outlook which too readily accepted the Nazi claim to be the only alternative to communism, the eager acceptance of pseudo-Christian doctrines especially with regard to the Jews, and the willing cult of the personality of a leader, were all significant factors which led churchmen to welcome with enthusiasm Hitler's take-over of power in January 1933. The subsequent Church Struggle, which began so soon afterwards, showed, however, that there still remained a courageous if limited minority who quickly realised the dangers of apostasy in the worship of the false gods of nationalism, racism or expediency. The triumph of National Socialism raised fundamental doubts about the exercise of power and the moral basis of modern society in a totalitarian state. If the churches had earlier failed to be alert to these issues, it was left to the efforts of such men as Martin Niemöller, Karl Barth, Dietrich Bonhoeffer and their followers to uphold the witness of the churches in what was to become this most fateful and tragic chapter in Germany history.

Notes

1 Klaus Scholder, *Die Kirchen und das Dritte Reich*, Vol. I, *Vorgeschichte und Zeit der Illusionen 1918–1934* (Frankfurt/Berlin/Vienna: 1977).

2   Jonathan R. C. Wright, '*Above Parties*'. *The Political Attitudes of the Protestant Church Leadership 1918–1933* (OUP, 1974.)

3   W. Reginald Ward, *Theology, Sociology and Politics. The German Protestant Social Conscience 1890–1933* (Berne/Frankfurt/Las Vegas: 1979).

4   Ernest G. Helmreich, *The German Churches under Hitler. Background, Struggle and Epilogue* (Detroit, Mich: 1979).

5   Kurt Nowak, *Evangelische Kirche und Weimarer Republik. Zum politischen Weg des deutschen Protestantismus zwischen 1918 und 1932* (Göttingen: 1981).

6   Friedrich-Martin Balzer, *Klassengegensätze in der Kirche. Erwin Eckert und der Bund der Religiösen Sozialisten Deutschlands* (Cologne: 1973).

7   Walter Bredendiek, *Zwischen Revolution und Restauration. Zur Entwicklung im deutschen Protestantismus während der Novemberrevolution und in der Weimarer Republik* (Berlin: 1969); *Irrwege und Warnlichter*, (Hamburg: 1966); *Zwischen Aufbruch und Beharrung. Der deutsche Protestantismus in politischen Entscheidungsprozessen* (Berlin: 1979).

8   Claus Motschmann, *Evangelische Kirche und preussische Staat in den Anfängen der Weimarer Republik. Möglichkeiten und Grenzen ihrer Zusammenarbeit* (Lübeck: 1969).

9   Jochen Jacke, *Kirche zwischen Monarchie und Republik. Der preussische Protestantismus nach dem Zusammenbruch von 1918* (Hamburg: 1976).

10   Jacke, *Kirche*, chs 1 and 2; Wright, *Above Parties*, ch. 2.

11   Scholder, *Die Kirchen*, p. 84.

12   K. Repgen, 'Über die Entstehung des Reichskonkordats-offerte im Frühjahr 1933 und die Bedeutung des Reichskonkordats'; *Vierteljahrshefte für Zeitgeschichte*, vol. 26, no. 4, (1978) pp. 497 ff; see also Scholder's reply, 'Altes und Neues zur Vorgeschichte des Reichskonkordats' in the same issue, pp. 552 ff.

13   Gordon Zahn, *German Catholics and Hitler's Wars* (New York: 1962), p. 73.

14   Rolf Hochhuth, *The Representative* (London: 1963).

15   Adolf Hitler, *Mein Kampf* (English trans., London: 1939), p. 239.

16   *Hitler's Secret Conversations 1941–1944* (New York: 1953), p. 664: Table talk for 30 November 1944.

17   For English translation of the Nazi Party programme, see M. Oakeshott (ed.), *The Social and Political Doctrines of Contemporary Europe* (New York: 1953), pp. 192–3.

18   Hitler, *Mein Kampf*, p. 289.

19   W. Breucker, *Die Tragik Ludendorffs* (Oldenburg: 1953), p. 107.

20   See Albrecht Tyrell, *Führer befiehl . . . Selbsterzeugnisse aus der Kampfzeit der NSDAP. Dokumente und Analyse* (Düsseldorf: 1969), pp. 149 f, 210 f.

21   Scholder, *Die Kirchen*, p. 123.

22   Peter D. Stachura, 'Who were the Nazis? A socio-political Analysis of the National Socialist *Machtübernahme*', *European Studies Review*, vol. 11, no. 3, July 1981, pp. 306–7.

23   Hans Buchheim, *Glaubenskrise im Dritten Reich: drei Kapitel nationalsozialistischer Religionspolitik*, (Stuttgart: 1953), p. 51.

24   Quoted in Buchheim, *Glaubenskrise*, p. 73; for further examples of the contacts between Nazi Party officials and sympathetic churchmen, see Nowak, *Evangelische Kirche*, pp. 312–20.

25   Quoted in Scholder, *Die Kirchen*, p. 273.

26   ibid.

27   ibid., pp. 124–44; Nowak, *Evangelische Kirche*, pp. 227–44.

28   Scholder, *Die Kirchen*, p. 539.

29   ibid., p. 150; but as Nowak has pointed out, the same restraint was not felt among the students. By 1930 a large proportion of the students of Protestant theology were already convinced supporters of Nazism or even Party members, Nowak, *Evangelische Kirche*, p. 304.

30   Uriel Tal, *Christians and Jews in Germany. Religion, Politics and Ideology in the Second Reich 1870–1914* (Ithaca, NY and London: 1975), ch. 5.

31 Richard Gutteridge, *Open Thy Mouth for the Dumb. The German Evangelical Church and the Jews 1919–1950* (Oxford: 1976), ch. 2.
32 Quoted in J. S. Conway, *The Nazi Persecution of the Churches* (London: 1968), p. 411.
33 Quoted in Gutteridge, *Open Thy Mouth*, p. 2.
34 ibid., p. 3.
35 See Eduard Lamparter, 'Evangelische Kirche und Judentum', in R. Geis and H.-J. Kraus (eds), *Versuche des Verstehens. Dokumente jüdisch-christlichen Begegnung 1918–1933* (Munich: 1966), p. 255.
36 Donald Niewyk, *The Jews in Weimar Germany* (Baton Rouge: 1980), p. 61.
37 Ian Kershaw, *Der Hitler-Mythos. Volksmeinung und Propaganda im Dritten Reich* (Stuttgart: 1980).
38 See Nowak, *Evangelische Kirche*, pp. 216–27.
39 M. Broszat, introduction to Kershaw, *Der Hitler-Mythos*, pp. 13–14.
40 See Conway, *Nazi Persecution*, pp. 334 ff.

9 National Socialism and Foreign Policy 1919–33

JOHN HIDEN

'If I have properly understood the National Socialist idea (of foreign policy)', Vernon Bartlett wrote in a study published in the year of the *Machtergreifung* and engagingly called *Nazi Germany Explained*, 'the conquest of territory has ceased to be important'.[1] The interest of this book lies not in its erroneous predictions but in its reflection of the uncertainty, especially amongst contemporary conservative and liberal observers, about what constituted 'National Socialist' foreign policy. Many examples exist of the early failure properly to understand the implications of what leading National Socialists but above all Hitler had said on the subject during the Weimar Republic. It was not quite true that *Mein Kampf* was an 'unread bestseller', ignored in most European countries with the singular exception of the USSR, as Karl Lange argued at the end of the 1960s.[2] Admittedly in Britain, which after all was crucial in Hitler's world view, the tendency of those conservatives who had actually heard of *Mein Kampf* to treat it as a youthful indiscretion mirrored the comforting assumption that no matter what National Socialists may have said and done out of office, they were to be seen, in keeping with their arrival to power in a coalition with the German Nationalists, essentially within the framework of the Weimar Republic's long-standing attempt to revise the Treaty of Versailles. In France, on the other hand, there existed a strong tradition of German studies and attention had been drawn to the warmongering paragraphs of Hitler's book; thus perceptions were dulled in this case less by ignorance than by a simultaneous interest in what struck the French Right as the better features of National Socialism, in particular its apparent success in lessening the class conflict, which had the effect of playing down the NSDAP's rearmament and racial policies.[3]

Just as appeasement in the 1930s had nourished illusions about 'moderates' in National Socialist foreign policy, so its failure, together with the outbreak of war over Poland in 1939, dramatically removed obstacles to the serious study of National Socialism and foreign policy before 1933. A full English edition of *Mein Kampf* had appeared in 1938 and the ensuing preoccupation with this work was in keeping with the sentiment expressed by Chamberlain in his broadcast at the outbreak of hostilities, that it was one man's war, Hitler's.[4] In 1939 Ensor's Oxford pamphlet, *Who Hitler is*, affirmed the 'unity and continuity of his

(Hitler's) main ideas', before describing the events of the 1930s, including measures against the Jews and the action against Austria, Czechoslovakia, Memel and Poland as 'logical steps towards realising these ideas. Not till we reach his recent compromise with Soviet Russia do we find any divergence from the long-charted course'.[5]

The latter event presented problems to the early analysts on the Left, who were less prone to giving undue weight to personalities and who had the definition of fascism by the Comintern Congress of 1935 to guide them: fascism was represented here as the open, terroristic dictatorship of the most reactionary elements of finance capital, which provided a key to the general implications of National Socialist foreign policy. As Laski argued in his foreword to Brady's, *The Spirit and Structure of German Fascism*, published in 1937, the 'inescapable outcome of its habits is war'.[6] Interestingly such observers were at one with conservatives and liberals in automatically relating the growing mass appeal of the National Socialists to the 'revisionism' of the Weimar Republic after 1919, if primarily bent on using this to show why the Junkers and industrial finance interests decided to 'use' Hitler. In truth the Left was in some disarray by 1945, after the bewildering series of events leading from condemnation of Hitler in the mid-1930s, to collaboration with National Socialist Germany in 1939 and finally to a joint campaign with the Allied Powers against the Third Reich.

Books on the immediate causes of the Second World War, either following Namier's classic Germanophobe account of a Germany bent on war, or the notion in Bullock's biography, of Hitler as a masterly opportunist, generally offered narrative accounts of the diplomacy of the 1930s; historians working on the policies of the Weimar Republic with the documentation captured during the war seemed equally reluctant at the other extreme to advance beyond the 1920s. In that sense the 1961 book by A. J. P. Taylor was a missed opportunity historiographically speaking, because unlike most of the diplomatic studies until then the work devoted a good third to the 1920s.[7] These pages contained interesting references to the fact that Hitler and Stresemann, the Republic's most celebrated Foreign Minister, had shared a 'continental' outlook, and that neither had challenged the 'western settlement', but such comparisons were never probed in depth. Taylor's main concern was to argue that the Führer embarked on war with the West in 1939 by accident, and he gave little weight to Hitler's conviction in the 1920s that there was an inescapable link between action taken in the East and what happened in the West. Aycoberry is, however, misguided in suggesting that Taylor's bestseller held back serious study,[8] although it received more public attention than Trevor-Roper's pioneering article on Hitler's long-term aims. Trevor-Roper developed Ensor's prewar thesis about the continuity of Hitler's foreign policy from the 1920s onwards by using material not only from *Mein Kampf* but also from Rauschning and from

Hitler's *Second Book*, originally written in 1928 but unpublished before the war.[9] The Oxford historian insisted on Hitler's long-held belief in *Lebensraum* in the East and in the need to solve the Jewish problem ruthlessly, in effect arguing that there *was* a National Socialist foreign policy before Hitler came to power and thereby coming into direct conflict with Taylor's contention that Hitler's utterances in the 1920s were best regarded as speculation.

As this debate stimulated historians to examine National Socialist views on foreign policy during the Weimar Republic, so pressure was applied from the other end of the interwar years, as it were, by the controversies over Fritz Fischer's study of German aims in the First World War, also published in 1961.[10] Fischer's work offered a more meaningful historical perspective for the study of National Socialism than that of the earlier Germanophobes: it stressed the 'continuity' of German policies betwen 1871 and 1945 and simultaneously forced scholars away from purely diplomatic accounts of 'foreign policy' by insisting on the crucial, indeed primary, influence of domestic factors on Germany's international relations after 1871. In this connection it is interesting to note that Trevor-Roper's article began with a consideration of *Mein Kampf* and tended to present Hitler's ideas in a vacuum by deliberately excluding his public comments (which he argued merely fuelled the notion of Hitler as opportunist) and concentrating only on his private remarks. By contrast, the newer work by Schubert, Jäckel and Kuhn gathered all available sources of Hitler's early statements – public, private and anonymous – to present a fuller picture of his foreign policy before and after the publication of *Mein Kampf*.[11] Such an approach raised more questions, if often indirectly, about the connections between National Socialist beliefs and others current in the Weimar Republic.

It quickly became apparent that such links were far more complex than earlier observers had supposed when equating Hitler's success with his more forceful espousal of the policy of revising the Treaty of Versailles. In the first place, this overlooked the importance of the distinction between moderate and anti-Republican revisionists. For the former, far from being insignificant, socio-political groups wedded to revision through 'fulfilment' of the peace terms, the avoidance of conflict with the Allied Powers became axiomatic. Hitler was a 'revisionist' like all Germans at the close of 1918, but his speech of 13 November 1919 confirmed how readily he accepted the idea of a war against his 'detested' France to achieve the overthrow of the Versailles settlement.[12] In itself, this hardly distinguished him from many anti-Republican revisionists on the Right, but his quest for allies in such a conflict compelled him to take issue at an early stage with extremist and moderate revisionist alike, as the case of Italy illustrates. His conviction, at the latest by 1 August 1920, that Italy should be Germany's essential ally, derived from his perception of the innate hostility between Rome and Paris, although after Mussolini's 'march on Rome' in 1922 he underpinned his strategic arguments by reference to the ideological compatibility between his movement and Italian fascism.[13] Moreover, Hitler had already passed the stage of 'speculation'; by September 1922 he had become part of the network of unofficial contacts fostered by Mussolini's henchmen in Germany, which ran like a 'red thread' as a counter-theme to official German–Italian relations.[14] Hitler's activity directly conflicted with official policy since not only did Wirth and Stresemann attach less weight to Italy as a power, but also with their constant need to preserve a domestic basis for a realistic foreign policy, they shunned closer collaboration with the fascists on these grounds.[15] Additionally Hitler's attempt from 1922/3 to argue for the abandonment of the Germans in the Tyrol to ensure the alliance with Italy, committed him to a politically unpopular path, even to anti-Republican revisionists.

The interaction between Hitler and his immediate contemporaries as a factor in forming his early views on foreign policy, which the example of Italy suggests, has been of secondary concern in much of the recent work elaborating the framework of his alliance system as a whole. Those historians who related Hitler's ideas to trends in Wilhelmine Germany and above all to the events in the second half of the First World War, have confirmed that the strategic lessons of that conflict helped to mould Hitler's plans for a network of alliances to restore Germany's power. The formative example of Germany's climactic victory in March 1918 at Brest-Litovsk suggested that securing a vast land base at Russia's expense was the necessary prelude to world power.[16] The reminder of the objective strategic realities for the Germany created in 1871 was an important corrective to the tendency to treat Hitler's foreign policy as something radically new in itself, but it did not explain the intensity of his obsession with a war for living space in the East to enable the German race to grow. Nor did it account for the fact that it was some time after Brest-Litovsk before Hitler clearly made his mind up to fight Russia with the help of England. Hildebrand, Jäckel and Kuhn all argued that this decision was not reached before 1923. The latter even felt that Hitler was undecided until he wrote *Mein Kampf*.[17]

The emphasis on the influence of power-politics in forming Hitler's ideas for alliances with Italy and England, still left a need to explain at what point ideological considerations began to affect the fabric of National Socialist foreign policy. Such influences were manifestly present when *Mein Kampf* saw the light of day. Jäckel's study admittedly suggested ways in which his beliefs modified his earliest reflections on foreign policy. In July 1920 Hitler had urged that: 'Any alliance between Russia and Germany can only come about if Jewish elements are removed', and before this, as early as 10 December 1919, he had wondered indignantly if it was right that the Russians should enjoy eighteen times as much land per head of the population as Germany had.[18] The historian is reduced in this instance to patching together somewhat scattered fragments, but they combine to create discomfort with Kuhn's assertion that, when talking about gaining land before 1923, Hitler was referring to the recovery of Germany's overseas colonies because he still expected conflict with Britain.[19] Nor does this argument take full account of the early development of Hitler's ideas on a hierarchy of races, which lay behind such remarks as that of 10 December 1919, that: 'The English have reason to be proud as a people'.[20]

It was the aim of Stoakes, in an article published in 1978, to resolve the disputes concerning the dating of Hitler's ideas on foreign policy by stressing ideological rather than strategic considerations as a determining factor. Whereas between 1919 and 1923 Hitler was supposedly still 'dreaming of restoring the splendour and glory of the Hohenzollern monarchy within its prewar frontiers',[21] Stoakes contended that during these years 'the Nazis were ... developing behind a carefully nurtured facade of conventionality many of the ideas which appear so novel in Hitler's autobiography'; further, that Hitler had fundamentally revised his previously well-disposed attitude towards Russia during 1920 because of his ideological 'insight' that the Jews were in fact the real force behind Bolshevism.[22] A welcome attempt was made to confirm that the Party's Russian expert, Rosenberg, influenced Hitler and that Ludendorff and Baltic Germans like Scheubner-Richter played an important role in causing Hitler to introduce into his view of Russia the concept of 'living space' for settlement in the East.[23] Previous accounts had argued on the whole that this notion occurred to Hitler only later, during his Landsberg imprisonment, when he was exposed to the visits of the geopolitician, Haushofer, although Erich Matthias had in fact doubted this explanation in a little-remarked piece in 1971, where it was implied that Hitler had never seriously considered postwar Russia as an ally.[24] That would reinforce objections to Kuhn's thesis that Hitler abandoned the idea of some agreement with Russia only in 1924, when objective realities confirmed that the Bolsheviks would remain in control and that the 'White' Russians were a spent force. H. A. Turner had in fact already used the document which forms a central plank in Stoakes's argument, namely the report by the co-owner of the Munich *Neueste Nachrichten*, Eduard Scharrer, after a meeting with Hitler in December 1922, when the latter affirmed: 'In foreign policy, Germany would have to adopt a purely continental policy avoiding damage to English interests. The destruction of Russia with the help of England would have to be attempted. Russia would provide sufficient land for German settlers and a wide field of activity for German industry. Then England would not interrupt us in our reckoning with France'.[25] As Stoakes concluded: 'Hitler had completed the transition from aggressive revisionist to territorial imperialist by the end of 1922, two years earlier than is usually assumed'.

This particular time-scale can be reinforced by referring to policies being developed by Weimar governments, although sustained questions on the relationship between early National Socialist views and such policies are still largely missing from much recent writing on the NSDAP's international goals. In this instance it seems odd not to give more weight to the controversy in the Weimar Republic about the whole question of Germany's relations between East and West. Both anti-republican and moderate revisionists gave varying degrees of support to the Soviet–German Rapallo agreement of April 1922. Surely a key point to keep in mind, therefore, is that Hitler's attack on the Weimar system on a broad front made it difficult for him not to oppose the sort of policy towards Russia favoured by the likes of Wirth, Rathenau and Stresemann. Hitler's ideas on Russia represented a clear alternative to their vision, as important to his developing criticism of the Republic as it was to his own determined effort to rally criticism of his own views in the NSDAP. This is one perfectly obvious yet barely emphasised reason why Hitler's policies towards Russia hardened at precisely the time when a republican strategy was being clarified towards the Soviet leaders. Such a context was bound to intensify Hitler's fear that Soviet Russia was 'a lead weight pulling us further down into the depths'.[26] Notwithstanding the highly dramatic accounts of the genesis of the Rapallo treaty in older studies, Germany's relationship with Russia in the 1920s was perfectly compatible with collaboration with the Western powers.[27] The very personalities and governments supporting the Rapallo agreement were closely associated with fulfilment and the actual course of Russo-German relations after the First World War was part of the painful evolution of a post-Versailles policy whereby Germany integrated its strategy between East and West.[28]

Hitler had in mind a much more dramatic development. It depended not on the reluctant but tacit acceptance by the Western powers of Germany's inevitable recovery of economic and therefore political supremacy in East Europe, which was Stresemann's vision and one after all shared by powerful elements even in his own party, but on 'English' support for a racialist and expansionist *Lebensraumpolitik* in the East. Too many questions have been left unanswered however, by the newer orthodoxy that 1923 was the turning-point when the British part of Hitler's foreign policy jigsaw fell into place. Such an explanation assumed that Britain's opposition to France's invasion of the Ruhr convinced Hitler that he did not automatically have to count on British aggression. The implications of 1923 for Hitler's policy towards Britain, whilst important, should not be exaggerated. The policy of fulfilment rested on the compulsion to accept that the Franco-British identity of interest was larger than their much publicised differences, whilst at the same time it sought to reduce the restraints imposed by that shared interest to manageable and acceptable proportions for Germany. Hitler was *not* unaware of this and it makes more sense to accept that his greater interest in winning Britain as an ally, which was actually clearly voiced at the end of 1922, was being reinforced by his anti-Russian stance. By 1923 he was looking primarily for arguments to reinforce this option, rather than for new directions; for justifications for ready-made decisions. Again, in this instance, his defence against ideological variations in his movement overlapped with the need to preserve a sustained attack on the foreign policies of Republican governments. Inevitably the republican policies leading from 1923 to the Locarno treaties, with their reaffirmation of Franco-British collaboration, stood in natural opposition to Hitler's determination to work for Britain's separation from France as a step towards a policy of aggression to Russia.[29] After all, in spite of the domestic criticism of Locarno on the right, the grudging support of it by even some of the DNVP and Stresemann's own DVP, together with the financial arrangements after the Dawes plan, inexorably promoted that interlocking of a European system of trade pivoting on Germany, which in turn pushed the revision of Germany's borders towards the most distant future.

A more dramatic alternative to the 'strategy of balance' implied by the Locarno agreements of 1925 on the one hand, and the Russo-German Treaty of Berlin in 1926, on the other, would be difficult to imagine than the full-scale public presentation of Hitler's foreign policy in these same years in his two volume autobiography. Whilst the first volume in 1925 stressed the need in general for an alliance with Britain, the second volume, published in December 1926, openly called for living space in the East at the expense of the Jews and Bolsheviks. The original idea of a revisionist war against France was now integrated with his expansionist plans for the East. The defeat of the arch-enemy France became the precondition of a successful campaign against Russia. Yet West German historians in particular have also increasingly wanted to emphasise the extent to which Hitler had already developed his overall foreign policy by arguing that *Mein Kampf*, together with his *Second Book* of 1928, contained the core of a 'programme', a concept which owed much to Trevor-Roper's earlier work but which clearly goes further.[30] Even the 'stages' in the programme have been outlined from close textual analysis. The need for an alliance with Britain to subjugate continental Europe and Soviet Russia meant the renunciation of colonies for the time being, but was merely the first 'stage'. Once Germany's continental base had been assured the second phase would inevitably involve expansion overseas and eventually the probability of an ultimate conflict with the United States for world supremacy. Germany's victory would be guaranteed only by making sure in between that its racial supremacy was developed and assured. Germany would ultimately enjoy dominance not merely of the continent but also of the globe.[31]

Objections to such a 'programme' were predictable enough: that it presented an over-schematic and too coherent a view of Hitler's aims; that Hitler's ideas were speculative because of the contradictions and unrealistic nature of some of them, notably his assessment of Britain and his underrating of the strength of the Russian commitment to Marxism, to say nothing of his at times dismissive remarks about the United States. Some of these reactions can be explained by the weight of the legacy of the older 'opportunist' thesis, which necessarily denied the existence of any long-term strategy and demanded as proof of this an impossibly exact relationship between the ideas of Hitler in the 1920s and the actions of the 1930s, perhaps most neatly exemplified by D. C. Watt's complaint in his recent introduction to *Mein Kampf* that: 'There are only [sic] two elements common to his words in *Mein Kampf* and his deeds in the period 1933–1941, the drive for living space and the attempt to reach an understanding with Britain and Italy'.[32] Such objections have long since been met by the growing recognition that the clarification of Hitler's foreign policy in the 1920s was not primarily to reveal a blueprint for later action but to uncover the most important driving forces behind that policy. As a result, much of the current work on early National Socialist foreign policy has come to accept that 'Hitler's ideas in this sphere are to be regarded as constituents of a coherent, if fundamentally irrational, programme'.[33] Much of the linked debate as to whether Hitler's programme was primarily 'continentalist', culminating in *Lebensraum* in the East, or 'globalist', must necessarily be of greater concern to those examining the outbreak and course of the Second World War. Much less effort has been made to use the newer evidence on early National Socialist foreign policy to re-examine the proposition that the movement automatically profited from it in its quest for power before 1933.

There is a central paradox here. On the one hand, the emphasis on the affinities between early National Socialist ideas and the traditional goals of Germany after 1871 seems at first glance to make it easier to explain the *Machtergreifung*, and to buttress the familiar argument that the partial identity between National Socialist aims and those of anti-republican revisionists was in itself sufficient to explain why those same élites deluded themselves that Hitler could be 'used' for their own purposes. 'Most of what passed for "Nazi" ideas on foreign policy', we are told, 'were in reality a re-hash of policies pursued by Germany between 1914 and 1918, cloaked in Hitler's stridently anti-semitic world view';[34] alternatively that Hitler's programme was not 'peculiar or unique, particularly since the roots of such ideas can be discovered in Wilhelmine and Bismarckian politics'.[35] Yet most of the Wilhelmine élites surviving into the Weimar Republic continued to advocate a policy of re-establishing Germany's borders of 1914, an aim which Hitler's policy was intended to make very much redundant.[36] Those same writers who have traced the 'roots' of Hitler's programme have simultaneously used it to differentiate Hitler's ultimate aims not only from those of moderate

Weimar revisionists but from the anti-republican élites.[37] In this respect Trevor-Roper was much more consistent in emphasising not only the divergence between Hitler's aims and those of the élites in industry, agriculture, politics and the army, but also his distaste for these discredited castes, who had had their chance and lost it.[38]

Nor has the long-standing argument about the NSDAP being careful to preserve a 'facade' of conventional revisionism ever properly accounted for Hitler's own conviction that he needed to offer new paths for the Germany of the future. His overriding concern from the mid-1920s was to advocate his ideas forcefully, otherwise he would hardly have bothered to set them out in *Mein Kampf* in the first place. Not only did the evolution of the ideas in that work reflect a deliberate conflict with moderate Weimar revisionists, not only did its proposals go beyond what even many anti-republican revisionists wanted, but also it expressed Hitler's determination to overcome resistance to his foreign policy within his own movement. By the mid-1920s, in keeping with the range of extremist and rightist groups who had helped to swell the movement, the NSDAP appeared to offer a range of foreign policy options for contemporaries. This too has been used to prop up the idea that National Socialism sought to 'disguise' its true intentions in this sphere by deliberately offering different things to different groups. In part such explanations reflect the influence of the current orthodoxy of Third Reich studies, with its stress on the co-existence of a variety of conflicting agencies in Hitler's Germany. Notwithstanding the investigation of the different National Socialist bodies active in the field of foreign affairs before and after 1933, however, notably by H. A. Jacobsen, only the occasional scholar has seriously disputed that when it came to foreign policy Hitler's role was supreme.[39]

The central importance of Hitler is precisely what newer research on his programme has restored, in spite of, or because of, our greater appreciation of its roots and of the varied postures developing within the early movement. This is manifestly not to argue that Hitler was National Socialism, but his aims in the field of foreign affairs self-evidently separated him from those on what Hildebrand called the 'moderate right' of the NSDAP, men like Ritter von Epp and Goering, whose ideas were akin to large sections of the Nationalist middle class as well as to the policies advocated by other parties of the Centre and right, like the DNVP and DVP. Even those NSDAP elements round the Party's farm leader, Walther Darré, differed in important respects from Hitler, for all their advocacy of a 'blood and soil' ideological doctrine of the conquest of land in the East for the benefit of, and recovery of, German farming. Unlike Hitler, they appeared at times to envisage the division between the land-power of Germany and the sea-power of Great Britain as a more or less permanent state of affairs.[40] At the other extreme, the policies of the 'socialist' wing of the movement were firmly resisted by Hitler.

Above all, if we accept the inescapable link between NSDAP attempts to overthrow the Republic and its foreign policy aims – the first being a precondition of the latter – then it must necessarily be odd to think of Hitler's foreign policy in the later 1920s as 'speculation'. On Hitler's terms, the very survival and even development of his movement at that time was an advance towards a new 'foreign policy', just as his determined effort to win followers for this was an integral part of the attack on the Republic as such. It required considerable and constant activity to launch the movement 'against the aimlessness and incompetence which have hitherto guided our German nation in the line of foreign affairs' and to encourage it 'to gather our people and their strength for an advance along the road that will lead this people from its present restricted living space to new land and soil, and hence to free it from the danger of vanishing from the earth or of serving others as a slave nation'.[41] Hitler's forceful defence of his programme before his own Party opponents and before the plurality of interest groups in the Weimar Republic should be stressed more strongly. First, this would put into proper perspective what overtures *were* made by the NSDAP to the political establishment at the end of the 1920s, by serving to remind us that any 'disguising' of foreign policy aims was mainly a consequence of divisions in the NSDAP. Secondly, it would bring out more clearly than is at present often the case, that the élites in Germany who helped Hitler into office could not fail to be only too well aware of the considerable risks entailed in combining their own revisionist drive with that of the NSDAP. The element of calculation on the part of the powerful establishment figures in trying to 'use' Hitler was more than outweighed by that of desperation in the last resort.

This in turn serves to underline how important the mounting domestic and international crisis after 1929 was in radicalising opinion at large in Germany, in helping to foster a widespread irrational mood and in bringing about a more rapid convergence between the revolutionary international aims of the Hitler movement and the increasingly desperate measures practised by late Weimar governments. The NSDAP's own part in exacerbating the effects of the crisis thereby brought it nearer to the 'making' of foreign policy. Not surprisingly there has been a growing debate on the 'transition' to the Third Reich, in which the dialogue between West and East German historians has been of particular interest. The continuing problem for many Western historians, of unravelling the strands of NSDAP policy from those of other Weimar parties and interest groups, is not central to the concerns of East German historians working on the Republic's foreign policy. In Marxist historiography, the whole notion of 'moderate' or 'peaceful' revisionism, exemplified by Stresemann's actions in bourgeois accounts, is a fiction; the concept of security is 'indivisible', and France could not have been given 'security' whilst Germany simultaneously left open options for

revision in East Europe. Such an explanatory framework provides the
key to the treatment of NSDAP policy during the crisis, which is
represented as merely the occasion for a predictable and inevitable shift
in the accent of policy-making towards military measures, thus providing a direct bridge to Hitler's policies after 1933. Wolfgang Ruge, for
example, examined the way in which as early as 1927 even prominent
Centre Party leaders, including Papen, were beginning to argue in favour
of Britain's anti-Bolshevik policies whilst at the same time paving the
way for agreement with Poland to further German economic penetration
of East Europe. Ruge could therefore draw a direct line from the
Polish–German liquidation agreement of 1929 to the first 'success' of
Hitler's foreign policy, the Polish–German non-aggression pact of 1934.
Similarly, for Ruge, Locarno was a step on the road to Munich and the
Second World War.[42]

Such arguments are more sophisticated than one would imagine from
reading the numerous dismissive references to East German scholarship
in so many Western accounts, and form part of an extended attempt to
demonstrate the anti-Bolshevik stance of not only the NSDAP but also
most other German parties. Significantly East German scholars have
accepted the more sweeping statements made by Western continuity
theorists in the early post-Fischer era, which are often cited with
approval by the Eastern bloc and have provided it with ammunition to
deny any essential differences between the hostility of Stresemann
towards Russia on the one hand, and Hitler on the other.[43] Moreover,
the East German blanket acceptance of the fundamental affinity between
Weimar revisionism and NSDAP policies serves to underpin the thesis of
the basic identity of interest between German monopoly capitalism and
the NSDAP. This in turn conforms with the long-established Marxist
argument that an 'alliance' existed in 1932 between industry, agriculture
and the NSDAP to exploit the market potential of East and South East
Europe to offset the crisis of capitalism.[44]

West German historians have come to share their Eastern colleagues'
interest in tracing the NSDAP's obsession with the economic prospects
of East Europe after 1929. What divides the two groups in the last resort,
however, is the East German insistence on the 'primacy of economics',
with its assumption that Hitler and the NSDAP functioned as the tools of
monopoly capitalism, although during the course of their exchanges with
the West, East German historians have been compelled to acknowledge
the different groupings within the 'capitalist' camp.[45] For the historians
of West Germany, the existence of Hitler's programme *before* he came
into extensive contact with leading industrialists and financiers is the
central plank of their argument against the primacy of economics in
National Socialist foreign policy. It may well be that the momentum of
this debate has pushed the 'programme' advocates further than they
might otherwise have gone in emphasising the priority of *political* and

ideological goals in NSDAP foreign policy. At any rate, in some of the
latest arguments on the subject the stress has been placed more on the
near autonomous nature of those foreign policy goals, and as a result it is
less easy to see them purely as a function of Germany's *domestic*
necessities; they cannot, in other words, be wholly explained in terms of
their power to integrate a divided German society and to buttress the
power of the establishment, as seemed to be the case prior to the First
World War.[46] This would help to account for a greater readiness to
accept the distinctions between NSDAP policies and Weimar revisionism than was the case when Hitler's programme was first seriously
elaborated in the 1960s, a point which has already been made. A Western
scholar like Salewski can share with Ruge the perception that 'security'
was bound to mean different things to France on the one hand, Germany
on the other, whilst wanting by contrast to reaffirm that during the years
of crisis, in spite of the convergence of aims:

> Hitler at any rate, and this is historically the essential difference to the
> security policy of the Weimar Republic, applied in a ruthless fashion
> the diplomatic, political and military instruments made available from
> Brüning to Schleicher, for a policy with which neither Brüning, Papen
> nor Schleicher, neither Groener nor Hammerstein, and probably also
> Blomberg, would have identified themselves.[47]

Such a distinction is preserved in Wollstein's book, one of the very few
extended studies of foreign policy at this critical juncture.[48]

The debate concerning the relative weight of economic and political/
ideological explanations for NSDAP foreign policy has been mainly
concerned with the 1930s. It would suggest, however, that attention be
redirected to the whole question of the economic dimension of Hitler's
early foreign policy. Hitler's concept of *Lebensraum* was never a foreign
policy goal alone, but was the basis for a future German economic order,
which Hitler had made quite clear to industrialists in 1927.[49] Yet both
Eastern and Western historians perpetuated the idea of Hitler's indiffer-
ence to economics, the one reducing his activity in this sphere to the
function of serving ruling élites, the other dismissing his ability to
understand economics and pointing to the absence of economic theory in
National Socialist ideology. Until very recently there was a striking
absence of serious study of the economic ideas of National Socialism,
although as they approached power the movement's leaders were
increasingly compelled to make pronouncements on economic matters.
When Turner tried to remedy the situation a few years ago he
concentrated on Hitler and tended to reduce his economic thought to a
basic drive to secure food for the race.[50] Barkai's interesting work
accepted Hitler's limited grasp of economics, but argued that the
Führer recognised its importance before going on to analyse the evo-

lution of distinctive National Socialist contributions to economic debate prior to 1933.[51] Of more direct relevance here is the stress on the importance of the Party in popularising the notion of autarchy during the crisis. The NSDAP's readiness to take seriously this and other ideas advanced by those economists who were regarded by contemporary experts as 'cranks', itself further distinguished the movement from other Weimar parties and interest groups. The NSDAP's propagation of the notion of a crisis-free economic order was a necessary, vote-catching, positive alternative to the Weimar policy of collaborating with the Western powers, criticised so bitterly and with such telling effect by the NSDAP during the crisis.

The fact that Western historians have increasingly joined East German scholars in studying the role of the East European states in the projected '*Krisenfest*' economy, or '*Grossraumwirtschaft*', stretching from the Atlantic to the Urals, has supplemented what slender evidence we have for Hitler's own earlier thoughts on the 'lands between' Germany and Russia. These were certain to be affected by his *Lebensraumpolitik* but their particular role was less systematically thought out in his writings and statements than that of Italy, Britain, France and Russia, an omission contrasting notably with the attention given to East Europe by Weimar governments.[52] NSDAP plans for economic hegemony in East and South-East Europe do not necessarily provide support for the notion that the movement was the tool of monopoly capitalism. If, like the foreign policy programme in general, due weight is given to the ideological dimension of the dream of a *Grossraumwirtschaft*, the NSDAP's reduction of the Eastern states to the level of subservient markets clamped into the German orbit went beyond the Wilhelmine vision of a gigantic *Mitteleuropa*, for all the affinities which some scholars have found.[53] Equally, whilst NSDAP ideas in this instance bore some resemblances to the policies and plans of key industrial and agrarian interest groups in the Weimar Republic, the ideological and strategic rationale of the NSDAP proposals ran contrary to the network of most-favoured-nation trade treaties carefully built up in the East by Weimar governments, often misguidedly seen as preparing the way directly for Hitler's later policies.[54] Similarly the question of German minorities living in East Europe, whose fate after 1918 had been directly linked with their readiness and ability to play a constructive role in the development of East–West trade, was transformed by Hitler's ideology into one about their potential contribution as agents of a disruptive and expansionist policy.[55]

As in other areas of NSDAP foreign policy before 1933, the reappraisal of its economic dimension promises to provide additional proof that the NSDAP succeeded not primarily because of any identification with 'revisionism'; there were affinities, not least because of the fact that many swelling the numbers of the movement formed part of the larger national reaction against the Peace Treaty. Success came ultimately, however, because under Hitler's influence dramatic alternatives were propounded to the difficult and essentially long-term revisionist strategy of Weimar governments. The widespread impatience inside Germany with which those governments had to contend from the outset, could only count decisively in the NSDAP's favour therefore, when the international and domestic foundations on which the policy had rested had collapsed with the onset of crisis. Hitler's prime concern then was not to fudge policy issues but to foster the militant nationalism in Germany as a launching pad for a programme which would draw a line under Germany's previous policies. The dire implications of this were not so much deliberately disguised by the movement as overlooked, both by the millions helping Hitler through the ballot box and by the played-out German élites who chose to gamble against the odds in admitting him to office. This was not the end of 'speculation' and the beginning of NSDAP 'foreign policy' as such, but a guarantee that the strategies evolved by the movement and by Hitler above all in the 1920s would be completed.

Notes

1   Vernon Bartlett, *Nazi Germany Explained* (London: 1933), p. 199.
2   K. Lange, *Hitlers unbeachtete Maximen. 'Mein Kampf' und die Öffentlichkeit* (Stuttgart: 1968).
3   P. Aycoberry, *The Nazi Question: An Essay in the Interpretation of National Socialism* (New York: 1981), p. 15.
4   On the publishing history of *Mein Kampf* see N. H. Baynes, *Hitler's Speeches*, Vol. I (OUP, 1942), p. 997; *Mein Kampf*, with an Introduction by D. C. Watt (London: 1969), pp. xv–xvi.
5   R. K. Ensor, *Who Hitler Is* (Oxford Pamphlet, 1939), p. 27.
6   R. Brady, *The Spirit and Structure of German Fascism* (London: 1937), p. 15; cf. E. Nolte, *Theorien über den Faschismus* (Berlin: 1967), pp. 52–5.
7   A. J. P. Taylor, *The Origins of the Second World War* (London: 1964 edn), pp. 22 ff, 98–9.
8   Aycoberry, *The Nazi Question*, p. 216.
9   H. Trevor-Roper, 'Hitlers Kriegsziele', *Vierteljahrshefte für Zeitgeschichte*, 8, 1960, p. 124. Roper testified to the influence of R. K. Ensor in this article.
10 F. Fischer, *Griff nach der Weltmacht* (Düsseldorf: 1961); cf. K. L. Jarausch, 'From Second to Third Reich. The problem of continuity in German foreign policy', *Central European History*, XII, 1979.
11 G. Schubert, *Anfänge nationalsozialistischer Aussenpolitik* (Cologne: 1963); A. Kuhn, *Hitlers aussenpolitische Programm* (Stuttgart: 1970); E. Jäckel, *Hitlers Weltanschauung* (Tübingen: 1969).
12 E. Deuerlein, 'Hitlers Eintritt in die Politik und die Reichswehr', *Vierteljahrshefte für Zeitgeschichte*, 7, 1959, p. 207; cf. context of Hitler's view in E. Laubach, *Die Politik der Kabinette Wirth* (Lübeck: 1968), pp. 78–9.
13 Jäckel, *Hitlers Weltanschauung*, pp. 33, 34; G. Weinberg (ed.), *Hitlers Zweites Buch* (Stuttgart: 1961), p. 187.
14 J. Petersen, *Hitler, Mussolini. Die Entstehung der Achse Berlin-Rom* (Tübingen: 1973), p. 10; A. Cassels, 'Mussolini and German nationalism 1922–5', *Journal of Modern History*, 35, 1963, p. 137.

15   *Akten zur deutschen auswärtigen Politik 1918–1945*, Series B (1925–33), (Göttingen: 1966), Vol. VII, pp. 565–6.

16   cf. A. Hillgruber, *Deutschlands Rolle in der Vorgeschichte der beiden Weltkriege* (Göttingen: 1967), p. 65. For a much older statement of this basic idea, see H. Behrend, *The Real Rulers of Germany* (London: 1939), p. 178.

17   Kuhn, *Hitlers Programm*, pp. 99–104, offered the formula: increased population– demand for living space–alliance with GB–rejection of colonies–Eastern expansion, for the chronological development of Hitler's ideas.

18   Jäckel, *Hitlers Weltanschauung*, p. 39.

19   Kuhn, *Hitlers Programm*, pp. 96–9.

20   Jäckel, *Hitlers Weltanschauung*, p. 35; on Hitler's early grudging admiration of GB, see also, R. H. Phelps, 'Hitler als Parteiredner im Jahre 1920', *Vierteljahrshefte für Zeitgeschichte*, 11, 1963, p. 318; Schubert, *Aussenpolitik*, pp. 86–7.

21   K. Hildebrand, *The Foreign Policy of the Third Reich* (London: 1973), p. 19.

22   G. Stoakes, 'The evolution of Hitler's ideas on foreign policy, 1919–1925', in P. D. Stachura (ed.), *The Shaping of the Nazi State* (London: 1978), p. 23.

23   ibid., pp. 24, 38. Stoakes follows W. Laqueur in many respects, *Russia and Germany: A Century of Conflict* (London: 1965); cf. H. E. Volkmann, *Die Russische Emigration in Deutschland* (Würzburg: 1966); to offset the tendency to think of Baltic Germans in general as 'Hitler's mentors', consult K.-H. Grundmann, *Deutschtumpolitik zur Zeit der Weimarer Republik* (Hanover-Döhren: 1977).

24   Hildebrand, for example, accepts Haushofer's influence as decisive, *Foreign Policy*, p. 19; but see E. Matthias, 'The western powers in Hitler's world of ideas', in A. J. Nicholls and E. Matthias (eds), *German Democracy and the Triumph of Hitler* (London: 1971), p. 169.

25   H. A. Turner, 'Hitlers Einstellung zu Wirtschaft und Gesellschaft vor 1933', *Geschichte und Gesellschaft*, 2, 1976, p. 94, which reinforces arguments for the concept of 'space' appearing earlier in Hitler's thoughts.

26   Stoakes, in Stachura (ed.), *Nazi State*, p. 31.

27   H. Graml, 'Die Rapallo Politik im Urteil der westdeutschen Forschung', *Vierteljahrshefte für Zeitgeschichte*, 18, 1970, p. 382, tries to perpetuate earlier comparisons between 1922 and the 1939 Nazi–Soviet pact, but cf. more realistic interpretations of K. Hildebrand, *Das Deutsche Reich und die Sowjetunion im internationalen System 1919–1932* (Weisbaden: 1977).

28   J. Hiden, *Germany and Europe 1919–1939* (London: 1977), pp. 89 ff; H. Pogge von Strandmann, 'Rapallo-strategy in preventive diplomacy', in V. Berghahn and M. Kitchen (eds), *Germany in the Age of Total War* (London: 1981), p. 143.

29   cf. W. Horn, 'Ein unbekannter Aufsatz Hitlers aus dem Frühjahr 1924', *Vierteljahrshefte für Zeitgeschichte*, 16, 1968, pp. 280 ff.

30   K. Hildebrand, *Das Dritte Reich* (Munich: 1980), p. 170; cf. also H. Holborn, 'Origins and political character of Nazi Ideology', *Political Science Quarterly*, 79, 1964, pp. 543, 545.

31   Hillgruber, *Deutschlands Rolle*, pp. 68 ff; 'England's place in Hitler's plan for World domination', *Journal of Contemporary History*, 9, 1974, p. 11; J. Henke, *England in Hitlers politische Kalkül* (Boppard: 1973).

32   Watt, 'Introduction' to *Mein Kampf*, p. xxxiv.

33   Stachura (ed.), *Nazi State*, p. 11.

34   Stoakes, in Stachura (ed.), *Nazi State*, p. 44.

35   Hildebrand, *Foreign Policy*, p. 20.

36   *Mein Kampf*, pp. 593, 595. 'The boundaries of the year 1914 mean nothing at all for the German future'.

37   Hildebrand, *Foreign Policy*, p. 18; Hillgruber, *Deutschlands Rolle*, pp. 71 ff.

38   Trevor-Roper, 'Hitlers Kriegsziele', p. 123; Holborn, 'Nazi Ideology', p. 553.

39   H.-A. Jacobsen, *Nationalsozialistische Aussenpolitik, 1933–1938* (Frankfurt: 1968); Wolfgang Michalka argues for the importance of other influences before and after

1933, in M. Funke (ed.), *Hitler, Deutschland und die Mächte*, (Düsseldorf: 1978), pp. 46–62.

40 Jäckel, *Hitlers Weltanschauung*, p. 52 stresses the similarities more, whilst Hildebrand, *Foreign Policy*, insists on the distinction between Darré and Hitler.

41 *Mein Kampf*, p. 590.

42 W. Ruge, 'Die Aussenpolitik der Weimarer Republik und das Problem der europäischen Sicherheit 1925–1932', *Zeitschrift für Geschichtswissenschaft*, 22, 1974, pp. 276, 290.

43 cf. M. Walsdorff, *Westorientierung und Ostpolitik. Stresemanns Russlandpolitik in der Locarno Ära* (Bremen: 1971), pp. 26–9; with W. Ruge, *Stresemann. Ein Lebensbild* (East Berlin: 1965), p. 226.

44 For a survey of the literature on this idea and for critical reactions against it, see H. A. Winkler, *Revolution, Staat, Faschismus. Zur Revision des historischen Materialismus* (Göttingen: 1978), pp. 71 ff.

45 Some insight into the debate in D. Eichholtz and K. Gossweiler, 'Noch einmal: Politik und Wirtschaft 1933–1943', *Das Argument*, 10, 1968, pp. 210 ff.

46 Hildebrand, *Dritte Reich*, p. 173.

47 M. Salewski, 'Zur deutschen Sicherheitspolitik in der Spätzeit der Weimarer Republik', *Vierteljahrshefte für Zeitgeschichte*, 22, 1974, pp. 138 ff.

48 G. Wollstein, *Vom Weimarer Revisionisms zu Hitler* (Bonn: 1973).

49 H. A. Turner, 'Hitler's secret pamphlet for industrialists, 1927', *Journal of Modern History*, 40, 1968, pp. 348 ff.

50 Turner, *Hitlers Einstellung*, p. 93; cf. J. Heyl, 'Hitler's economic thought. A re-appraisal', *Central European History*, 6, 1973, pp. 83–96.

51 A. Barkai, *Das Wirtschaftssystem des Nationalsozialismus. Der historische und ideologische Hintergrund* (Cologne: 1977), pp. 25, 37, 39, 53–5.

52 Hiden, *Germany and Europe*, pp. 113 ff; Hiden 'The Baltic problem in Weimar's Ostpolitik 1923–1932', in Berghahn and Kitchen (eds), *Germany in the age of total war*, pp. 151 ff.

53 cf. E. Lederer, 'Gegen Autarkie und Nationalismus', in J. Kocka (ed.), *Kapitalismus, Klassenstruktur und Probleme der Demokratie in Deutschland 1910–1940* (Göttingen: 1979), pp. 199 ff.

54 H. J. Schröder overlooks crucial differences in his 'Deutsche Südosteuropapolitik 1929–1936. Zur Kontinuität deutscher Aussenpolitik in der Weltwirtschaftskrise', *Geschichte und Gesellschaft*, 2, 1976, pp. 5–31. For more general treatment of these ideas see R. Frommelt, *Paneuropa oder Mitteleuropa. Einigungsbestrebungen im Kalkül deutscher Wirtschaft und Politik 1925–1933*, (Stuttgart: 1977).

55 cf. J. W. Hiden, 'The Weimar Republic and the problem of the Auslandsdeutsche', *Journal of Contemporary History*, 12, no. 2, 1977, pp. 273–89, with A. Komjathy and Rebecca Stockwell, *German Minorities and the Third Reich. Ethnic Germans of East Central Europe between the Wars* (London: 1980).

10 Ideology, Propaganda, and the Rise of the Nazi Party

IAN KERSHAW

The role of Nazi ideology and propaganda in the rise of the NSDAP is less obvious than it initially may seem. According to Hitler the contribution of ideology and propaganda to the growth of mass support was straightforward: the role of propaganda was 'to see that an idea wins supporters', 'to force a doctrine on the whole people'.[1] In reality things were less simple. The problems attached to defining the Nazi 'doctrine', how it was conveyed to the masses, and especially how it was received are complex.

The half-century since Hitler's appointment as Chancellor has produced a massive literature on Nazi ideology, but no signs of any unanimity about its essential character. The difficulties are partly definitional, depending upon whether 'ideology' is taken to be a composite and distinctive grouping of interrelated beliefs constituting a political philosophy or doctrine, or whether it is understood rather as an amalgam of characteristic attitudes and beliefs underpinning, produced by and reflecting socio-political culture. Even more so, the difficulties stem from the prevalent features of the Nazi 'doctrine' – a paradoxical concoction of conservative and radical elements without any basis in the intellectual rigour of a rational philosophy, a cynical 'catch-all' programme offering a rag-bag of contradictions in which it is hard to distinguish 'idea' from 'presentation of idea'. Finally, discussion of Nazi ideology has inevitably been influenced, consciously or not, by current political and ideological positions. Studies of Nazi ideology have, not surprisingly therefore, produced diametrically opposed interpretations. Nazi ideology has been regarded by some as genuinely revolutionary in content,[2] and branded by others as quintessentially counter-revolutionary.[3] Leading historians have seen Nazism as 'dynamic nihilism devoid of ideological commitment'[4] and Hitler as an opportunist without principles or ideology seeking power for power's sake,[5] while others have distinguished Nazism from Italian and other forms of fascism on the grounds of its theoretical basis in a doctrine of race[6] and have interpreted Hitler as a politician driven by a remarkably consistent and coherent, if hateful and repulsive, ideology.[7] Nazi ideology has also commonly been put forward as the outgrowth of specifically German intellectual currents rooted in reactions against the French Revolution, a uniquely German phenomenon;[8] while, irreconcilably opposed to this, it has been viewed in class terms as merely the German manifestation of the extreme chauvinistic, anti-socialist forces common to most European nations as a product of acute imperialist rivalries before and after the First World War, gaining political weight in conditions of a crisis in the dominant bourgeois ideology.[9]

Until recently, the role of propaganda has seemed less controversial. If surprisingly few works have concentrated exclusively on analysing propaganda in the pre-1933 period,[10] a proliferation of detailed regional studies of the rise of the Nazi Party has, during the past two decades, generally emphasised the crucial role of propaganda and has thoroughly examined its organisation and content. Less work has been done on the more difficult questions relating to the processes of dissemination and reception of propaganda, whose effectiveness has often been presumed more than demonstrated. In the past few years there have been signs of a more critical assessment of the role and effectiveness of propaganda. Recent work in 'grassroots' social history has tended to reject an over-easy emphasis on manipulation 'from above' and has laid weight rather on the need for detailed examination of the processes of mobilisation 'from below' in an attempt to comprehend the social as well as the overtly political determinants of receptivity to Nazism.[11] Revision of the importance attached to propaganda has in the mean time proceeded so far as to suggest that the generally assumed massive success of Nazi propaganda before 1933 is no more than a myth.[12]

It seems, therefore, a suitable time, fifty years after the 'seizure of power', to attempt briefly to take stock of the role of ideology and of propaganda in the rise to power of the NSDAP, by concentrating on the deceptively simple questions of how important the 'idea' of Nazism was to the growth of the movement, and whether the role of propaganda in the creation of the mass movement has been exaggerated.

I Ideology and Mobilisation

The establishment of the main contours of Nazi ideology and of the 'market' for the ideology provides a necessary starting-point.

The dominant features of Nazi ideology comprised: the central notion that sovereignty resided in the 'racial people', the basic premiss which provided underlying legitimation to all social imperialist claims; the idea of a 'national community', in which the divisiveness of class conflict would be transcended by massive emphasis upon national consciousness and unity; militant anti-Marxism, levelled at the nation's main ideological enemy and the threat to society's private property economic base; the unquestioning acceptance of leaders selected not through birth or rank but through achievement and ability, a meritocracy in which the best, the most able, and the strongest should rightly rise to the top; and extreme chauvinism and glorification of militarism and war, in which military values of blind obedience, discipline, manliness, sacrifice, hardness, and ruthlessness, were inculcated into civilian life, German national virtues elevated above all others, and war extolled as the peak of human experience. Rejection of liberal democracy as the negation of most of these values was automatic. Populist anti-capitalism and a form of pseudo-socialism were exploited propagandistically, but were not taken seriously by the dominant forces in the Nazi leadership, were inevitably dropped eventually, and cannot be regarded as intrinsic to the ideology.[13]

The features of Nazi ideology just listed were reducible to one overriding principle: the unchallengeable primacy of the nation above all else, within Germany and in the world outside. It was a principle which the Nazis voiced in its most radical and uncompromising form, but hardly one to which they could stake an exclusive claim. 'Nazi ideology' was neither something which the Nazis invented, nor something peculiar to the Nazis.

Though some of the strands which went to make up Nazi ideology had a longer history, the basic components of the creed were essentially a product of the populist imperialism of the Wilhelmine era. The spread of racist and social-Darwinist philosophies – themselves part of the ideological baggage of imperialism – and the popularisation by neo-conservatives of anti-democratic ideas, not least the notion of a new Reich to be brought about by 'conservative revolution' from above, provided the pseudo-intellectual background within which Nazi 'theory' developed.[14] But the history of ideas alone can do little to explain the mass appeal of Nazism. Political and social factors have to be taken into account in explaining the emergence of an available 'market' for the ideology.

This 'market' had its beginnings in Wilhelmine Germany, in the mobilisation for the first time of a populist, radical Right, rabidly chauvinist and anti-socialist in character, and providing the earliest manifestation of a mass popular opposition on the Right, which rejected the 'status-quo politics' of conservative, bourgeois rule, and sought the renewal of the nation through the pursuit of radical nationalistic policies at home and abroad.[15] This mobilisation of predominantly middle-class strata in Wilhelmine Germany produced, therefore, a potentially destabilising political force represented for the time being in the mass membership of anti-Marxist, imperialist pressure groups. Paramilitary organisations of ex-Front soldiers like the *Stahlhelm*, anxious for an attempt to reverse the changes of 1918, also helped the continued purveyance, in the crisis-ridden postwar atmosphere, of an extreme nationalist, anti-socialist ideology. The dynamic right-wing radicalism of the *völkisch* groups and paramilitary organisations found only an uncomfortable home within the bourgeois parties of the Weimar Republic, organised around their party cliques and upholding the power base of the traditional dominant élites. Even the German National People's Party, itself with many fascistic characteristics, could only uneasily accommodate the new strength of the populist forces on the radical Right. The fickle behaviour of voters on the centre and Right (except the Catholic *Zentrum*) even before the rise of the Nazis illustrates the lack of political anchorage of vast numbers of middle-class Germans – stridently nationalist, increasingly detesting the 'Marxist' Republic, but not picturing their ideal in a return to the class-ridden, privileged world of the Kaiser.[16] If the bourgeois parties could scarcely contain the restless, largely negative energy of the 'new Right', the Marxist parties, speaking a language of undiluted class warfare and 'dictatorship of the proletariat', discarded any chance of integrating the radical, untrammelled forces of middle-class protest into a left-wing revolutionary movement and pushed them instead even further in the direction of outright anti-socialism under the nominally class-neutral slogan of the 'national community'. This slogan was ideally placed to integrate the heterogeneous middle class on an ideological plane into a movement which could promise to defend sectional interest while claiming to stand above it.[17]

Wide sections of the German middle class – but also not insignificant numbers of the proletariat who had not been 'schooled' in the Marxist parties and mistakenly hoped to find a path through Nazism to a bright, new world – were therefore ideologically 'available' for right-wing populist mobilisation. Lacking a fixed political home and sharing the same ideological prejudices as the Nazis, they became prime ballot-fodder for the NSDAP. There was, however, little or nothing specifically Nazi about the 'idea' of Nazism behind the mobilisation. It amounted to little more than an onslaught on the whole fabric of the 'Marxist' Republic coupled with a chiliastic, pseudo-religious vision of a 'national awakening' – a political, social, and moral new start for Germany.[18] What distinguished the Nazis from their right-wing rivals was less the idea itself than their presentation of the idea (which I will come to later in this paper) and the emphases they attached to it. Two emphases stand out: 'struggle' and 'leadership'.

The notion of 'struggle' was intrinsic to every aspect of Nazi ideology. The word *Kampf* was an ever-present component of the Nazi vocabulary. Hitler's book was called *Mein Kampf* ('My Struggle'), and after the 'seizure of power' the entire pre-1933 period was referred to as the *Kampfzeit*, the 'time of struggle'. 'Struggle' meant fighting to the death against internal and external enemies of the nation. It was the fight for the nation's future, for its survival, the fight to get rid of Versailles, the Republic, the Marxists, the Jews. It also meant the struggle of the individual for advancement and social mobility: the chance to prosper in the *Leistungskampf* of daily life. To interpret politics, and life itself, as struggle, as Hitler did in *Mein Kampf*, distinguished the Nazi philosophy from that of their right-wing rivals. It meant the Nazis could claim a *totality* for their *Weltanschauung* which no other party could match. In place of party politics the Nazis offered the mortal struggle of *Weltanschauungen*, in which there were no half-ways.

The theme of 'struggle' was closely linked to the second element which distinguished the Nazi 'idea': the emphasis on leadership. The notion of heroic leadership was a common component of right-wing thought in the 1920s.[19] In an ideological climate which was largely the product of imperial rivalries and war, the qualities seen in the coming *völkisch* leader, necessarily a man from the people, reflected struggle, conflict, the values of the trenches. He was to be hard, ruthless, resolute, uncompromising, and radical. He would be ruler, warrior and high priest alike. The society he would rule would be one based upon authority and leadership in which subordinate leaders would earn their right to command and direct through their own qualities, shown by coming out on top in struggle and competition. The ideology was an extreme strain of the weight attached in social and economic norms to competition, the right of the best and strongest to thrive. There was, therefore, nothing specifically Nazi about belief in a *Führerprinzip*. But the way in which the *Führerprinzip* was made into the organisational premiss of the NSDAP by the mid-1920s and especially the rapid growth from this period of a fully blown Führer-cult attached to Hitler increasingly set the NSDAP apart from other parties and organisations.[20] Hitler was more and more portrayed as not just another party leader, but as *the* Leader for whom Germany had been waiting, the embodiment and inspiration of the ideological struggle, missionary and prophet, a man who could not simply be ranked alongside Germany's contemptible *Politiker*. It was not for nothing that the NSDAP now came commonly to be dubbed '*die Hitlerbewegung*' ('the Hitler Movement') and its members '*die Hitler*' ('the Hitlers'). The Hitler-myth became, therefore, a distinguishing feature of Nazi ideology and an overriding integrative factor incorporating 'idea' and movement. In this sense, Hitler *was* the ideology, he was the movement. The 'total' claims of the Nazi ideology were interpreted as residing in Hitler's 'vision'. And yet, paradoxically, Hitler's 'vision' can do little to explain Nazism's popular appeal. We must now turn to consider the relationship of Hitler's *Weltanschauung* to Nazi mobilisation of the masses.

Contrary to earlier interpretations of Hitler as 'an opportunist entirely without principle', Eberhard Jäckel's meticulous re-reading of the central Hitlerian texts demonstrated a high degree of ideological consistency and cohesion, however base the principles, contained in the coupling of fanatical anti-Semitism with the aim of conquest of

Lebensraum, synthesised in a Darwinistic, racially determined under-standing of the historical process as one of eternal struggle in which the strong survive at the expense of the weak.[21] Since Hitler became increasingly unchallengeable as the fount of ideological orthodoxy within the movement, there are obviously grounds for regarding his *Weltanschauung* as the core of Nazi doctrine. Remarkable though it may seem, however, there is little to suggest that Hitler's personal ideological fixations had much to do with Nazism's mass appeal.

The theme of winning *Lebensraum* in the east, for instance, played no role whatsoever in Nazism's mass appeal. It is hardly surprising that grandiose visions of German domination of Europe had little direct relevance to the social and political conditions of the Depression in Germany. Foreign policy, in fact, was no more than a sub-theme in Nazi propaganda of this period. Very few Nazi meetings were devoted to foreign affairs, and then only to use the allegedly shameful mishandling of past foreign policy (above all of course the signing of the Versailles Treaty) as a stick with which to beat Weimar governments and as an explanation of current domestic economic ills. The future was spoken of only in the vague sense that a united Germany would once more become a world power to reckon with, or that Germany would once again gain colonies overseas. More remarkable than the unimportance of *Lebensraum* as a main motivating force is the limited role played by anti-Semitism – the central plank in Hitler's *Weltanschauung* – in activating support for the NSDAP.

In the light of the spread of racial anti-Semitism in the half-century before the Nazis came to power, Hitler's paranoia about Jews, and the terrible events which took place during the dictatorship, it is more than understandable that many (especially Zionist) historians have considered anti-Semitism to be both the essence of Nazism and the key to its success before 1933. This view, deriving from a 'pedigree of ideas' approach to the rise of Nazism which concentrates on the spread of racist literature and theories from the mid-nineteenth century onwards, considerably exaggerates the importance of anti-Semitism in bringing Nazism to power. Though supporters of the NSDAP could hardly have been unaware of the anti-Semitism of the Party and its leader, a considerable amount of evidence points towards the conclusion that anti-Semitism was quite secondary to Nazism's electoral success – something which was 'taken on board' by the majority of Nazi supporters rather than representing a prime motivating factor behind their backing for the NSDAP.

Anti-Semitism was almost certainly a more important motivating force for the early activist core of the NSDAP, which had been drawn heavily from other *völkisch* organisations, than it was for recruits in the Party's 'mass phase' after 1929–30. However, even among *alte Kämpfer* – according to Peter Merkl's ranking of 'main ideological theme' in his analysis of the Abel material – only about one-eighth saw anti-Semitism as their most salient concern, while what he calls 'strong ideological antisemites' comprised only 8·5 per cent of the total sample.[22]

In the transformation from *völkisch* sect to mass party, anti-Semitism played no more than a secondary role. Areas such as Middle Franconia, parts of Hesse and Westphalia, and stretches of the Rhineland, where anti-Semitism was a leading feature of the NSDAP's campaigns, formed exceptions. A lengthy tradition of anti-Semitism in such areas had much of its source in the dominance of local trade and rural credit by a relatively large and widely dispersed Jewish population. In Franconia the baleful influence of Julius Streicher, Jew-baiter in chief of the Nazi Party, both reflected the prevailing regional importance of the 'Jewish Question' and also guaranteed a high priority to anti-Semitic agitation in the area. In most parts of Germany, however, even where the NSDAP did disproportionately well at the polls, there was little history of outright hostility towards the Jews going beyond latent prejudice, and anti-Semitism was not usually a particularly striking feature of Nazi propaganda. Though anti-Semitism probably played a more important motivating role for certain more 'ideologically' inclined social groups such as teachers and students, it came in the Depression period to be generally relegated to a role as backcloth to appeals made directly to economic interest and as a leitmotiv for other propaganda themes.[23] Even contemporary Jewish sources accepted that Nazi success was not primarily due to anti-Semitism, adding however the significant rider that people's rejection of anti-Semitism evidently did not go far enough to deter them from supporting an obviously anti-Semitic party.[24]

The centrality of anti-Semitism to Hitler's own *Weltanschauung* is clearly, then, not mirrored by its significance for the mass of Nazi voters or even Party members. The strength of Hitler's own ideological position was that his chiliastic vision was not reducible to the level of everyday social and political conflict and could therefore act without danger as the legitimating touchstone for quite disparate, antagonistic groups within the movement whose actual social motivation and aims were often wholly contradictory. But, as Martin Broszat has pointed out, Hitler's 'secret vision' was not regarded as altogether suitable for mass propaganda.[25] Hitler has to be seen, in fact, not as the ideological motivator of Nazism's mass following, but rather as the symbol, the representative figure whose popular image embodied the broad ideological prejudices and aspirations of the masses.

The main appeal of the NSDAP, as most studies of the rise of Nazism have emphasised, lay less in anti-Semitism than in its claim to be the most powerful adversary of Marxism and the most radical and forthright exponent of the belief in national and social renewal (the 'national community' idea, which was itself of course in essence outrightly anti-Marxist). Allen's conclusions drawn from his micro-study of

'Thalburg' have been amplified by analyses of the spread of Nazism in widely differing regions. People were drawn to Nazism first and foremost because it was an anti-Marxist party, by which was generally understood primarily an anti-SPD party. Secondly, the Nazis' claim to fervent patriotism and avid militarism won them respectability and widespread support in 'Thalburg'. Though the Nazis had no exclusive purchase on nationalism and though the town had always been nationalistic, the commitment to nationalism and militarism was increased by the advent of the NSDAP on the political scene, and Nazi manipulation of nationalist (and religious) symbols won them much middle-class backing.[26] A combination of destroying Marxism and establishing a strong Germany supported by a healthy 'national community' was also the main attraction for new recruits to the Party membership. According to Peter Merkl's categorisation of the Abel material, some two-thirds of the Party members, ranked by their chief object of hostility, were anti-Marxists; over a half of the respondents looked forward to a 'nation reborn' and free of 'the system'; while the main ideological theme of about a third was the idea of a 'national community', and a further third were prompted mainly by nationalist, revanchist, super-patriotic, and German–romantic notions.[27]

Seen in these banal terms as the renewed evocation and widened popularisation of long-standing extreme chauvinistic, anti-Left feelings, Nazi ideology emerges neither as the culmination of uniquely German intellectual trends (though these naturally coloured the expression of the ideology), nor as a distinctive theoretical race doctrine (though race-hatred was subsumed as an important component within the ideology), but as the extreme formulation and continuation of a branch of imperialist ideology, adapted within the framework of German 'national' and 'political culture' to petty bourgeois aspirations.[28] To view Nazism as a distinctive doctrine is both misleading in itself, and cannot explain Nazism's popular appeal. Hitler himself had little patience with the view that a mass following could be won through ideological concepts. His view was blunt and simple: 'Comprehension is a shaky platform for the masses. The only stable emotion is hate.'[29] Nazi Party members – and even less so the millions of voters drawn to the NSDAP between 1930 and 1933 – were indeed seldom attracted by a clear understanding and conscious acceptance of a Nazi ideological programme or doctrine. In itself this is nothing unusual. It is common for a theoretical understanding of a party's ideology, also on the political Left, to *follow* an initial commitment to the party. In the case of Nazism, however, theoretical grasp of the doctrine neither preceded nor followed the commitment to the Party. There was, in effect, no theoretical understanding to be had. The 'ideology' of Nazi supporters comprised essentially an amalgam of phobias, resentment, and prejudice coupled with vague expectations of a better future through Nazism. A recent analysis of the motivation of *alte*

Kämpfer in Hessen-Nassau, for example, emphasises (perhaps over-emphasises) the lack of reflection and political conviction involved in joining the NSDAP.[30] Conan Fischer's study of the ideology of rank-and-file SA men also demonstrates a particularly low level of ideological comprehension.[31] Direct evidence of motivation on the part of Nazi voters is hard to come by. Their reasons for voting Nazi have largely to be inferred. But it is unlikely that they derived from a deep understanding of the fine points of Nazi ideology.

The nature of the German social and political structure, and in particular the form of bourgeois ideology which developed in the imperialist period provided the clear potential, in crisis conditions for that socio-political system, for a *Sammlung* of the Right to be created under a popular nationalist, anti-Marxist banner. That the NSDAP should be able to convince millions of Germans that it alone was the legitimate exponent of ideas held generally on the Right, can only be explained through the style of its politics and not the content of its ideology.

II   Propaganda and Mobilisation

Until recently the importance of propaganda to the rise of Nazism seemed obvious and was largely uncontested. After all, Hitler had devoted some of the more original pages of *Mein Kampf* to revealing his vital interest in propaganda in contrast to his lack of interest in the motivating force of ideas as such;[32] following his precepts, the NSDAP attached such great weight to propaganda that even acute financial difficulties did not deter it from an extraordinary level of activity; contemporaries – even outright enemies of the Nazis – could not help but be impressed by the organisation, the skilful manipulation and psychological success of the appeal to raw emotion; and historians have generally been as impressed as contemporaries by the decisive role played by propaganda in mobilising the masses and undermining the Republic.

This consensus has now been challenged. Partly influenced by the current scholarly preoccupation with *Alltagsgeschichte* ('the history of everyday life') and mainly based upon detailed local studies of the ways in which existing social and political structures accommodated Nazism, there has been a conscious attempt to 'demythologise' Nazi appeal, to try to comprehend the attractions of Nazism in terms of rational social and political choices of an electorate, and, rather than concentrating so heavily upon the output and content of propaganda, to evaluate a wide variety of responses to Nazi agitation. The awakened interest in the processes of mobilisation at the 'grassroots level' during the rise of Nazism has built, too, upon recent work on political mobilisation in Wilhelmine Germany which itself has reacted strongly against the usual emphasis upon manipulation from above misleading people as to their 'real' interests. The case for a revision of the conventional picture of the importance of propaganda to the rise of the NSDAP has been put in its most forthright fashion by Richard Bessel, who goes so far as to claim that contemporaries and historians alike have been misled by what he calls the 'myth' of Nazi propaganda.[33]

Bessel's aim is to question the assumption that the success of the NSDAP in mobilising the support of millions can be ascribed to the manipulation of the masses by a well-functioning propaganda machine. Leading historians of different persuasions have, alleges Bessel, held superlative Nazi propaganda techniques responsible for 'conning' millions of German voters into the apparently irrational decision to support the NSDAP. Against this interpretation he argues that the success of the NSDAP was due primarily to factors quite independent of the Party's propaganda techniques, which were neither in method nor in theme markedly different from those of the Party's right-wing competitors. Social and political culture, and not propaganda, played the crucial role in his view. The class and confessional patterns of Nazi support challenge the assumption 'that the German people were swept away by Nazi propaganda'. Rather, he asserts, the main role of propaganda was in determining the behaviour of Party activists; the Nazis themselves were the main victims of their own propaganda. As far as the mass of voters was concerned, propaganda merely reinforced sympathies among people well-disposed anyway towards the Nazi message, and was therefore preaching to the converted. The decision to support the NSDAP was, then, not irrational, but 'based on rational (if confused) consideration of what [people] perceived to have been their interests' and was primarily a result of the 'failure of the Weimar political system to satisfy their perceived needs'. By about 1930 there was for them little alternative to giving their support to the NSDAP.[34]

Though, in rather overstating the case he is attacking, Bessel sets up something of a 'straw man' to knock down and at the same time exaggerates the extent of his 'revision', his article does raise important points, in particular about the role of propaganda in the electoral breakthrough of the NSDAP, and about the extent to which people chose the Nazi Party on quite 'normal' and 'rational' grounds of what they saw as the best safeguard of their material interests rather than being drawn by the great 'ideals' of national salvation and the alluring promises of 'millenarian' politics. The following discussion focuses on these two questions.

The scale of the NSDAP's gains in the 1930 *Reichstag* election took even the Nazis by surprise. It was the breakthrough from being largely a protest party, to a party with a real possibility of taking power. It would indeed be an oversimplification to attribute the scale of the Nazi victory to the brilliance of the Party's propaganda techniques. There was, in fact, no straightforward correlation between propaganda activity and electoral success. The Nazis performed well electorally in some places where the level of propaganda agitation had been low, and conversely did badly in some areas where a sophisticated campaign had been carried out. Class, religion, and (mainly linked to these) strength of existing political loyalties determined, as is well known, the general preconditions for the relative success or failure of the NSDAP. Where circumstances favoured the Nazis, success could come without the aid of a massive propaganda campaign. In the Swabian district of Günzburg, for example, the NSDAP held in 1930 only half as many election meetings as the SPD. Even a Hitler speech here made no great impact (in contrast to the Führer's repeat visit two years later). And though a spectacular 'propaganda action' had been carried out earlier in the year, it had apparently not been hugely successful. Yet despite the limited propaganda effort in this locality, the NSDAP made massive gains and in fact scored its greatest successes in the small communities which had been relatively neglected in its campaigns as far as meetings, marches, and the usual propaganda razzmatazz was concerned.[35]

As this example suggests, the mechanisms by which people were 'converted' to Nazism frequently had little to do with direct exposure to Nazi propaganda methods. Recent studies have, therefore, quite rightly pointed to the need to examine carefully the ways in which Nazism began to penetrate the social infrastructure of a community. An important role was often played here by the close network of middle-class clubs and associations (*Vereine*) in providing a social framework of petty bourgeois life in which Nazism was acceptably blended into existing local tradition and, once established, rapidly expanded through social contact and influence.[36] A key role was often played here by the personal example set by local worthies and 'social insiders', particularly in provincial towns and country districts. In 'Thalburg', for instance, the Nazis took a big leap forward when the Party started to gain the support of prominent figures in the town.[37] In remote country areas, persuasion to support the Nazi Party was more likely to come from neighbours and friends, from talk at the market, in pubs and clubs, than it was from attendance at Nazi rallies and meetings. In villages where the peasant leaders and other figures of local economic and social influence were won over to the NSDAP, further converts followed rapidly. It often needed only a small push by one or two prominent individuals, themselves convinced Nazis, to produce a local landslide.[38] Conversely, where the local representatives of the NSDAP were 'social outsiders', were 'upstart nobodies', or enjoyed dubious reputations, the Party faced considerable difficulties in gaining acceptance as a serious political choice. The 'anti-church' image made penetration of Catholic country districts, where the social and political scene was dominated by the local *Zentrum* or BVP establishment, a particular problem.[39]

Acknowledgement of the importance to the rise of Nazism of 'informal agitation', based upon personal contact and social networks, is, however, no reason to play down the significance of the Party's methods of direct agitation to the Nazi success of 1930. Rather, the important role of 'informal agitation' testifies itself to the success of the Party in creating an attractive and distinctive image for the NSDAP.

All studies of the rise of Nazism point to the years 1925–9, when the NSDAP was electorally in the wilderness, as the crucial period in the organisational development of the Party, when networks of local groups of activists unrivalled by any other party of the Right were built up. An astonishing level of agitation could be sustained by only a small Party membership, providing that the membership contained a high proportion of activists and that there was tight political organisation. In Lower Saxony new propaganda techniques such as the saturation of a single district over the course of a weekend showed big success rates. In the 1930 campaign the use of speakers was for the first time centrally controlled; detailed directives were sent out; and special novel propaganda methods were employed. Jeremy Noakes's conclusion was that the 1930 campaign was one of exceptional skill carried out by a formidable propaganda machine which gave the NSDAP a considerable advantage over the rapidly improvised campaign of the other bourgeois parties.[40] What the Nazis achieved above all was the creation of an image: that of a vigorous, dedicated, and youthful party of force, drive, and *élan*. The image, rather than any specific point of the Party programme, was often the attraction.

By the time of the Depression the Nazis were, in fact, making others sit up and take notice. Whereas in 1928 the bourgeois press had largely ignored the Nazi campaign, by 1930 the brownshirts were forcing themselves regularly onto the front pages. And the more the enemies of the Nazis felt it necessary to report their activities in order to condemn them, the more the propaganda image of the NSDAP as a party which could neither be ignored nor suppressed was taking effect. In the Ruhr district, for instance, not one of the NSDAP's happiest hunting grounds, a Dortmund newspaper, drawn increasingly to ever-more fierce denunciation of the Nazis, was forced to concede in the summer of 1930 that 'the organisation, activity, and will to power which inspires the Nazis deserves the strongest recognition. The flag-bearers of the Party have for years not been prevented from going into the most far-flung villages and casting their slogans to the masses in at least a hundred meetings a day in Germany'.[41] The astonishing energy of the Party could not be gainsaid: in the run-up to the 1930 election there were no fewer than a thousand meetings of the NSDAP held in Upper Franconia and a similar number in adjacent Middle Franconia.[42] This high level of agitation carried out through meetings, rallies, publications, and – not least – street violence not only put the Nazis on the political map, but also had wide ripple effects. Like it or not, the Nazis were now an inevitable element of the daily political debate. Their propaganda had given them a presence and projected a sustained image of action and vitality even in areas where no meetings were held, where the local Party was still in its beginnings. The conversion of local worthies to Nazism and their subsequent personal and social 'indirect propaganda role' is unthinkable without the direct propaganda which made them aware of Nazism in the first place. Above all it was the growing feeling of strength and purpose attached to the Party– a direct creation of agitational methods in the first instance – which persuaded many 'respectable citizens' that this was a party that mattered.

If the themes of Nazi propaganda were little different from those of the DNVP and their other right-wing rivals, the presentation of the themes, the style of Nazi meetings, the scurrilous scandal propaganda, the violence and the flamboyance, all struck contemporaries as a new phenomenon, something different from old-style bourgeois politics. The Nazis created a new form of political confrontation with a type of organisation which was not a conventional political party but a fighting movement – as an independent political force rather than merely a paramilitary structure like the *Stahlhelm*, also a *novum* on the bourgeois political scene. To imply that Nazi propaganda was not new in 'any way other than its quantity'[43] flies in the face of the mass of contemporary non-Nazi opinion and furthermore misses the point that even the very *quantity* of Nazi propaganda amounted, in terms of the image created, to a *qualitative* distinction from other bourgeois parties. Based on their public image, the DNVP, DVP, and the various right-wing interest-organisations increasingly appeared puny competitors of the Nazis. Faced, in the rapid polarisation of class conflict in late Weimar Germany, with the question as to which party had any hope of getting Germany back on its feet again, the answer seemed more and more obvious.

The claim that historians have concentrated on explaining the rise of Nazism in terms of the 'mystification of the masses' who were 'conned', 'seduced', 'hypnotised', and 'entranced' by 'those political snake charmers Hitler and Goebbels',[44] and have thereby ignored the 'rational' motivation of material self-interest is a puzzling one, since practically all detailed analyses of the spread of Nazism in specific localities or regions have laid great stress upon the NSDAP's appeal to economic interest and have emphasised strongly the class composition of the Party's support. From the beginning of the NSDAP's meteoric rise, ideological slogans of 'national community', 'anti-Marxism', and 'anti-Semitism' served, in fact, to legitimise and justify hard individual, sectional, and class interest. One symptom of the growing failure of the Weimar bourgeois parties to portray themselves as anything more than narrow, sectional interest representations was the proliferation and expansion of 'interest-parties' and 'interest-organisations' in the later 1920s. The NSDAP was able to latch onto this disintegration into pure interest politics by projecting itself as a party which could incorporate each real sectional interest within a powerful movement capable of looking after the interests of each by looking after the interests of all. Two organisational and propagandistic developments of the Party during this period were of fundamental importance here. One was the reorientation of propaganda towards the rural and provincial *Mittelstand* in 1927–8, enabling the Party increasingly to tap the wave of elemental anger and bitterness arising from the onset of the crisis in the rural economy. The second was the development, especially from 1930 onwards and running alongside the Party's appeal to the submerging of individual good within the common good of the nation, of special subsections of the Party designed to attract and cater for particular sectional interests.[45] It was a conscious attempt to appeal through propaganda directed at sectional interest and material well-being, always of course within the umbrella framework of 'national renewal'. No other party could match the NSDAP's range or scale of middle-class interest-group propaganda. It was an important point in its favour.

An illustration of the NSDAP's appeal as a 'super-interest-party' is provided by Zdenek Zofka's detailed analysis of the collapse of the *Bayerischer Bauernbund* (BBB) at the hands of the Nazis in Günzburg (Bavaria). Alongside the *Bayerische Volkspartei*, the BBB had traditionally dominated this overwhelmingly Catholic, agricultural area, but was by the early 1930s already in an advanced stage of dissolution and was losing votes not only to the Nazis, but also on all sides. Supporters of the BBB were, in fact, becoming increasingly aware that in a crisis of such magnitude their little, provincial party of peasant interest-representation could offer them nothing, and that their only hope lay with a big and powerful party. The crucial propaganda weapon of the Nazis was to suggest that they were just that 'big party' which, in standing 'above interest' as the advocate of a 'national community', could offer farmers the certainty of a new society in which their interests would have pride of place. The Nazi profile among peasant leaders in the area had superficially therefore little or nothing to do with the classic hallmarks of Nazi ideology, but amounted first and foremost to the belief that the Party was well-disposed towards farmers. This generalised party image, embracing as it did the movement's militancy, radicalism, and strength, was far more important than specific promises of agricultural reform. The image was bolstered by the Party's overt anti-socialism, seen in the area not as abstract symbolism but as a clear commitment to defend the interests of primary producers, whereas the SPD and the trade unions had only looked after the interests of the consumers. The appeal of the NSDAP in Günzburg, therefore, was – especially after 1930 – primarily rational and practical, determined by sectional interest, rather than affective and emotional. Zofka focused his analysis on peasants, on the older rather than younger generation of Nazi voters, and on the 'bandwagoners' of 1931–3 more than on the earlier converts. In each case, arguably, this enhanced the 'rational' choice of the Nazi option. Yet even 'rational' Günzburg experienced its moments of delirium. Even here the Hitler cult was something which transcended ordinary 'rational', 'interest-group' mentality. Hitler's second visit to Günzburg in the autumn of 1932 was greeted with 'almost hysterical enthusiasm' and may well have tipped the balance in the election campaign in this district which, quite untypically for Germany as a whole, recorded an increase in the Nazi vote in the November election of 1932.[46]

The economic motivation of material self-interest is obviously a vitally important element of the support for Nazism. But it is not the whole story. Explanations of the appeal of Nazism which exclude the emotional, irrational side of Nazi propaganda fall in danger of 'over-normalising' the attractions of Nazism, of failing to reflect the extraordinary atmosphere of Depression politics in Germany. In small towns the passion of the revivalist meeting, fired by clever exploitation of national and religious symbolism, coexisted with 'rational' economic motives.[47] Among young people in particular, the appeal of Nazi propaganda was often highly emotional and had little to do with direct material interest. And for not a few who found their way into the NSDAP, the conversion had indeed a mystical dimension:

> On April 20 1932, in Kassel, for the first time I heard the Führer Adolf Hitler speak in person. After this, there was only one thing for me, either to win with Adolf Hitler or to die for him. The personality of the Führer had me totally in its spell.[48]

This is not exactly the language of 'rational' politics. Probably most Nazi supporters found their way to the movement for more prosaic reasons. But the importance of the Führer-cult as the fulcrum of Nazi propaganda appeal cannot be doubted. Alongside the susceptibility to irrational, mystical appeals to race and nation, it was a product of the political culture of the German bourgeoisie. And the greater the apparent threat to order, authority, unity, and status posed by the industrial working class became, the greater was the readiness to look for the embodiment of all these qualities in a single, great, popular leader. But that that leader should have been Hitler, and that these feelings should have become such a potent political force even in the depths of an economic crisis was due primarily to the conscious 'marketing' of the Hitler cult by Goebbels's propaganda apparatus.[49] The Führer-cult demonstrates that the effectiveness of Nazi propaganda depended *both* upon an 'ideologically available' stratum of the population in favourable (that is, crisis-ridden) economic and political conditions, *and* upon skilful and sustained manipulation of the existing ideological predisposition by determined and energetic methods of agitation. If the notion of a population wholly manipulable by a propaganda machine functioning at the behest of extreme groups of capitalists is one end of the spectrum which is difficult to accept, it is also going altogether too far to play down almost to disappearance-point the contribution made to the rise of the NSDAP by masterful demagogic exploitation and propaganda manipulation of a socio-psychological mood of panic in the German middle class which cannot be explained by economics alone.

That the decision to support the Nazis was, as Bessel points out, the product of the failure of the Weimar political system to support the voters' perceived needs, seems axiomatic, but begs the question of what the Nazis themselves contributed to the growing sense of awareness of a failed political system and why they should be its main electoral beneficiaries. To stress the part played by social and political culture in the rise of the NSDAP is also correct, but insufficient as an explanation of Nazi success. Being well disposed towards certain parts of the Nazi message was not the same thing as being a Nazi. The propaganda of the NSDAP was not 'preaching to the converted' when it persuaded people with similar ideological leanings to the Nazis to vote for the NSDAP rather than for the DNVP or the DVP, or those who had never voted before to cast their ballot for the NSDAP. It was, in fact, doing an extremely effective job of political mobilisation in ensuring that the Nazi Party cornered the right-wing vote – something which no other single party or organisation had managed either in the empire or in the Weimar Republic.[50] Finally, that there was no obvious alternative to the NSDAP by the turn of the 1930s testifies not to the unimportance but to the unquestionable success of Nazi propaganda. It had made the NSDAP seem indispensable – for millions the only conceivable way out of national crisis. The importance of propaganda to the rise of the Nazis, far from being a myth, can hardly be overstated.

By the July election of 1932 the high-point of propaganda effectiveness had already been reached. The barrage of propaganda which had set in with the first presidential election in March continued, but it was now increasingly a matter of maintaining the presence through emphasis on pageantry, display, marching, and entertainment evenings. The political fronts, as the Nazis themselves recognised, were by mid-summer 1932 as clearly defined as they were going to be under a parliamentary system. In pro-Nazi areas like Franconia the swastika was now the overwhelmingly dominant political symbol.[51] The Nazi vote in such areas was often as high in July 1932 as it was to be even in the March election of 1933. With the partial exception of the DNVP, the other bourgeois parties had been demolished. On the other hand, the Nazis had recognisably failed to break down the two major political blocs of the working-class and Catholic parties. The SPD, KPD, and *Zentrum* had in the mean time learnt much from Nazi propaganda tactics, and though their own propaganda was narrower in scope and – except for the KPD – defensive in nature, aimed at holding on to their own supporters rather than winning new converts, it could build not only upon strong organisation but also on a close mesh of social ties which were almost impenetrable to the Nazis.

It is hardly surprising that Nazi propaganda failed to maintain its momentum and prevent a drift away from the NSDAP in the November election of 1932. In the fifth major election campaign of the year, the NSDAP found it difficult to sustain the extraordinary tempo of the first half of 1932. The propaganda machine was close to breaking-point by the time of the election setback in November. Though it managed one last show of strength in the Lippe state elections of January 1933, Hitler was appointed Chancellor at a time of propaganda failure, not success. The propaganda had, however, already done its job in creating a mass movement which, in the political stalemate of autumn 1932, could not be left out of consideration.

The NSDAP still had in early 1933 the direct support of fewer than one in two Germans. But this figure is somewhat misleading. The potential was there for a much wider consensus to be attained if Nazi aims could now be put across as national goals rather than in the language of party politics. The appointment of Goebbels as Reich Propaganda Minister on 13 March 1933 marked the beginning of the new task of propaganda, that of uniting the entire people behind the Nazi leadership. From its previous role as a Party instrument, focusing exclusively upon getting the NSDAP into power, propaganda now had to be converted into a new role as an instrument of rule.

Notes

1 A. Hitler, *Mein Kampf* (Munich: 1943 edn), p. 652.
2 For example, E. Weber, 'Revolution? Counter-Revolution? What Revolution?', in W. Laqueur (ed.), *Fascism. A Reader's Guide* (Harmondsworth: 1976), pp. 488–531; as revolutionary anti-modernist, H. A. Turner, 'Fascism and Modernization', in his *Reappraisals of Fascism* (New York: 1975), pp. 117–39; and as a revolutionary, despite reactionary aspects of its ideology, J. Noakes, *The Nazi Party in Lower Saxony, 1921–1933* (Oxford: 1971), pp. 249–50.
3 Most Marxist accounts take this line. For the most recent DDR studies, which stress the bourgeois (not petty bourgeois), counter-revolutionary, anti-proletarian essence of Nazi ideology, functioning in the service of the most extreme sections of 'the ruling class', cf. esp. the contributions by K. Gossweiler, J. Petzold and W. Ruge to the collection of essays, D. Eichholz and K. Gossweiler (eds), *Faschismus-Forschung. Positionen, Probleme, Polemik* (East Berlin: 1980); and K. Pätzold and M. Weissbecker, *Geschichte der NSDAP* (Cologne: 1981).
4 M. Broszat, *German National Socialism 1919–1945* (Santa Barbara: 1966), p. 89.
5 For example, A. Bullock, *Hitler. A Study in Tyranny* (Harmondsworth: 1962 edn), p. 804. This view goes back to the influential interpretations of Hermann Rauschning, *Revolution of Nihilism* (New York: 1939) and Konrad Heiden, *Der Führer* (London: 1944).

6   Eugen Weber, *Varieties of Fascism* (New York: 1964), pp. 141–3, distinguished the 'theoretical doctrine' of National Socialism from the 'cheerful pragmatism' of Mussolini and Degrelle. Klaus Hildebrand, *Das Dritte Reich* (Munich/Vienna: 1979), pp. 139–40, sums up the argument (which leans heavily upon the distinctiveness of the Nazi race doctrine) that Nazism was qualitatively different from fascism.

7   cf. E. Jäckel, *Hitlers Weltanschauung. Entwurf einer Herrschaft* (Tübingen: 1969).

8   G. Mosse, *Crisis of German Ideology: Intellectual Origins of the Third Reich* (New York: 1964) might be taken as representative of this approach.

9   A different slant to the DDR approach (as typified in the works listed in n. 3 above) is provided by some Western Marxist writers, such as R. Kühnl, *Formen bürgerlicher Herrschaft* (Reinbek bei Hamburg: 1971), and especially the sophisticated theoretical work of N. Poulantzas, *Fascism and Dictatorship* (London: 1979, Verso edn).

10 The only comprehensive attempt, so far as I can judge, though limited in its source base and conclusions and extremely dated in its conceptual approach, is the thesis by H. Balle, 'Die propagandistische Auseinandersetzung des Nationalsozialismus mit der Weimarer Republik und ihre Bedeutung für den Aufstieg des Nationalsozialismus', (Phil. F. Diss., University of Erlangen, 1963). Apart from a number of detailed studies of the Nazi press, works specifically concentrating on propaganda before 1933 are practically confined to ch. 1 of Z. E. B. Zeman, *Nazi Propaganda* (Oxford: 1964) and chs 1–2 of E. K. Bramsted, *Goebbels and National Socialist Propaganda* (Michigan: 1965). Neither work is at its best on the pre-1933 period.

11 For the most recent example of this type of approach, see R. Koshar, 'Two "Nazisms": the Social Context of Nazi Mobilisation in Marburg and Tübingen', *Social History*, January 1982, pp. 27–42. Apart from the rather misleading implication that there were two types of Nazism, whereas in fact only the outward forms of Nazism in the two towns were slightly different, it must unfortunately be said that this essay promises more than it can deliver: the conclusion seems to amount (p. 42) to little more than that 'in the specific geographical setting discussed here, a dynamic interplay between the various manifestations of "fragmentation" and a wider social hegemony of the middle classes occurred'.

12 R. Bessel, 'The Rise of the NSDAP and the Myth of Nazi Propaganda', *Wiener Library Bulletin*, 33, 1980, (= New Series, nos 51/52), pp. 20–9.

13 cf. esp. Franz Neumann, *Behemoth* (London: 1942), Part One, sections IV–VI, in particular pp. 140–1. See also Kühnl, *Formen bürgerlicher Herrschaft*, pp. 84–99. For the view that socialism and anti-capitalism were 'principal components' of Nazi ideology before 1933, cf. P. D. Stachura, 'The Political Strategy of the Nazi Party, 1919–1933', *German Studies Review*, 3, 1980, 274.

14 cf. e.g., Mosse, *Crisis*, and also his *Germans and Jews* (London: 1971); P. Pulzer, *The Rise of Political Anti-Semitism in Germany and Austria* (London: 1964); F. Stern, *The Politics of Cultural Despair* (Berkeley, Calif: 1961).

15 cf. G. Eley, *Reshaping the German Right. Radical Nationalism and Political Change after Bismarck* (New Haven, Conn: 1980), esp. ch. 5; and his essay, 'The Wilhelmine Right: How it Changed', in R. J. Evans (ed.), *Society and Politics in Wilhelmine Germany*, (London: 1978), pp. 112–35.

16 The instability of the right-wing and 'liberal' vote was well demonstrated by H. A. Winkler, 'Extremismus der Mitte? Sozialgeschichtliche Aspekte der nationalsozialistischen Machtergreifung', *Vierteljahrshefte für Zeitgeschichte*, 20, 1972, pp. 175–91.

17 cf. M. Broszat, 'Soziale Motivation und Führer-Bindung des Nationalsozialismus', *Vierteljahrshefte für Zeitgeschichte*, 18, 1970, pp. 394, 393–6.

18 For a different view, see B. M. Lane and L. J. Rupp, *Nazi Ideology Before 1933* (Manchester: 1978), p. xi.

19 cf. K. Sontheimer, *Antidemokratisches Denken in der Weimarer Republik* (Munich: 1962, 4th edn), pp. 268–83.

20 cf. I. Kershaw, *Der Hitler-Mythos. Volksmeinung und Propaganda im Dritten Reich* (Stuttgart: 1980), ch. 1.

21   Jäckel, *Hitlers Weltanschauung*; cf. now also the mammoth edition of Hitler's early writings: E. Jäckel (ed.), *Hitler. Sämtliche Aufzeichnungen, 1905–1924* (Stuttgart: 1980).

22   P. H. Merkl, *Political Violence Under the Swastika. 581 Early Nazis* (Princeton, NJ: 1975), pp. 33, 453.

23   cf. Noakes, *Nazi Party*, pp. 209–10; G. Pridham, *Hitler's Rise to Power: the History of the NSDAP in Bavaria, 1923–1933* (London: 1973), pp. 237–8.

24   A. Paucker, *Der jüdische Abwehrkampf gegen Antisemitismus und Nationalsozialismus in den letzten Jahren der Weimarer Republik*, (Hamburg: 1969, 2nd edn); pp. 194–5. See now also the recent study by D. L. Niewyk, *The Jews in Weimar Germany* (Manchester: 1980), ch. 3.

25   cf. Broszat, 'Soziale Motivation', pp. 400, 402 ff.

26   W. S. Allen, *The Nazi Seizure of Power. The Experience of a Single German Town, 1930–1935* (New York: 1973, paper edn), pp. 26, 28, 132–6, 274–6.

27   Merkl, *Political Violence*, pp. 32–3, 453, 522–3. The SA men in the sample differed little from Party members in their main ideological leanings: cf. Merkl, *The Making of a Stormtrooper* (Princeton, NJ: 1980), p. 222.

28   Based on Poulantzas, *Fascism*, pp. 252–3.

29   Cited in Broszat, *German National Socialism*, p. 57, from Hitler's speech to the *Hamburger Nationalklub* in 1926.

30   C. Schmidt, 'Zu den Motiven "alter Kämpfer" in der NSDAP', in D. Peukert and J. Reulecke (eds), *Die Reihen fast geschlossen* (Wuppertal: 1981), pp. 32–4.

31   C. Fischer, 'The SA's Rank and File Membership in the early 1930s. Social Background and Ideology', unpubl. paper delivered to the German Social History Seminar, Norwich, 1979, p. 9.

32   Especially Book I, ch. 6, and Book II, chs 6, 11.

33   See n. 12 above.

34   ibid., pp. 22–8.

35   Z. Zofka, *Die Ausbreitung des Nationalsozialismus auf dem Lande* (Munich: 1979), pp. 76–9, 91–2, 343–4. Bessel, Rise of the NSDAP, p. 23 cites the example of Neidenburg in East Prussia, where despite little Nazi organisation to speak of before 1931 the vote for the NSDAP in the 1930 election rose to 25·8 per cent, well above the national average. On the other hand, E. Faris, 'Take-Off Point for the National Socialist Party: the Landtag Election in Baden, 1929', *Central European History*, 8, 1975, pp. 166–8, attributes the Nazi 'take-off' in Baden not to general propaganda, but to meticulous organisational work at the local level and to determined 'local effort' in canvassing.

36   cf. Koshar, 'Two Nazisms', pp. 32–6.

37   Allen, *Nazi Seizure*, pp. 25–6.

38   R. Heberle, *From Democracy to Nazism. A Regional Case Study on Political Parties in Germany* (Baton Rouge: 1945), pp. 109–11.

39   cf. Wolfgang Kaschuba and Carola Lipp, 'Kein Volk steht auf, kein Sturm bricht los. Stationen dörflichen Lebens auf dem Weg in den Faschismus', in Johannes Beck, Heiner Boehncke, Werner Heinz and Gerhard Vinnai (eds), *Terror und Hoffnung in Deutschland 1933–1945. Leben in Faschismus* (Reinbek bei Hamburg: 1980), pp. 119–34, for an example of a locality where, on social and religious grounds, the Nazis found great difficulty in establishing themselves.

40   Noakes, *Nazi Party*, pp. 94–5, 99, 140–2, 145–6, 148–51.

41   Cited in W. Boehnke, *Die NSDAP im Ruhrgebiet, 1920–1933*, (Bad Godesberg: 1974), p. 147.

42   R. Hambrecht, *Der Aufstieg der NSDAP in Mittel und Oberfranken (1925–1933)* (Nuremberg: 1976).

43   Bessel, 'Rise of the NSDAP', p. 27.

44   ibid., pp. 22–3, 28–9. Such loaded expressions themselves illustrate Bessel's rather artificial, overstated recapitulation of the alleged argument he is challenging. His own case, on the other hand, is usually hedged with cautious qualifications, as, for

example, in his comment that Nazi propaganda 'did not exist *solely* for the seduction of the masses' and his wish to avoid the claim 'that the propaganda had *absolutely no effect* upon its recipients' (ibid., p. 27, my italics).

45 cf. Noakes, *Nazi Party*, pp. 104–7, 162 ff; D. Orlow, *The History of the Nazi Party, 1919–1933* (Newton Abbot: 1971), chs 5–6; P. D. Stachura, 'Der kritische Wendepunkt? Die NSDAP und die Reichstagswahlen vom 20. Mai 1928', *Vierteljahrshefte für Zeitgeschichte*, 26, 1978, pp., 66–99.

46 Zofka, *Ausbreitung des Nationalsozialismus*, pp. 89–90, 96, 105–15, 115–16, 154, 341–50.

47 Allen, *Nazi Seizure*, pp. 133–4, 275 f, 297; Noakes, *Nazi Party*, pp. 123 f, 220 f; Zofka, *Ausbreitung des Nationalsozialismus*, p. 80.

48 Merkl, *Political Violence*, p. 539.

49 cf. Kershaw, *Der Hitler-Mythos*, ch. 1.

50 Bessel, 'Rise of the NSDAP', pp. 24, 28.

51 Hambrecht, *Aufstieg der NSDAP*, p. 209.

Notes on Contributors

JOHN S. CONWAY is Professor of History at the University of British Columbia, Canada. He is the author of numerous articles on the German churches in the twentieth century, the Vatican and on the Holocaust, and also of *The Nazi Persecution of the Churches 1933–1945* (1968), which has been published in German, French and Spanish editions. Professor Conway is currently working on Christian–Jewish relations since 1945.

DICK GEARY is Head of the Department of German Studies at the University of Lancaster. He is the author of *European Labour Protest 1848–1939* (1981) and has also written articles in British, Italian and German academic journals on the history of the German Labour Movement and Marxism. Dr Geary is Review Editor of the *European Studies Review*.

MICHAEL GEYER is Associate Professor of History at the University of Michigan, USA. He is the author of articles on German militarism and his study *Aufrüstung oder Sicherheit. Die Reichswehr in der Krise der Machtpolitik 1924–1936* was published in 1980. A further study, *Deutsche Rüstungspolitik, 1890–1980*, is due to appear in 1983.

GEOFFREY J. GILES is Assistant Professor of History at the University of Florida, USA. He was previously involved in comparative and historical research on higher education at Yale University, where he published several papers and articles about various European and Canadian universities. Dr Giles has published a number of essays about students in Nazi Germany in recent books, and has completed a manuscript on students and professors at the University of Hamburg during the Third Reich.

JOHN HIDEN is Senior Lecturer in European Studies at the University of Bradford. His publications include *The Weimar Republic* (1974), *Germany and Europe 1919–1939* (1977), an English translation of Martin Broszat's *The Hitler State* (1981), and articles on Weimar Ostpolitik, German–Baltic relations, and German minorities during the 1920s in various scholarly journals and anthologies. Dr Hiden is currently preparing a joint study entitled *Explaining Hitler's Germany: Historians and the Third Reich*.

IAN KERSHAW is Senior Lecturer in Modern History at the University of Manchester. His publications include *Der Hitler-Mythos. Volksmeinung und Propaganda im Dritten Reich* (1980), and articles on Nazism. His book, *Popular Opinion and Political Dissent in the Third Reich. Bavaria 1933–45*, is to be published this year.

PETER D. STACHURA is a Lecturer in History at the University of Stirling. He has published numerous articles in British, German and American scholarly journals and anthologies on topics including the Nazi and German Youth Movements, and the leadership, electoral character, political strategy and social composition of the Nazi Party. Dr Stachura is also the author of *Nazi Youth in the Weimar Republic* (1975), *The Weimar Era and Hitler 1918–1933* (1977), *The Shaping of the Nazi State* (editor, 1978), *The German Youth Movement 1900–1945: An Interpretative and Documentary History* (1981), and *Gregor Strasser and the Rise of Nazism* (1983).

JILL STEPHENSON is a Lecturer in History at the University of Edinburgh. Dr Stephenson has contributed articles on German women during the 1920s and 1930s to academic journals and anthologies, and is the author of *Women in Nazi Society* (1975) and *The Nazi Organisation of Women* (1981). She is presently engaged on a regional study of Württemberg in the Weimar and Nazi eras.

Index